# THE LOGIC OF PRAGMATIC THINKING

## From Peirce to Habermas

*Edmund Arens*

*translated by david smith*

HUMANITIES PRESS
New Jersey

P
99.4
.P72
A7413
1994

First published 1994 by Humanities Press International, Inc.,
Atlantic Highlands, New Jersey 07716.

©1994 by Edmund Arens

**Library of Congress Cataloging-in-Publication Data**
Arens, Edmund, 1953–
[Kommunikative Handlungen. English]
The logic of pragmatic thinking : from Peirce to Habermas /
Edmund Arens ; translated by David Smith.
p.   cm.
Includes bibliographical references and index.
1. Pragmatics.   2. Semiotics.   3. Discourse analysis.   4. Jesus
Christ—Parables.   I. Title.
P99.4.P72A7413   1993
401'.41—dc20                      92-33235
CIP

A catalog record for this book is available from the British Library.

Printed in the United States of America

*To Helmut Peukert*
*my teacher and friend*

# Contents

# Abbreviations

Complete publication information can be found in the Bibliography.

| | |
|---|---|
| BB | Schmidt, *Bedeutung und Begriff* |
| CES | Habermas, *Communication and the Evolution of Society* |
| CV | Wittgenstein, *Culture and Value* |
| HTW | Austin, *How to Do Things with Words* |
| KHI | Habermas, *Knowledge and Human Interest* |
| KK | Habermas, *Kultur und Kritik* |
| LC | Habermas, *Legitimation Crisis* |
| LSS | Habermas, *On the Logic of the Social Sciences* |
| MCCA | Habermas, *Moral Consciousness and Communicative Action* |
| OC | Wittgenstein, *On Certainty* |
| PG | Wittgenstein, *Philosophical Grammar* |
| PI | Wittgenstein, *Philosophical Investigations* |
| SA | Searle, *Speech Acts* |
| Stud | Wunderlich, *Studien zur Sprechakttheorie* |
| T | Wittgenstein, *Tractatus logico-philosophicus* |
| TCA | Habermas, *The Theory of Communicative Action* |
| ThdG | Habermas, "Theorie der Gesellschaft oder Sozialtechnologie?" |
| TP | Habermas, *Theory and Practice* |
| TRS | Habermas, *Toward a Rational Society* |
| TT | Schmidt, *Texttheorie* |
| VB | Habermas, "Vorbereitende Bemerkungen zu einer Theorie der kommunikativen Kompetenz" |
| Wth | Habermas, "Wahrheitstheorien" |

# ═══ *Preface* ═══

This book emerged out of an attempt to contribute to the unfolding of pragmatic theory, bringing together those traditions in Anglo-American and Continental thinking that are devoted to pointing out the structure and orientation of language and action. The history of pragmatic theory formation is sketched here, beginning with Charles Sanders Peirce's semiotics and pragmatism up to Karl-Otto Apel's transcendental pragmatics and Jürgen Habermas' universal pragmatics. I maintain that through a systematic reconstruction of the history of pragmatic theory formation, the logic of pragmatic thinking becomes evident.

This project is deeply inspired by the thinking of Karl-Otto Apel and Jürgen Habermas. I had the privilege to study with them for a couple of years at the University of Frankfurt. They sharpened my understanding of pragmatics and helped me to find my way through the difficult problems of pragmatic theory formation. Therefore, I first of all want to express my thanks to both of them.

My studies of pragmatic thinking are part of a theological doctoral dissertation which I did at the University of Münster. Johann Baptist Metz and Karl Kertelge were my advisers there, and I want to thank them for their interest in and the stimulation of my work. The dissertation project has been made possible by a grant provided by the Study Foundation of the German People. I owe my gratitude to the foundation.

The preparations for the American edition were completed during a visiting semester at Union Theological Seminary in New York City. I wholeheartedly thank the former academic dean and current president, Holland Hendrix, for inviting me to teach at Union. My best thanks also go to Peter Van Ness, whom I was able to join in teaching a doctoral seminar that touched on several of the issues discussed here. In order to write a new introduction and an afterword I made use of my Heisenberg Scholarship, an invaluable research opportunity given to me by the German Research Foundation, to which I want to express my deep appreciation.

Many thanks go to Stephen Bronner, who strongly supported the publication of an American edition of my work, and to Eduardo Mendieta, who in many respects helped it get realized.

I thank David Smith for his difficult task of translating the book into English. I would like to express my special gratitude to the World Association for Christian Communication in London for financing the translation. It was above all the concern of Michael Traber and Philip Lee to get my work translated, and I thank both of them for all they have done for me and my book.

I express my appreciation to Ken Estey for correcting the "Teutonic" English of my new Introduction and Afterword, and to Marc Mullinax, without whose expertise in handling computers I would have been lost. Finally, I would like to acknowledge the helpful and reliable work of Karen Napolitano Starks in editing my manuscript.

This book is dedicated to a person with whom I studied at the University of Münster; he acquainted me with the different theories of language and action, introduced me to Apel's and Habermas' philosophy, and for two decades has been my teacher, friend, and most inspiring conversation partner: Helmut Peukert.

# Introduction
## The Formation of
## Pragmatic Theory

This book presents and discusses the development of pragmatic thinking. It does this by integrating the diverse approaches to pragmatic theory, including theories of signs, of texts, and of language, communication, and action. A systematic reconstruction of the various approaches shows their interconnection and reciprocal criticism. It leads to an explanation of the logic of pragmatic thinking.

The approaches to and conceptions of pragmatics existing so far provide much, often unrelated material. Yet this material has striking similarities and provides elements and aspects for integration and systematization. The material includes outlines, systematic expositions, and individual studies of the branch of semiotics, linguistics, and philosophy that in the present century has become increasingly developed as basic not only to individual scientific research but also to fundamental debate in the sphere of scientific theory as a whole. In fact, it has penetrated even more deeply and has come to embrace the theory and reconstruction of human action as such. In recent years, a number of fundamental assumptions with varying approaches and emphases have been made about theories of signs, communication, and action. Despite the variations of these approaches, they have pointed to the irreducible nature of the subjects of the process of research and the formation of pragmatic theory, the fundamentally threefold character of the relationship of signs, and the act-character of human interaction and language as the indispensable condition of the possibility of knowledge.

In a systematic reconstruction of the history of the formation of pragmatic theory, I consider these fundamental assumptions from the point of view of a theory of communicative action or universal pragmatics. The fundamental aspects of this theory have been elaborated by Jürgen Habermas. In this survey, I look first at Habermas' universal pragmatics as pointing in the same direction as Karl-Otto Apel's transcendental pragmatics, despite the differences between them that will later have to be discussed in greater detail.

The theory of communicative action, which I, in common with Helmut Peukert, regard as an integration of the theory of language and action into a normatively based interaction theory, does not sufficiently integrate or give a high enough value to all the pragmatic approaches that are discussed here. Therefore, it will be necessary to extend this reconstruction more systematically. My review of the relevant stages in the formation of a pragmatic theory provides a clear guideline and the necessary material for this continuation. My outline of the history of pragmatically oriented philosophy, semiotics, linguistics, and speech and action theory also supplies the categories that can be used to describe the program of pragmatics. This outline also presents and examines in depth the approaches and emphases in each approach as each stage in the history of the development is reviewed.

I will not necessarily look at these stages in chronological order, but will rather consider them according to their special position, focal point, or emphasis in the formation of theory. There are, in my opinion, five subgroups in this process of formation, which can be summarized as follows:

• The pragmatically integrated semiotics of the threefold character of the relationship of signs. The work of Charles Sanders Peirce laid the foundations for this, and his work was continued by different representatives of American pragmatism. It found its most elaborate expression in the behavioristic semiotics of Charles William Morris.

• Approaches to a pragmatically oriented materialistic linguistic theory, as represented in the now almost forgotten work of Valentin N. Vološinov or of Utz Maas, who will be discussed in the context of speech act theory.

• The later writings of Ludwig Wittgenstein and, following him, ordinary language philosophy, with special emphasis on the speech act theory of John L. Austin, John R. Searle, Dieter Wunderlich, and Utz Maas.

• The approach of Siegfried S. Schmidt toward a linguistic theory of the text.

• Projects such as those by Karl-Otto Apel and Jürgen Habermas to evolve a transcendental or universal pragmatic philosophy.

Chapter 1 traces the development of a pragmatically integrated semiotics from Charles Sanders Peirce to Charles William Morris. In 1.1, it shows how Peirce laid the foundations for the formation of a pragmatic theory. On the one hand, he gave birth to the pragmatic movement in American philosophy. On the other hand, he developed a three-dimensional semiotics which increasingly has become the basic theory of logic, language, and science. My aim in this section is to demonstrate the interconnections between Peirce's semiotics of the threefold relationship of signs and his pragmatism. First, I sketch his foundations of semiotics in the triadic relationship of signs and his explication of the categories, based on a logic of relations. Then I outline Peirce's pragmatism, starting with his "Pragmatic Maxim" as the determining factor for the classification of meaning and leading to his concept of habit.

I then show the fundamental aspects of Peirce's pragmatic theory of semiotics, of the three-dimensional character of the relationships of signs and pragmatism, as a theory of meaning in his doctrine of the interpretants. I consider this doctrine as a normative concept of interpretation, including the normatively right habits reached at in the long run by the community of investigators.

In 1.2, a brief outline of the reception of Peirce's ideas by American pragmatism follows, including William James' empirical reduction of Peirce's normative concept of pragmatism in terms of a naturalistic and pluralistic view of pragmatism (1.2.1). John Dewey's conception is sketched in 1.2.2 as an instrumental pragmatism that implies, in particular, questions about values but reduces their normative dimension to that of factual existence. Josiah Royce's absolute or idealistic pragmatism (1.2.3) is regarded as an important continuation of Peirce's conception. It points toward a most significant philosophy of sign-mediated interpretation, related to a community of interpretation in which an infinite process of interpretation is taking place. George Herbert Mead's constructive pragmatism (1.2.4) genetically extends Royce's concept of the community of interpretation and unfolds it in terms of a theory of social processes of sign-mediated interaction. This has been a most valuable contribution to pragmatic thinking.

A pragmatic integration of semiotics is achieved by Charles William Morris (1.3), who considers his behavioristic semiotics to be the unifying principle of the pragmatic movement. He manages to unfold a pragmatically integrated three-dimensional semiotics by explaining its aspects and distinguishing a variety of signs. Nevertheless, Morris' conception of pragmatism and semiotics faces certain insuperable difficulties, which will be pointed out as the aporias of his behavioristic approach.

Chapter 2 deals with the approach to a pragmatically oriented materialistic linguistic theory undertaken by the Russian philosopher Valentin N. Vološinov. Vološinov's materialistic conception of language as sign-mediated social interaction is presented along with his semiotic theory of ideology (2.1). Both are directed against an objectivized as well as a subjectivistic conception and point to the sign community as the place in which linguistic interaction takes place. Vološinov has outlined the tasks confronting a pragmatically based theory of signs, ideology, language, and literature, and he has, in various respects, anticipated a pragmatic theory of texts.

The pragmatic philosophy of the late Ludwig Wittgenstein, the ordinary language philosophy deeply inspired by him, and speech act theory are discussed in the third chapter. The first section (3.1) is devoted to Wittgenstein's pragmatic language-game theory, which is shown as a breach with his early attempts to construct an ideal language. The later Wittgenstein's focus on ordinary language is then examined as aiming at a description of the multiplicity of language games and showing their interwovenness with the multiplicity of forms of life. I discuss Wittgenstein's explanation of meaning in terms of use as well as his concept of rules and grammar. I try to show that his rejection of reflection in the name of therapy and description leads to aporias in his concept of philosophy.

In 3.2, I sketch John L. Austin's approach to speech act theory. He is on the track of the double structure of language, which is later developed by John R. Searle in his systematic outline of speech act theory (3.3). From my point of view, Searle's conception, despite its significance for the formation of an encompassing pragmatic theory, runs into difficulties. They result from his semantically oriented self-understanding, which misses the fundamentally pragmatic structure of speech act theory. The following section (3.4) is devoted to Dieter Wunderlich's further development of speech act theory in the framework of linguistic pragmatics, in which he points to the historical, contextual, and sequential character of speech acts. Finally, in 3.5, I outline Utz Maas' theses about a reconstruction of speech act theory in terms of an action theory of language.

Chapter 4 focuses on the contribution of a pragmatic textual theory, in which I present Siegfried J. Schmidt's plan for a theory of texts. Schmidt locates his theory in the framework of what he calls communicative act games. Starting from Schmidt's departure at a pragmatically oriented theory of meaning, I highlight his category of communicative act game and discuss his concept of textuality and text. The importance of Schmidt's work lies in the fact that he points out the textuality of all linguistic action, which necessarily takes place by means of texts and thus requires a theory of texts as an indispensable element of a comprehensive pragmatic theory.

Karl-Otto Apel and Jürgen Habermas are dealt with in the following chapters. Apel's conception of transcendental pragmatics and Habermas' universal pragmatics are presented in chapters 5 and 6. In chapter 6, Karl-Otto Apel's transcendental pragmatics is unfolded as a reflection about the conditions of the possibility and validity of linguistic communication. I sketch Apel's claim to reach at a transformation of Kant's transcendental philosophy in terms of a transcendental linguistic pragmatics or transcendental semiotics. This transformed transcendental approach provides the philosophical foundations of any pragmatic theory. Starting from Apel's points of contact with the pragmatic semiotics of Peirce and Morris, the language-game model of the late Wittgenstein, and Austin's and Searle's speech act theory, I focus on Apel's criticism and further development of these positions in view of his transcendental pragmatic philosophy of the communication community. Apel's approach shows the synthetic power of bringing together important stages in the formation of a pragmatic theory.

Yet he is primarily devoted to reflection on the question of the conditions of the possibility and validity of communicative agreement, thus laying the foundations for pragmatic reflection.

While Apel directs every philosophical tendency on the royal highway of transcendental reflection, Habermas' approach tries to integrate the most diverse areas of scientific theory and philosophical reflection within an all-embracing theory of communicative action. The central core of this theory, from my point of view, is Habermas' universal pragmatics, aiming at an identification and subsequent reconstruction of the universal conditions of possible agreement, which unfolds the infrastructure of human action. I discuss Habermas' concept of action and especially the conditions of communicative action, the forms of colloquial communication, and the validity claims implied in speech. I focus on the task of universal pragmatics to reveal that the validity claims that are assumed in communicative action are at the same time universal conditions of possible understanding. I want to reconstruct them as providing the normative foundation of interaction by which factual interaction and norms of interaction are assessed, criticized, and challenged. Habermas' theory is directed at the normative basis of the formation of a pragmatic theory. In this respect it shows a great deal of similarity with Apel's approach. Apel too claims to provide the foundations of pragmatic thinking, by transcendental reflection. Habermas claims to do this by scientific reconstruction. That is why these claims have to be confronted with one another.

In the concluding chapter, 7, I trace an integrative pragmatic theory with the confrontation of universal and transcendental pragmatics with regard to their claims to provide the foundations for pragmatics. In this, I propose a fundamental pragmatic theory that integrates the reflective elements of both universal and transcendental pragmatics, as a basis for the formation of a pragmatic theory by which Habermas' claim to identify and reconstruct the universal conditions of possible agreement can, in my view, most suitably be met. On this reflective and fundamental pragmatic basis that I elaborate, I then present the theory's elements and the areas of research that should result from my reconstruction of the history of the formation of a pragmatic theory. At the same time, I also integrate the elements into a coherent whole. Thus the logic of pragmatic thinking becomes evident.

My Afterword, written for the American edition, first summarizes the achievements or basic insights of pragmatic thinking. Then I deal with recent developments of pragmatic thinking, covering especially Apel's and Habermas' work in discourse ethics. Finally I address the challenges that the emergence of American neo-pragmatism poses to Apel and Habermas. I sketch some of the concerns of its representatives, who include Richard

Rorty, Richard Bernstein, and Cornel West. By either explicitly or more implicitly challenging a universal or transcendental pragmatic conception, they are themselves engaged in dealing with the characteristics, the elements, the shape, and the logic of pragmatic thinking.

# 1

# A Program of Pragmatically Integrated Semiotics: From Peirce to Morris

## 1.1 CHARLES SANDERS PEIRCE: SEMIOTICS AND PRAGMATISM

### 1.1.1 PEIRCE'S SEMIOTICS OF THE THREEFOLD RELATIONSHIP OF SIGNS

Charles Sanders Peirce, the founder of American pragmatism,[1] laid the foundation stone of the formation of a pragmatic theory by following and debating with Kant's transcendental philosophy.[2] Also, by defining his pragmatic maxim of the elucidation of meaning, he provided an impetus, on the one hand, for the "pragmatic movement in American philosophy"[3] and, on the other, for semiotics, which were increasingly becoming the basic theory of logic, language, and science. For a long time, the connection between pragmatism and semiotics in Peirce's work remained obscure, especially as he provided insufficient information about that connection himself.[4] This situation was rectified with the appearance of J. J. Fitzgerald's *Peirce's Theory of Signs as Foundation for Pragmatism*, in which the connection was systematically investigated. Following Fitzgerald, I shall explore the fundamental "interconnections"[5] between the two. I shall also follow Fitzgerald's way of proceeding, which corresponds closely to Peirce's own method, and look first at Peirce's semiotics and then at his pragmatism, turning finally to his doctrine of interpretants, in which the two are closely linked.

Peirce's theory of signs is set out in his three classes of signs (icon, index, and symbol), their relation to the three fundamental categories (firstness, secondness, and thirdness), and the three classes of interpretant (immediate, dynamic, and ultimate), which are related to the other two.

Peirce defines a sign as "anything which is related to a Second thing, its Object, in respect to a Quality, in such a way as to bring a Third thing, its Interpretant, into relation to the same Object, and that in such a way as to

bring a Fourth into relation to that Object in the same form, *ad infinitum*"
(2.92).[6] Elsewhere, he says that the sign has "as such, three references: first,
it is a sign to some thought which interprets it; second, it is a sign for some
object to which in that thought it is equivalent; third, it is a sign, in some
respect or quality, which brings it into connection with its object" (5.283).
References to "medium," "object," and "interpretant" constitute the sign as
a "triadic relation"[7] to an object in a definite sense with regard to an
interpreter. This threefold dimension is constitutive for every sign as a sign,
and Peirce establishes this principle with his three fundamental categories.
As an "illustration" of these, he "performed a 'transcendental deduction' of
three types of signs parallel with the three kinds of inferences . . . in the
sign-relation (semiosis) as provisionally the 'highest point' of his 'transcendental logic.'"[8]

The controversy about the status of Peirce's doctrine of categories thus
comes into contact with the foundations of semiotics. There is general
agreement among those who have attempted to interpret Peirce's teaching
that, in his dispute with the Kantian transcendental deduction of the table of
categories, he transcendentally deduces—and especially in his "New List of
Categories" (1.545–1.559), published in 1867—the three fundamental categories of knowledge (quality, relation, and representation).[9] What is, however, still disputed is whether, in the deduction based on the logic of relations
that he makes later in "One, Two, Three: Fundamental Categories of
Thought and of Nature" (1.369–72 and 1.376–78), he definitively replaces
the first three categories or whether this is an attempt to go beyond both by
means of a phenomenological foundation.[10] On the one hand, there is the
aporia of a phenomenological foundation, and, on the other, the insufficiency
of a failure to find a justification in favor of a pragmatic verification. In view
of these two factors, I would, with Apel, insist on both the necessity and the
possibility of a justification in the logic of relations of the categories that can
be illustrated phenomenologically. This is provided for Peirce in the formal
structure into which he is able to integrate completely every possible (sign)
relation and by means of which he is in a position to prove the irreducibility
and sufficiency of the triadic relation. The fact that the doctrine of categories
is verified in the analysis of phenomena is based on the adequacy of the logic
of relations.

Logic, Peirce claims, is "another name for semiotic . . . the quasi-
necessary, or formal, doctrine of signs" (2.227). He defines logic as "the
science of the general necessary laws of Signs and especially of Symbols"
(2.93). A formal doctrine of signs, which defines the general necessary laws of
those signs, can, however, be found in Peirce's doctrine of the three fundamental categories.

Peirce makes a distinction between three categories of firstness, secondness, and thirdness as the "three kinds of elements that attentive perception can make out in the phenomenon" (8.265) (phenomenological access). He also defines them as the conditions of the possibility of analyzing processes of perception, knowledge, and interpretation as sign processes. They are abstractions from the totality of these processes in the sense of an abstractive and generalizing analysis into constitutive elements. It is important to consider these three categories separately now.

"Category the First is the Idea of that which is such as it is, regardless of anything else. That is to say, it is a Quality of Feeling" (5.66). For Peirce, firstness is the dominant element in phenomena to which we apply the idea of freshness, life, and freedom, because it denotes spontaneity without relationship. Firstness is a pure quality, applied to the consciousness. It is pure feeling and pure possibility. Peirce speaks in this context of "may be" (1.304), which is thought of as not yet embodied in reality or as an abstraction from a material manifestation in something that goes together with secondness.

"Category the Second is the Idea of that which is such as it is as being Second to some First, regardless of anything else, and in particular regardless of any Law, although it may conform to a law. That is to say, it is Reaction as an element of the Phenomenon" (5.66). Elements which are as they are in relation to a Second, but are independent of a Third, are seen by Peirce as to be demonstrated in the "otherness" (1.296) of conflict, action and reaction, cause and effect, and crude violence. Secondness as a collision represents one aspect of secondness. Its other manifestation, which is related to the first, in Peirce's opinion, is the existence of the individual in the concrete. Peirce wrote in a letter to William James that the category of secondness was "an experience. It comes out most fully in the shock of reaction between ego and non-ego" (8.266).

Connected with the concrete individual is the Here and Now, the presence of what is experienced at the moment as abstracted from history and as distinct from the "may be" or the "might be" (1.304) of the pure possibility, in other words, that which "happens to be" (6.367), the factual existence of that which is such as it is as distinct from and in opposition to that which is different.

"Category the Third is the Idea of that which is such as it is as being a Third, or Medium, between a Second and its First. That is to say, it is Representation as an element of the Phenomenon" (5.66). Phenomena in which this category of thirdness appears are those implying representation, universality, continuity, and law. Firstness is pure quality and pure possibility, and secondness is experience, factual existence, and reality. Thirdness, however, is concept and necessity. It is analogous to the "might be" and the "happens to be" and is the "would be" of "what would, in the long run, occur under certain circumstances" (6.327).

Why are these three fundamental categories both sufficient and necessary for an analysis of all phenomena and for the determination of the process of signs? Peirce's answer to this question is: "It is a priori impossible that there should be an indecomposable element which is what it is relatively to a second, a third and a fourth. The obvious reason is that which combines two will by repetition combine any number" (1.298). In other words, relationships in any grade of complexity can be formed from dyads and triads, although these cannot, for their part, be reduced either to each other or to another.[11] The fruitfulness of the approach based on the logic of relations can be seen in an analysis of the sign process. Peirce's subdivision of signs "in terms of the categories involved"[12] into three classes—icon, index, and symbol—points clearly to the phenomenological relevance of basing semiotics on the logic of relations.

Peirce defines the icon as a category in the following way: "An Icon is a Representamen whose Representative Quality is a Firstness of it as a First. That is, a quality that it has qua thing renders it fit to be a representamen" (2.276). It is a sign "which refers to the object that it denotes merely by virtue of characters of its own" (2.247), that is, *qua* similarity (see 3.362) between the bearer of the sign and the object denoted.[13] Peirce's examples of icons are portraits or diagrams. On the basis of what is conventionally involved in them, it is clear that these are not purely iconic, and this in itself indicates that there are in reality no pure icons. "In terms of the categories, an icon is a First, and firstness is only an aspect of the phaneron. There are no pure firsts in existence."[14]

Peirce goes on to define the index as a category in the following way: "An Index, or Seme . . . is a Representamen whose Representative character consists in its being an individual second" (2.283). He makes a distinction between genuine indices and indexically employed linguistic signs. Indices are signs that direct attention toward the objects (see 2.285), with which they have either an existential relationship or a relationship that is mediated by rules and conventions. (These are degenerated indices as indexical symbols.)

Finally, Peirce defines the symbol as a category as follows: "A Symbol is a law, or regularity of the indefinite future" (2.293). A law is for its part thirdness. As distinct from both the icon and the index, the symbol is only connected with its object by an "association of ideas or habitual connections" (1.369). As a third, it is abstract and universal. Insofar as it can be applied to much that is individual and can incorporate itself into it, it also implies secondness and firstness, since thirdness does not exist without a quality that can manifest itself as a possibility and a fact of incorporation.

A sign "stands for something" (1.339) that it denotes, its object. It is a sign of that object in relation to an interpreter of the sign, on whom it has an effect by producing or modifying an "idea." The effect produced by the sign process, the triadic semiosis (see 5.848), in the interpreter Peirce calls the interpretant. An interpretant must, if it is to be a sign that is capable of interpretation, be produced triadically. It is in any case not necessarily a sign (see 8.332). Peirce requires the interpretant as a sign to be related to the object in the same way as the sign itself (see 2.303). This points to the possibility of an infinite process of interpretation, in which the interpretant is related to the object in the same perspective as the sign, the interpretant of the interpretant as the interpretant and the sign, and so on *ad infinitum*.

Peirce also attempts to specify the possible effect on an interpreter. To do this, he introduces a subdivision of the interpretant into the immediate, the dynamic, and the ultimate. The immediate is "the interpretant as it is revealed in the right understanding of the Sign itself" (4.536), "the Quality of the Impression that a sign is fit to produce, not . . . in any actual reactions" (8.315). This immediate interpretant, then, is the quality of the impression made by the sign, that which is immediately produced by the sign, and at the same time also the ability of the sign itself to be interpreted, the possibility of its "interpretability,"[15] quite apart from any interpreter in the concrete.

Unlike the immediate, the dynamic interpretant is "the actual effect which the Sign, as a Sign, really determines" (4.536). Peirce subdivides the dynamic interpretant into the emotional, the energetic, and the logical.[16] The real effect of the dynamic interpretant, then, is differentiated into "the first proper significate effect of a sign . . . a feeling produced by it," a "feeling of recognition" that is equal to the emotional interpretant (5.475), the effect in form of a muscular or spiritual activity produced by the sign that is equal to the energetic interpretant, and finally effect as the production of a new sign that is equal to the logical interpretant. The last of these, which at the same time points to the possibility of an infinite semiosis, represents, at the level of secondness, a transition in the direction of the ultimate interpretant. The latter is that "which would finally be decided to be the true interpretation if consideration of the matter were carried so far that an ultimate opinion were reached" (8.184). It is not a real effect, but one that the sign would produce in any understanding if the process of interpretation were continued for long enough. This interpretant does not represent a sign that is included within the process of infinite semiosis. On the contrary, it prepares the way for the process of interpretation to reach a definitive end, which consists in the formation of that habit of behavior that is not factual (secondness) but normatively correct (thirdness), and to which a process of interpretation that brings itself to an end would lead. It is not possible to decide definitively whether this normatively correct "habit" is acquired in individual cases, because each interpretant that is factually formed as a non-ultimate and definitive logical interpretant can always be called into question again in the course of any subsequent interpretation. To that extent, then, a fallibility that is critical of meaning is constitutive for Peirce's understanding of the problem. In this, he dissociates himself from a fallibility that is universally critical by rejecting as meaningless the question as to whether there can be true knowledge, as such, of a reality existing as being in itself, and replacing it by the question about reality as the factor that is obviously in accordance with the consensus of the "community of investigators" in the "ultimate opinion" (see 5.407f.).[17]

### 1.1.2   THE "PRAGMATIC MAXIM" AS THE DETERMINING FACTOR IN THE DIRECTION FOLLOWED BY PEIRCE'S PRAGMATISM

The concept of the "habit" of behavior occupies a central position in Peirce's pragmatism or pragmaticism, as he began to call his method of elucidation of meaning from 1904 onwards. In 1877, in "The Fixation of Belief" (5.358–5.387), a work that helped lay the foundations of pragmatism, he took everyday linguistic usage as his point of departure and insisted that we always distinguish between a state of conviction and one of doubt and tend to move from the second, insofar as it occurs, to the first. We strive to reach a state "of there being established in our nature some habit which will determine our actions" (5.371). The aim of our inner struggle against doubt, which ends when that doubt ceases, Peirce claims, is to acquire an opinion in the sense of a firm conviction as the basis for our future behavior. There may be different methods leading to the establishment of a conviction,[18] but only the method of (experimental) science can in the long run provide the certainty of conviction that is based on reality. That method must be founded on a continuous process of research that will bring everyone's experiences together in "the one true conclusion" (5.384).

In "How to Make Our Ideas Clear" (5.388–5.410), published in 1878 and described by one scholar as one of the "birth certificates" of pragmatism,[19] Peirce considers conviction that is oriented toward behavior in terms of meaning. Because, in his view, the only function of thought is to establish modes of behavior and action, we merely have to determine what modes of behavior a thought produces in order to develop the meaning of that thought, since what an object means consists simply in the modes of behavior that it involves. This leads Peirce to the view that there is no distinction of meaning "so fine as to consist in anything but a possible difference of practice" (5.400). In the following well-known definition of the pragmatic maxim, the rule is: "Consider what effects, that might conceivably have practical bearings, we conceive the object of our conception to have. Then, our conception of these effects is the whole of our conception of the object" (5.402).

In opposition to a verificatory interpretation of this maxim, which takes as its point of departure an assumed equation of convictions as "habits of action" with observable behavior, and regards this as an early version of the verification principle, Fitzgerald appeals to a later self-interpretation by Peirce, and objects that Peirce in fact never identified habits of behavior and convictions with observable behavior.[20] He insists that Peirce's concept of action, in which thought is implied—"thought is essentially an action" (5.397)—shows that convictions as "habits of action" cannot be reduced to what is externally perceivable. The concept of sense perception, in Fitzgerald's opinion, has to be approached within the framework of Peirce's theory of reality as knowable, in the sense of a result of research undertaken by the unlimited community of investigators in the light of judgments made about perception that form part of that process.

In his lectures on pragmatism given in 1902, Peirce proposed a revised understanding of the pragmatic maxim: "Pragmatism is the principle that every theoretical judgment expressible in a sentence in the indicative mood is a confused form of thought whose only meaning, if it has any, lies in its tendency to enforce a corresponding practical maxim expressible as a conditional sentence having its apodosis in the imperative mood" (5.18). What is important here in comparison with the definition of 1878 is the restriction to theoretical judgments, which presupposes a distinction that was not present in the earlier formulation between "theoretical" and "practical."[21]

Pragmatism as a theory of meaning, then, is the object of logic, and Peirce defines the place of the latter in his construction of a system of sciences. In that system, philosophy is a branch of the theoretical sciences and is divided into three fields—phaneroscopy or phenomenology, normative science, and metaphysics. Normative science, "which investigates the universal and necessary laws of the relation of Phenomena to Ends" (5.121), is further subdivided into aesthetics, ethics, and logic. It is in the relationships between these three branches of science, Peirce says, that "we begin to get upon the trail of the secret of pragmatism" (5.130). He claims that logic is based on ethics, which is in turn based on aesthetics, and both are related to an ultimate aim or ideal which they have in common (see 5.130). Insofar as this is the case, he concludes, with regard to pragmatism, for which the meaning of a symbol is to be found in "how it might cause us to act" (5.135), that this or that aim exists, but that he has "to inquire what an ultimate aim, capable of being pursued in an indefinitely prolonged course of action, can be" (5.135). This aim exists as an unchangeable reality because it is otherwise not ultimate, and it "should accord with the development of the agent's own esthetic quality" (5.136), "the development of concrete reasonableness" (5.3), toward which we move in hope and strive in research—the rationalization of the universe.

In the "whetstone theses" of the 1903 lecture on pragmatism, Peirce poses the question of central importance, concerning the relationship between judgment about perception and abductive conclusion, as the process in which an explanatory hypothesis on the basis of the supposition "that something might be" (5.171) is formed. He answers this question by suggesting that what is *in sensu*, that is, a judgment about perception, is, insofar as it always contains universal elements, that is, by virtue of its character as interpretation, an extreme case of abductive conclusion. The judgment about perception therefore comes, on the basis of the supposition "that something might be," to the conclusion which is mediated by interpretation of the phenomena that there is something definite that is, unlike the abductive conclusion, absolutely certain for it.

Following the "whetstone theses," Peirce completes his identification of pragmatism with the logic of abduction by showing that the pragmatic maxim, "which only proposes a certain maxim, must render needless any further rule as to the admissibility of hypotheses to rank as hypotheses." Also, because "nothing but such considerations has any logical effect or import whatever" (5.196), the whole field of admissible hypotheses, which means also that of the logic of abduction, can be included in this.

As part of his preparation for a discussion of the purpose of abduction, Peirce sets out three conditions for good, meaningful abduction: 1) it must explain the facts; 2) it must lead to the establishment of a habit of positive expectation that is exempt from disappointment; and 3) it must be accessible to experimental verification. In the case of this third condition, it should be borne in mind that verification is not limited for Peirce to what can be or is perceived by the senses, especially since this implies not only secondness but also thirdness. This leads him to observe that the pragmatic maxim "ought to take a satisfactory attitude toward the element of thirdness" (5.206). There are three possible positions for the recognition of thirdness: 1) it should not be experimentally verifiable; 2) it should be experimentally verifiable but not directly perceptible; 3) it can be directly perceived. Of these three positions, Peirce finds only the third acceptable, because only it recognizes that laws are active in reality, and thirdness cannot simply be regarded as effective only in abduction, which would create a deep gulf between reality and our knowledge of reality. This gulf is prevented from occurring if the third position is accepted. That position combines the reality and perceptibility of thirdness. Its maxim is: "The elements of every concept enter into logical thought at the gate of perception and make their exit at the gate of purposive action; and whatever cannot show its passports at both these two gates is to be arrested as unauthorized by reason" (5.212).

### 1.1.3   THE DOCTRINE OF INTERPRETANTS AND PRAGMATISM

According to Peirce, pragmaticism[22] is a "method of ascertaining the meanings of words and concepts" (5.465). It maintains "that the total meaning of the predication of an intellectual concept is contained in an affirmation that, under all conceivable circumstances of a given kind . . . the subject of the predication would behave in a certain general way" (5.467). If these claims are valid, then "the problem of what the 'meaning' of an intellectual concept is can only be solved by the study of the interpretants, or proper significance effects, of signs" (5.475). The interpretant is "the proper significance outcome of a sign" (5.473).

In his subdivision of interpretants and his discussion of them, Peirce regards the status of the logical interpretant as particularly important in that it acts as a bridge between the doctrine of interpretants and pragmatism. If the logical interpretant were an intellectual sign, it would also have to have a logical interpretant itself. It would therefore be drawn into the process of infinite semiosis and would consequently not be able to represent the ultimate logical interpretant of the sign. A "mental effect" completing the process of interpretation "that is not a sign, but is of general application, is a habit-change" (5.476). A change in habits of behavior, however, can only be brought about in three ways. It can take place 1) by new experiences enforced on the intellect, 2) by repeated muscular activity, or 3) by mental trial and error.

By what, however, are logical interpretants developed? Peirce provides a description of the process of their formation which leads him, via conjectures based on judgments about perception (the first logical interpretant) and thought experiments constructed on that basis, to a modification of the interpreter's consciousness, for which the logical interpretant, as a triadic factor, produces "at least, in all cases, a sufficiently close analogon" (5.485). The conditions of universality and conditionality that are valid for logical interpretants are only fulfilled precisely by habit. "Therefore there remains only habit, as the essence of the logical interpretant" (5.486). The fact that a habit is universal as the disposition to act in a certain way under certain conditions (and not as actual behavior as secondness) is the result of its belonging to the category of thirdness. The fact, moreover, that a habit is conditional is connected with the fact that it comes into play under certain conditions. (If this or that is the case, it comes into operation.) Finally, it is not in any sense necessary for every habit to be the result of a process of investigation or research (the ultimate logical or definitive interpretant is bound to be the one that will suggest itself as the result of the continuous process of research conducted by the "community of investigators"), but this scientific process undoubtedly leads to a series of habits, and in this follows a path that corresponds to the non-scientific process of habit-formation (thought experiments, the formation of hypotheses, and "verification" in the judgment of perception). Peirce is therefore able to conclude: "The real and living logical conclusion" (reached as the result of experiments in the inner world) "is that habit; the verbal formulation merely expresses it."

The concept, Peirce continues, "somewhat partakes of the nature of a verbal definition and is as inferior to the habit, and much in the same way, as a verbal definition is inferior to the real definition. The deliberately formed, self-analyzing habit—self-analyzing because formed by the aid of analysis of the exercises that nourished it—is the living definition, the verifiable and final logical interpretant" (5.491).[23] This "final logical interpretant," as the normatively correct effect in all interpreters, consists in the habit that is aimed at in the course of an unlimited process of research undertaken by the unlimited "community of investigators," both consensually and at the same time with an adequate interpretation of the facts in view, within a coherent framework of interpretation. It is worth noting in this context that this adequate interpretation is what Apel calls the aspect of the evidence of correspondence.[24]

What has to be kept strictly separate from this is the factual habit-formation (at the level of non-ultimate logical interpretant) which is achieved in various ways in the process of research and investigation, and which can be withdrawn to the "would be" that aims at the normatively correct and be carried further in the process of continued criticism of the norm of the counter-factual. Peirce does not, then, reduce the ultimate logical interpretant to factual dispositions of behavior and habits that can be observed. On the contrary, he sees habit-forming interpretation as normative in the sphere of ultimately valid interpretation within the unlimited community of interpretation functioning as a regulating principle. This is in accordance with his idea of a fallibility that is critical of meaning, in the light of which any factually formed habit can be criticized.

At the level that he had reached in his writings by 1907, Peirce had come to identify the explanation of meaning that he had been aiming at, in his pragmatic maxim, with the pragmatic peak of three-dimensional semiotics via the doctrine of interpretation in the ultimate logical interpretant. In the light of this, it is justifiable to ask with Fitzgerald whether the pragmatic effect constitutes the entire meaning of an intellectual concept, as several of Peirce's statements would seem to indicate.[25] Peirce made a distinction "between that which a term *nominat*—its logical breadth—and that which it *significat*—its logical depth" (5.471). On the basis of this, Fitzgerald has suggested, a distinction can be made between "pragmatic meaning" and "internal" or "iconic meaning" or "significance."[26] It is also possible to say that the pragmatic meaning presupposes an internal meaning and consequently that, without internal meaning, there can be no pragmatic meaning. Whereas there are signs, however, such as works of art, that have no pragmatic meaning, intellectual concepts are bound to have one. Internal meaning (or significance) therefore has priority over pragmatic meaning and, what is more, it has priority because, as the meaning of symbols, the pragmatic meaning is based on the presence of an icon, which is the foundation of the internal meaning. The priority of internal meaning is rooted in the process of elaboration of the ultimate logical interpretant, with the aid of thought experiments that are carried out "in terms of icons."[27] It is also rooted in the necessity of iconic meaning for the intercommunication between members of the unlimited community of investigators.

This priority of internal meaning can be regarded as a marking off of the space available to possible pragmatic meaning or as a drawing of frontiers for the territory of interpretation as an objective frame of reference. It also refers to the explanation of pragmatic meaning within the boundaries marked off by the previously given objective frame of reference—and it is precisely here that, in the sense of the theory of truth, the aspect of the evidence of correspondence and of a consensus theory of truth which is stressed by Peirce, whereas it is not by Habermas,[28] is found. At the same time, this priority also opens a space for the process of interpretation which can be used for the elaboration of the meaning that is relevant to the object and, at the same time, normatively correct in the consensual exploration of those habits of behavior and action to which such interpretation is ultimately bound to lead. In this, what has to be retained is the aspect of the normative correctness of habits with regard to all factually oriented and functioning ones, which is directed toward the consensus of the unlimited community of research and investigation or the unlimited communication community that includes the community of research. These factually oriented and functioning habits have to be measured against that normative correctness, and, subject to the conditions of an explanation of meaning based on an objective frame of reference and oriented toward the consensus of the unlimited communication community, they can be formed within the framework of an adequate linguistic system.

## 1.2 THE RECEPTION OF PEIRCE'S IDEAS BY AMERICAN PRAGMATISM

In the foregoing sections, I used Peirce's doctrine of interpretants to outline the fundamental aspects of his pragmatic theory of semiotics of the three-dimensional character of the relationship of signs in its combination of the theory of signs and pragmatism as a theory of meaning. Before going on to consider what Apel has called Morris' "program of pragmatically integrated semiotics,"[29] I would like to outline how Peirce's teaching was received by American pragmatism. The principal figures in this movement are William James, John Dewey, Josiah Royce, and George Herbert Mead. Within the context of my study, the only really relevant factor is how these thinkers assimilated Peirce's ideas and what new points of view they introduced.

## 1.2.1 WILLIAM JAMES

After dedicating his collection of essays, *The Will to Believe*, to Peirce, who was at the time of their publication almost completely unknown, William James went on to make pragmatism famous by his "California Address"[30] of 1898. In this lecture, he used the word "pragmatism" for the first time and called Peirce's "principle of practicalism—or pragmatism, as he called it . . . the clue or compass"[31] to his own thought. Referring to Peirce's "How to Make Our Ideas Clear," he introduced the latter's pragmatic maxim with the characteristic extension that "the effective meaning of any philosophical proposition can always be brought down to some particular consequence in our future practical experience."[32] The effect of the concept as actual, practical behavior, the effect, in other words, that can be experienced by the senses and verified in the reaction of the interpreter, is, in James' opinion, that with which pragmatism is sharply contrasted. In his lecture on pragmatism, he claimed that there is no logical connection between pragmatism and the "radical empiricism" that he had developed.[33] In saying this, especially in his pragmatic theory of truth, he was clearly including the pragmatic method, which as such achieves "no particular results,"[34] within his radically empirical conception, and in this way was moving toward a naturalistic and pluralistic view of pragmatism. He also had a strongly nominalistic and pluralistic orientation, and these two tendencies in his thinking led him to develop a theory of truth and meaning that differed widely from Peirce's.

In addition to this, James' pragmatism was less firmly based on a misunderstanding of Peirce's ideas than has been suggested.[35] It contains an independent conception, one source of which can be found in Peirce's work. James differs most clearly from Peirce in his reduction of truth to factual "veri-fication"[36] and of meaning to perceptible behavior that is effective in practice and in the subjectivistic and relativistic consequences of empiricism. Apart from the world views of subjects guided by the "will to believe," which continue to gain ground and become practically effective in action,[37] there is no objective criterion of the truth of their convictions and the correctness of their behavior. All that can be regarded as true and right is what is verified in the struggle of truths. Peirce protested against this in the name of his normative theory of truth, which criticizes both the reduction of meaning to factual effectiveness in behavior and action and the reduction of truth to factual validity.[38]

James' pragmatism, then, can be described as following the pragmatic maxim of Peirce in its empirical reduction and therefore as non-semiotic and reduced, from Peirce's view, to two-dimensionality. It remained decisive and most influential in the decades that followed.

## 1.2.2 JOHN DEWEY

John Dewey defined pragmatism as "the doctrine that reality possesses practical character and that this character is most efficaciously expressed in the function of intelligence."[39] In this, he is clearly referring to both Peirce and James. He is oriented toward the first especially with regard to his logic of research, and toward the second in respect of his theory of truth. The form of pragmatism that Dewey developed can be described as instrumentalism. It implies, in particular, questions about value. In this, it is characteristically distinct from the pragmatism of the other American members of the movement.

Dewey, who was described as "the most outstanding axiologist of the pragmatic movement,"[40] provides with his doctrine of the practical character of reality a conception of pragmatism as a theory of actual reality that goes beyond Peirce's and James' methodical pragmatism. He comes to this view of reality by evolving a naturalistic theory in which the objects that are known and are to be known are constructed and reconstructed. This theory includes pragmatism, with a conscious renunciation of ultimate aims of action and definitive statements, within a "means-and-ends continuum" as leading to action. In this way, situations that have become problematical are transformed into situations that are no longer so, that is, situations in which practical action is not frustrated.[41]

This situational determination of theory, ethics, and teaching is certainly closely related to Peirce's *The Fixation of Belief* and his "critical logic," and takes its methodical apparatus from Peirce. The emphasis on the dynamic creativity of the problematical situation itself, however, in which the principles have to be developed in debate with it,[42] restricts Peirce's normative logic of research to processes of adaptation that are related to the situation and therefore revert from thirdness to secondness. Dewey undoubtedly makes a distinction that is comparable to Peirce's between "experience" and "knowledge,"[43] but, despite this, because he fails to recognize the necessity of a normative foundation for the process of research, he eliminates what has to be counterfactually postulated as true or correct.

Dewey therefore relates pragmatism to the satisfaction of actual and "natural" needs. The pragmatist, in the "creative valuation" of these natural needs, has a "mediation of impulse"[44] by means of thought as "reflection upon the way in which to use impulse to renew disposition and recognize habit,"[45] and should use this as a contribution to the creative growth of human possibilities and, ultimately, also to reality itself. The question of the ultimate aim is not involved in this process: "Not perfection as a final goal, but the everenduring process of perfecting, maturing, refining is the aim in living. Growth itself is the only moral 'end.'"[46] Ideas play a part in this process, functioning as plans of action,[47] and they can be verified in the ways in which those actions are carried out in order to solve problems. This means that, in Dewey's as in James' pragmatism, truth is determined by the situation. A judgment is true if it is a judgment of fact, goodness, or praxis that is related to concrete action and directs that action correctly. "Correctly" here means in accordance with the goal that is aimed at, and is constituted in the reconstruction of the situation itself in experience enforced by the failed action.[48] This initiative, based on the "control of ideas by facts,"[49] has obviously to be regarded, in contrast with Peirce's pragmatism, the three-dimensional semiotics of which is not accepted by Dewey, as a naturalistic reduction to factual existence (secondness) and an elimination of thirdness together with its normative implications.

The enormous influence that Dewey exerted, in his almost seventy years of research and teaching, on the pragmatic movement as a whole and on Morris in particular is sufficient justification for this outline of the essential theses found in his instrumental pragmatism.

### 1.2.3   JOSIAH ROYCE

In the second volume of his late work, *The Problem of Christianity*, Josiah Royce provided in 1913 a philosophy of interpretation which, although it was inspired by and conceived in terms of Hegelian idealism, contains astonishing parallels with Peirce's pragmatism. It is also an independent continuation of Peirce's work, which is why it has been accredited with the paradoxical subtitle "Idealistic Pragmatism."[50] Royce himself describes his own dialectical position, which in fact amounts to what has been called "an attempt at a synthesis of absolutism and pragmatism,"[51] as "absolute pragmatism."[52] In this synthesis, he combines an idealistic insistence on the existence of the absolute—which establishes reality, recognizes *totum simul*,[53] and interprets and therefore guarantees truth—with a pragmatic theory of the subject, society, and history as an infinite process of interpretation that culminates, in the unlimited community of interpretation, in the absolute.

Royce's theory, moreover, is clearly oriented toward Peirce's theory of signs. He takes over the latter's theory of the triadic sign process and thereby sees the subject as constituted by interpretation[54] and society as a synchronic, but history as a diachronic community of interpretation. In this, the present self, or the contemporary interpreters in all three dimensions, interpret the past with the future in view. This enables him to make "a hermeneutic transformation," "which took Peirce's semiotics as its starting point."[55] Taking Peirce's central theory of knowledge, that "interpretation always involves a relation of three terms,"[56] he provides a critique of the "dualistic view of the cognitive process,"[57] which, using the formal dichotomy of "perception" and "conception," he regards as determinative for the whole philosophical tradition, including James' version of pragmatism.[58] This critique is based on Royce's introduction of a third class of processes of knowledge that combines the other two, the processes of interpretation.

Royce clarifies the need for these processes by his "banknote parable." The cash value (which is analogous to "perception") corresponding to the nominal value (which is analogous to "conception"), in the case of exchange into foreign currency, is not directly convertible into an equal cash value, but has to be found interpretatively by means of a "process of interpreting the cash values"[59] on the basis of the relationship between the nominal and the cash value that is in force in the country in question.

Sign-mediated processes of interpretation not only bridge the gap between the "perceptions" and the "conceptions" of individual knowledge. They also constitute a community—the "community of interpretation," as Royce calls it.[60] This community is manifested both in the "community of scientific observers"[61] and in the human community of interpretation as a whole. It is present both synchronically and diachronically and combines the two communities, forming them into a "world of interpretation."[62] Royce insists that "an interpretation is real only if the appropriate community is real, and is true only if that community reaches its goal."[63] The reality and truth of interpretation, Royce believes, are guaranteed in the access of what is real to the unlimited community of interpretation, which will take the world as a whole as an "indefinitively complex Sign"[64] to its ultimate and definitive interpretation. Royce is consequently able to define his fundamental thesis in the following way: "The world is an interpretation of the problem which it presents."[65] This means that he is only able to see the unlimited community of interpretation as something real and effective in the mirror of divine interpretation, because he has no concept of habit analogous to Peirce's that enables him to express the possible realization of a definitive interpretation. He is prevented from achieving this by his idealism, which was already criticized by Peirce in the latter's assessment of *The Religious Aspect of Philosophy*. That idealism is so concentrated on thirdness, Peirce claims, that, like Hegel, Royce, "almost altogether ignores the Outward Clash."[66] What is of fundamental and lasting importance in Royce's philosophy of interpretation for the formation of a pragmatic theory is his social and historical reshaping of Peirce's semiotics in a hermeneutically oriented, triadic understanding of subject, society, and history.

## 1.2.4 GEORGE HERBERT MEAD

According to Morris, George Herbert Mead "provided a matrix for a significant expansion of pragmatism in the form of the 'philosophy of the act.'"[67] His "constructive pragmatism"[68] is to be found above all in his writings on social philosophy and psychology, and especially in the arguments that he used in *Mind, Self, and Society* against Watson's behaviorism.[69]

He is strongly oriented towards James' and Dewey's concept in his questioning of the theory of truth and science,[70] but he also develops an independent theory of identity and roles in which he outlines the emergence of the self as the bearer of identity from interaction in society. He uses Dewey's theory of the correlativity of stimulus and reaction[71] and James' distinction between "I" and "Me" as a means of describing the two aspects of discriminated personal existence.[72] In this way, he arrives at his own conception of the Ego that constitutes a person's identity by means of assuming the role of the other, to the extent of the "'generalized other' as the attitude of 'the whole community.'"[73]

Mead presents the intersubjective constitution of identity arising from interaction as a "process of self-conditioning"[74] that develops via the "significant symbol" of "vocal gesture."[75] In the process, the Ego implicitly causes the same reaction in itself, by means of the "vocal gesture", that it would cause explicitly in any *alter*, and can decide, in anticipation of the reactive attitude that would occur in an *alter*, to react in that way. The special importance of the vocal stimulus lies in the fact "that the individual can hear what he says and in hearing what he says is tending to respond as the other person responds."[76] It is by "vocal gestures," then, that we take "the attitude of the other persons into our own conduct."[77] This means that language is the social mechanism with which a "universe of discourse," as a "system of common or social meanings," is created.[78] That "universe of discourse" will be meaningful and valid for all those who act, and what will be constituted in it is a common world, based on the structure of social activity in which those who are concerned will participate in the simultaneous acceptance of everyone's perspectives.

Mead calls the product of this process that is related to the Ego the "Me," to distinguish it from the "I" as the "individual reflection of the general systematic pattern of social or group behavior."[79] The "I" receives its form from the "Me" that is guided by conventions and attitudes and therefore expresses social control. In this way, the "I" represents individual reactions to the attitude of society and is therefore the place where institutionalized claims made on the individual can be broken, developed further, and ultimately transformed in a rejection of the assumption of roles. That is why "an aspect of innovation" forms part of the "I."[80]

Mead, however, undoubtedly neglected this creative aspect of the "I" to a very great extent in favor of what is contained in the "Me" in the assumption of institutionalized expectations of role. This neglect led him to make statements of the kind described by Goffman as ideals of "total institutions."[81] One such pronouncement, for example, is: "The unity and structure of the complete self reflects the unity and structure of the social process as a whole."[82]

Seen in the light of Peirce's teaching, Mead's quasi-behavioristic orientation in the direction of the secondness of the factual existence of society, in
the "Outward Clash" of the previously existing datum of the "generalized
other," becomes clear in the claims made by the "I" but dominated by that
datum. What is more, Mead's position, especially as taken further both in
Morris' behaviorism and in the action theory of symbolic interactionism,[83] is
ambivalent. This is evident from the fact that the interpretation of his theory
of self-consciousness as a reflective relationship with one's own possibilities
(which have to be explored in the thought experiment),[84] which has been
provided by Tugendhat and closely follows Peirce, has several points of
departure in his work. If we accept Mead's pragmatic understanding of the
objective relativism of the "philosophy of sociality,"[85] it is possible to give his
position a pragmatic foundation by means of a theory that merges perspectives as processes of social interchange in which signs are interpreted.

Agents should therefore be consensually in agreement with regard to the
perspectives that they would choose to accept as communal, regardless of their
distinctive individual perspectives. They should also agree about the modes of
action they would decide to follow with those perspectives in mind.[86]

Despite its ambivalent form, Mead's contribution is indispensable for any
pragmatic semiotics. Although it is basically a tendentiously behavioristic
reduction, it performs the valuable function of genetically extending Royce's
concept of the community of interpretation, and in this way it also describes
how the social process of the interpretation of signs emerges as the result of
interaction and comes about in cooperative action by means of the language
of gestures and sounds.[87]

## 1.3   CHARLES WILLIAM MORRIS'
BEHAVIORISTIC SEMIOTICS

### 1.3.1   THE PRAGMATIC MOVEMENT IN THE PERSPECTIVE
OF MORRIS' WORK: BEHAVIORISTIC SEMIOTICS
AS UNIFYING PRINCIPLE

In his fundamental work on the theory of signs, *Foundations of the Theory of
Signs*, Morris states clearly: "'Pragmatics' must . . . be distinguished from
'pragmatism' and 'pragmatical' from 'pragmatic.'"[88] His conscious choice of
the term "pragmatics" for "the science of the relation of signs to their
interpreters" as a branch of the discipline of semiotics, however, expresses an
intention to "signalize the significance of the achievements of Peirce, James,
Dewey, and Mead within the field of semiotic."[89] In his later works, he
discusses semiotics within its systematic context of the pragmatic movement,
and expresses the opinion that the function of behavioristic semiotics is to act
as the organon of that movement. He calls it the central, unifying principle of

the pragmatic movement and one of its most original contributions.[90] The other unifying themes are: 1) a theory of behavioristic investigation, 2) a consideration of axiology in terms of preferential behavior, and 3) the semiotic doctrine of the reality of possibility, existence, and law. Morris believes that, together with these other themes, the "central unifying principle" can integrate the movement as a whole and give it a specific philosophical orientation.[91] Morris describes this direction in bold outline as follows: from Peirce's metaphysical idealism via James' radical empiricism to the empirical naturalism of Dewey and Mead, with which Morris, on his own admission, is very closely linked.[92]

Morris regarded Peirce as the central figure in the history of semiotics. In his view, Peirce combined semiotics and pragmatism because he understood "that a sign gives rise to an interpretant and that an interpretant is in the last analysis a 'modification of a person's tendencies towards action.'"[93] This combination led Peirce to move tendentiously, Morris thought, in the direction of behavioristic semiotics. At the same time, however, he believed that Peirce's "metaphysical rationalism," which arose from his metaphysical trust in logic, prevented him from finding a consistently behavioristic explanation of the sign process. Peirce's account of sign is "embedded in the metaphysics of his categories . . . and in the metaphysics of his view of mind."[94] Insofar as it can be applied to scientific semiotics, Peirce's understanding as expressed in the concept of the interpretant could be stated in a behavioristic conception of the interpretant.

Both James and Dewey contributed significantly, in Morris' opinion, to the development of a pragmatic methodology of verification: James with his theory of truth, which is in principle semiotic, and Dewey with his theory of investigation. Together with Mead's theory of action, James' and Dewey's theories were, according to Morris, the supporting pillars of the pragmatic movement. In this, Mead consistently changed both James' and Dewey's methodologies of research and investigation, in his own theory of objective realism, into a theory of action, thus extending pragmatism to make it a "philosophy of the act."[95] Morris concludes that Mead's special contribution consisted in the emphasis that he gave to the fundamentally social character of non-linguistic and linguistic signs.[96] This emphasis, Morris thought, was compatible with Peirce's purely logical analysis. It validated that analysis genetically, making a scientific semiotic theory possible in its social and behavioristic understanding and in opposition to Peirce's idealism. On this basis, Morris set out to develop a behavioristic conception of semiotics.

### 1.3.2 MORRIS' CONCEPTION OF THREE-DIMENSIONAL SEMIOTICS AS BEHAVIORISM

In *Foundations of the Theory of Signs*, Morris outlines his behavioristic semiotics; he develops this approach in *Signs, Language, and Behaviour*, which Klaus has rightly called "a little encyclopaedia of neo-positivistic and behaviouristic linguistic philosophy."[97] All later research into semiotics has built extensively on Morris' teaching in this book, and all attempts to form a theory of semiotics have had to struggle with it. In his third and later work on semiotics, *Signification and Significance*,[98] Morris takes his semiotic beginnings further and makes a connection between his theory of signs and a theory of values.

In *Foundations of the Theory of Signs*, the author defines the framework, in categories of semiotics, as an empirical form of behaviorism and introduces the fundamental terminology. "Semiotic has a double relation to the sciences: it is both a science among the sciences and an instrument of the sciences."[99] As a science, it has two tasks. In the first place, it develops the foundations of every formal science. At the same time, it also has the function of uniting and integrating the sciences. It does this, on the basis of its behavioristic and biological orientation, by incorporating its own integrated disciplines of sociology, psychology, and the human sciences into the project of scientific integration. Semiotics also regards signs as functional in that it understands them as functioning within sign processes. The latter consist of three components: 1) the bearer of the sign or "sign vehicle," that is, that which brings about the sign; 2) the designate, that is, that to which the sign refers, what it signifies; and 3) the interpretant, that is, the effect that is brought about in an interpreter by the sign and through which the sign vehicle appears to the interpreter as a sign. If there is an element from among the class of objects that designates the sign to which it refers, then the sign also has a denotate in addition to a designate.

Several two-dimensional relationships, according to Morris, can be abstracted from the three-dimensional relationship of signs, consisting of the sign vehicle, the designate, and the interpreter.[100] These are: 1) "the relation of signs and the objects to which the signs are applicable" as the "semantical dimension of semiosis" that is investigated by semantics; 2) the "pragmatical dimension" of the "relation of signs to interpreters," that is, the dimension of the object of pragmatics; and 3) the "syntactical dimension" which is analyzed by syntactics, that is, the dimension of the "formal relation of signs to one another."[101]

These three aspects of semiotics can be divided, like the science of semiotics itself, into a pure and a descriptive sphere. Pure syntactics are the most highly developed branch of semiotics, thanks to the work done by Carnap in the field of logical syntax. According to Morris, pure syntactics have the task of investigating language as a multitude of objects which can be combined and from which statements, by means of rules of transformation, can be derived from given statements. Pure semantics, on the other hand, presuppose syntactics, but have to be abstracted from pragmatics. They have the task of elaborating the semantic rules as the conditions under which "a sign is applicable to an object or a situation."[102]

Finally, there are pure pragmatics. These aim to develop a language in which the pragmatic dimension of the sign process can be expressed as a theme. Their task is also to discover the "pragmatical rules," which "state the conditions in the interpreters under which the sign vehicle is a sign."[103] Descriptive syntactics, semantics, and pragmatics apply meta-linguistically formulated syntactical, semantical, and pragmatical rules to "concrete instances of signs."[104] Pure semiotics as meta-language provide the formal logical structure for the analysis of natural languages and for the construction of scientific languages. "Considered from the point of view of pragmatics, a linguistic structure is a system of behaviour,"[105] with which the speaker designates situations in his habitual usage and in this way disposes the interpreter (who may be himself or another person) to react to the sign. In the same way, "a language in the full semiotical sense of the term is any inter-subjective set of sign vehicles whose usage is determined by syntactical, semantical, and pragmatical rules."[106]

Morris, then, regards the intersubjectivity of the experience of the person using the sign as rooted in the form of his individual reaction to the sign. His use of the sign, moreover, is determined by that form of reaction and is always more or less intersubjectively established. For him, this means that the meaning of a sign is consequently always completely determined by the establishment of its rules of usage and that it will always be possible to ascertain that meaning by objective research and investigation. Because the concept "meaning" is so vague, Morris introduces the term "analysis of signs" for this behavioristic research.[107]

Apel has correctly pointed out that it is not possible to speak of pragmatically integrated semiotics in Morris' *Foundations*. This is, on the one hand, because the three aspects of semiotics are regarded by him as "equally legitimate points,"[108] and, on the other, because designation and denotation are "subsumed under the semantic relation without taking into account their dependence on the 'deixis.'"[109] Morris does, however, provide pragmatically integrated semiotics in his *Signs, Language, and Behaviour*, where he develops the three semiotic disciplines consistently within a study of semiotics that is orientated toward behaviorism. He describes pragmatics as "that portion of semiotic which deals with the origin, uses, and effects of signs within the behaviour in which they occur; semantics deals with the signification of signs in all modes of signifying; syntactics deals with combinations of signs without regard for their specific significations or their relation to the behaviour in which they occur."[110]

What Morris says in *Signs, Language, and Behaviour* marks an important difference from what he said previously in *Foundations*. In the first place, he stresses the extensive implications of pragmatics, which he sees as including the production, use, and reception of signs. Secondly, he enlarges the scope of semiotics. From having seen it before as a one-sided designative model, he now regards it as a science of the relation of signs to situations, embracing all modes of signification.

This science of signs is at the same time placed on a biological foundation. It is, in other words, developed scientifically within the framework of behaviorism. What disposes an organism to react behavioristically is valid as a sign. Morris differs from the earlier behaviorists, with their theories of substitute stimuli based on Pavlov's teaching,[111] in that he regards the sign of an object as a "preparatory stimulus" in the sense of a disposition on the part of an organism to react to a sign in a similar way, as that object itself would produce reactions. Morris consequently lists as conditions that have to be fulfilled for anything to be a sign: "If anything, A, is a preparatory stimulus which in the absence of stimulus objects initiating response-sequences of a certain behaviour-family causes a disposition in some organism to respond under certain conditions by response-sequences of their behaviour-family, then A is a sign."[112] Within the framework of semiotics as a part and organon of empirical behaviorism, then, Morris introduces the fundamental concepts of interpreter, interpretant, denotate, and significate. What he has in mind here is the behavior of an organism that, as the interpreter of a sign in its disposition to reactive behavior, denotes to the interpretant if its reaction-sequence can be concluded, something—the denotate—that is made possible by the fact that the sign signifies something, in other words, has a significate.[113]

As an integrative definition of the concept "language" on this basis, Morris names five criteria: 1) it is composed of four signs; 2) each sign has a corresponding signification for many different interpreters; 3) the signs that constitute a language have to be "comsigns," that is, they must have the same signification for the organism that produces them as they have for other organisms; 4) they must also be plurisituational, in other words, they must be able to refer to many different situations with the same signification; and finally, 5) they must constitute a system of mutually connected signs with restrictions of combination. Morris summarizes this definition in the terse sentence: "A language is a system of comsign-families."[114] He regards the concept "comsign" as analogous to Mead's "significant symbols."[115]

Morris understands the semantic dimension of the sign process as that of the signification of signs in all their modes of signification. At the same time, he also distinguishes, after the principal factors which become effective in the behavior of signs: 1) the environment in which the organism acts, 2) the needs of the organism, and 3) the way the organism reacts in order to satisfy those needs. Designative, appreciative, and prescriptive components of signification constitute, in accordance with the dominance of their appearance, the designative, the appreciative, and the prescriptive modes of signification.

Another mode of signification, according to Morris, is the formative mode. In that mode, signs which signify in the formative mode dominate signs which are composed of other signs and whose signification they modify.

There are also five sign elements in the classes of signs, which Morris classifies in accordance with their mode of signification. These are the identificators, which dispose the interpreter "to direct his responses to a certain spatial-temporal region";[116] the designators; the appreciators; the prescriptors; and the formators. These signs influence the behavior of their interpreter in different ways. The identificators determine the place toward which behavior is directed. The designators prepare that behavior for objects with definite characteristics. The appreciators draw attention to objects with their relevance for the needs of the organism in mind. The prescriptors reinforce tendencies to react with certain response-sequences rather than with others; and the formators, which modify the behavior that is signified by other signs through their logical connection, form the last class of signs. To these five classes of signs Morris adds a class of statements (ascriptors). He classifies the ascriptor statements, according to the mode of signification that is dominant in them, as designative, appreciative, prescriptive, and formative.

Apart from classifying signs according to their mode of signification, Morris also classifies them according to their primary usage. If they are employed for the purpose of information of the organism, he speaks of an informative use of signs. If they are used for the selection of privileged objects, their employment is valuative. When their primary task is to stimulate certain reactions or response-sequences, he calls that use incitive. Finally, signs are used systematically when their function is the organization of behavior in a determined whole that is brought about by signs.

Four kinds of adequacy correspond to these four primary uses of signs. Morris regards informative adequacy as the power of conviction, valuative adequacy as effectiveness, incitive adequacy as the power of persuasion, and systematic adequacy as correctness. He consequently sees the question of the truth and reliability of signs as a question as to whether or not the ascriptor in which the sign is employed denotes. If it does denote, then it represents a T-ascriptor. If the ascriptor does not denote, then it is called an F-ascriptor. There are, moreover, both T- and F-ascriptors in all four modes of signification.[117] In this way, Morris builds up an apparatus for his behavioristic semiotics. It is his development and application of this apparatus that I shall consider in the following section.

## 1.3.3 SEMIOTICS AS LOGIC—SEMIOTICS AS SCIENTIFIC DISCOURSE—APPLIED SEMIOTICS

The distinction found in the *Foundations* between pure and descriptive semiotics is explained in *Signs, Language, and Behaviour* as a distinction between semiotics as logic and semiotics as scientific discourse. In the case of the first, that is, semiotics as logic, Morris treats semiotics as the construction of a language on the basis of natural language in which sign processes are discussed.[118] In the case of the second, that is, semiotics as scientific discourse, Morris regards semiotics as the empirical research and investigation of a definite form of sign behavior which constitutes semiotics as a natural science of human behavior, and in which the categories that are made available by pure semiotics are employed.

In applied semiotics, the science of semiotics is used as an instrument and a technique "concerned with improvement of reading, speaking, individual and social health, educational techniques, and intercultural communication."[119]

Morris' classification of the specializations of language, which he called types of discourse, comes, in accordance with the status of their categories, within the sphere of pure semiotics. In other words, he regards the classification of specializations of language, and their illustration by types of discourse that are in fact available, as a descriptive semiotic contribution to the construction of pure semiotics. With the formal definition, which had still not been reached, of types of discourse which were possible in semiotics, pure semiotics were no longer dependent on the use of everyday material as illustrative examples.

Morris therefore believed that he was in a position to provide a pure semiotic logical structure of possible types of discourse. At the same time, however, he had to depend on examples of everyday language for illustrative material in order to confirm and amplify that structure empirically and descriptively. It was his aim to make himself independent of this kind of illustration as his research into pure semiotics progressed.

Morris succeeds in classifying types of discourse by combining the mode of signification that is dominant in each complex of signs with its primary use. This classification according to mode and usage has both the advantage of a quantitative analysis of the kinds of ascriptors that appear in a complex of signs and the advantage of a classification of types of discourse viewed in the perspective of their usage. The classification of types of discourse on the basis of this combination of mode and use provides Morris with sixteen specializations of language, which he illustrates by examples.[120] His sixteen principal types of discourse can accordingly be understood through other supplementary examples of types of discourse that are possible in semiotics. The aim of pure semiotics, as we have seen, is to define these types of discourse without depending on illustrations, and thus in terms of pure semiotics.

Morris includes scientific discourse together with the other types of discourse in his set of sixteen. What is clear from his discussion of this particular type of discourse as "the most specialized form of designative-informative discourse"[121] is his orientation toward a deductive and nomological model aiming at a unification of the sciences, including descriptive semiotics as a scientific discourse.

As a scientific discourse about legal, mythical, political, metaphysical, and other kinds of discourse, semiotics have a task of scientific description, that of the modes of signification and usages of signs that are in fact employed in those discourses. In that task of description, use is made of the classification of types of discourse established by pure semiotics.

Having defined Morris' aims in this way, I conclude with a summary of the status that he accords to semiotics. As pure, semiotics is concerned with the elaboration of the formative discourse of semiotics, of the terminology and methodology that embraces all semiotic disciplines, analyses of discourse, and applications, and has to be unified in a behavioristic language. As descriptive, semiotics investigates the specializations of language in the scientific discourse of semiotics. Finally, as applied, semiotics contributes with an educational intention to the improvement of scientific communication and to communication outside the sphere of science. It is "both a phase in the unification of science and an instrument for describing and furthering the unification of science."[122] As such, it integrates humanistics within its descriptive field, that is, the descriptive investigation of those types of discourse which constitute the humaniora.[123] Finally and for these reasons, "it is indeed a prologomena to any future philosophy, demanding that philosophy make clear the nature of its signs and the purpose of its discourse."[124]

### 1.3.4 APORIAS IN MORRIS' BEHAVIORISTIC SEMIOTICS

Morris' approach raises a number of questions pointing to at least five apparently insuperable difficulties. These are: 1) How can signs that do not bring about behavior that can be directly observed be explained in behavioristic categories? 2) How can Mead's explanation of the identity of the meaning of symbols be expressed behavioristically? 3) From what source can a behaviorist take the categories to distinguish between the significate and the denotate? 4) Can the questions about the truth and reliability of signs be satisfactorily answered within the framework of a behavioristic paradigm? Finally, 5) Can Morris adequately express the pragmatic dimension of the sign process? I will deal with each of these questions in turn.

1) Morris clearly introduces the concept of disposition in an attempt to overcome the difficulties presented by a form of behaviorism oriented exclusively toward the causal chain of stimulus and response, as an observable structure of effect, by interposing a mediating factor. This can be seen as a "logical construction consisting of intersubjectively observable data,"[125] and it should make clear the extent to which signs can be understood in the categories of behaviorist theory even if they do not bring about behavior that is directly reactive. They dispose us toward an attitude of response, and this

behavior is brought about subject to a number of additional conditions.

But this information does not provide us with any explanation. As such, a disposition, as a "mental" readiness to react, eludes all questioning by behaviorists.[126] It also lacks any kind of behavioristic criterion for ascertaining similar dispositions which should constitute the identity of meaning in anything different from the same behavior. In the case of the latter, however, the advantage of introducing the concept of disposition is lost. A failure to have recourse to the same behavior will inevitably result in the persistence both of the unanswerable behavioristic question regarding the criterion for ascertaining the identity of readiness to react and of the question concerning the criterion for ascertaining the identity of the meaning of signs.

2) Mead explains the identity of the meaning of symbols with the help of the concept of the intersubjectivity of expectations of behavior by all those who are potentially involved in the sign process. Morris, on the other hand, finds identity of meaning in the fact that the behavior that can be observed to follow the sign has the same form. The observer can measure the identity of meaning against the identity of form of the behavior of the interpreter of the sign. But in that case, against what can the interpreter himself measure that identity of meaning? According to Morris, he can only ascertain the identity of meaning if he adopts the standpoint of the observer. But will that standpoint be sufficient to enable him to ascertain that identity?

Morris reduces regularization to regularity[127] and believes that an instance for the ascertainment of rules for behavior mediated by signs can be found in the observation of regularity of behavior. It is, however, not possible to ascertain regularity or identity of form simply by observation. These presuppose a "selective point of view"[128] by the observer which cannot itself be observed but which, as its condition, precedes the possibility of that condition. That is why Morris is only able to operate with the concept of identity of form and has to disregard the reflection which has entered into that concept and which is concerned with the points of view that are presupposed and that have to be selected for the attribution of an identity of form. The aporia resulting from a simple observation of an identity of form in behavior is made all the more obvious by the fact that Morris can neither include nor grasp as a reality the necessity of a preceding reflection with behavioristic categories.

3) According to Morris, the term "significate" means a "kind of object"[129] that is given with the sign or a class of objects whose real elements, if they are in fact present, represent the denotates. But how, then, is a discourse about classes of objects possible from the point of view of behaviorism? Is it possible, from that point of view, to go beyond an ascertainment of the appearance of empirical sign processes (that is, of the attribution of denotates) to make statements about classes of objects and classes of signs which can be empirically justified?[130] As a behaviorist, Morris is in principle not in

a position to do this. He depends on an affirmation of reactions to signs and complexes of signs and on the fact that men attribute them to objects (denotation and denotates). The signification and the significates lie outside the scope of his empirical investigation. He can only take them into account as a specialist in logic (semiotics) who is able to presuppose the concept of class reflectively and understand both classes of objects and classes of signs as abstractions from an intersubjectively valid use of signs.

4) Morris makes a distinction between the effectiveness of signs as the adequacy of their truth and reliability. A sign is reliable to the extent that it denotes something in the various situations in which it appears. A sign complex is true (T-ascriptor) if it denotes. Against what, however, can the truth be measured, according to Morris, in the four kinds of ascriptors? Morris' reply to this question is that it can be measured against the adequacy "underlying 'factual' components."[131] This simply means that it should be measured against the factual nature of the correctness that forms the basis of the adequate effectiveness of behavior of the needs of the organism which are signified and denoted by the sign complex. Morris is certainly not in a position to provide a criterion for these needs. In his biological orientation, he refers only to the "'paradigm' of a biological judgement of organic functions."[132] He has recourse to this paradigm as a basis, which is presumably value-neutral, for an empirical and scientific judgment of the truth of signs (or sign complexes), which is also value-neutral. He is not able to recognize a normative criterion of truth. He makes the truth and reliability of the truth of signs (and sign complexes) dependent on factual verification through behavior which satisfies the needs of the organism and which is brought about by the sign. In doing this, he submits to the "naturalistic fallacy" of reducing normative truth to the factual effectiveness of behavior (with Peirce, from thirdness to secondness). He is therefore not able, within the framework of his particular approach, either to include or to solve the problem both of the authenticity of needs and the legitimacy of modes of behavior and of its validity as a normative question.

5) Morris gives the pragmatic aspect of the sign process a central position in his semiotics. It is, however, valuable to compare his concept of the interpretant, which in his teaching is oriented toward the interpreter of the sign and is seen as a disposition toward reaction, with Peirce's concept of the interpretant. What is particularly striking is that Morris omits the habitual last logical interpretant and only considers the energetic interpretant. If this omission is seen from the point of view of Peirce's teaching, Morris is clearly reducing the thirdness of the disposition to behavior, which is present in an ultimately valid interpretation of a sign, to a factually acquired disposition that can be observed in its real effects (that is, secondness). This means that the positive achievement made by Peirce's interpreta-

tion, namely, a normatively correct understanding of the meaning of signs as a pragmatic guide to action for every interpreter, is lost. It is also reduced to a scientific explanation of the pragmatic effect of signs on behavior. The latter is clearly an aporia insofar as, seen in the perspective of a methodical approach, it is as impossible to grasp the reality of a change in interpretation as it is to consider the problem of the correct meaning.

# *Notes*

1. See the overviews by Murphy, *Pragmatism*; Rosenthal, *Speculative Pragmatism*.
2. See Apel, *Peirce*.
3. See Morris, *The Pragmatic Movement*.
4. In a letter to Ladd-Franklin, written about 1904, Peirce was more explicit than almost anywhere else about the connection between semiotics and pragmatism. "Pragmatism is the only result of my study of the formal laws of sign, a study guided by mathematics and the familiar fact of everyday experience and by no science whatsoever" (see Ladd-Franklin, *Peirce*, p. 720). He has been criticized above all by Alston, *Peirce*, about the lack of clarity concerning this connection. Alston consequently set about the task of clarifying it by reconstructing Peirce's arguments. Many interpreters of Peirce, because of this obscurity, have failed to grasp this fundamental connection and have discussed either his theory of signs or his pragmatism.
5. Fitzgerald, *Theory*, p. 10.
6. Peirce's *Collected Papers* are quoted as usual by indicating volume and paragraph. For the problem involved in Peirce's definition, see Greenlee, *Concept*, p. 24.
7. Walther, *Zeichenlehre*, p. 49.
8. Apel, *Towards a Transformation*, p. 84f.
9. See Murphey, *Development*, pp. 55–94; Apel, *Peirce*, p. 41.
10. Fitzgerald has pointed to a phenomenological foundation by regarding the "explication" of the fundamental categories as the "principal task of phaneroscopy" (*Theory*, p. 24, see also p. 28). Peirce seems to take a similar foundation as his point of departure in 8.213 and 5.43.

    Apel, *Peirce*, p. 109, see 115ff., with reference to von Kempski, *Peirce*, correctly draws attention to the aporia to which a phenomenology (in Peirce's case, a phaneroscopy) as a *prima philosophia* can lead. He has also pointed to the conclusions drawn by Peirce from his elaboration of the formal logic of relations (1903), as "the formal condition for the possibility of philosophy—as the phenomenological analysis of categories" (p. 123). He goes on to enlarge on "the advantages for the phenomenological analysis of the sign function that are provided by the guidelines of the logic of relations" (p. 123). If I understand Apel's arguments correctly, he is saying that Peirce gives his phenomenology a semiotic foundation, that is, in the logic of relations, with the result that it is not possible to derive his doctrine of categories from a phenomenological perspective. All that is provided is the formal basis for a categorial distinction between phenomena. The fruitfulness of the latter is also illustrated by a phenomenological analysis.

11. In his lectures on pragmatism given in 1907, Peirce in fact declares: "Less obvious, yet demonstrable, is the fact that no indecomposable concept has a higher valency than three." He goes on to explain that "careful analysis shows that to the three grades of valency of indecomposable concepts correspond three classes of character or predicates." He then argues, however, that "since the demonstration of this proposition is too stiff for the infantile logic of our time . . . I have preferred to state it problematically, as a surmise to be verified by observation" (5.469). This sounds as though Peirce is failing to provide a foundation in favor of pragmatic evidence, as Rorty, "Pragmatism," and Bernstein, *Praxis*, suggest. I think, however, that a failure to provide a foundation only applies to this lecture, in which he is not in fact discussing the logic of relations. It is worth noting that he says in the following sentence: "The little that I have contributed to pragmatism . . . has been entirely the fruit of this outgrowth from formal logic" (5.469). Here he is referring to his logic of relations, which he develops elsewhere (see 3.45–3.149). In any case, we are bound to recognize that Peirce was not always convinced that it was possible to provide a foundation for the categories by a logic of relations. In a letter to William James, for example, he writes: "Phenomenology has no right to appeal to logic, except to deductive logic," and insists that it has to be based on phenomenology (8.297). In the light of this ambivalent position, it is obviously not possible to regard a foundation for the categories by a logic of relations as a permanent and principal element in Peirce's understanding of the question or as a decisive point of view in a systematic reconstruction of his argument, in which the triadic relation that is analyzed and regarded as non-reducible by Peirce in the example of giving has the character of a paradigm. See Feibleman, *Introduction*, pp. 86, 105–110; Murphey, *Development*, pp. 151ff., 303–313.

12. Fitzgerald, *Theory*, p. 48.

13. See Greenlee's discussion of the problem of the "theory of resemblance" (*Concept*, p. 73) and his defense of the "similarity of discernibles" as their basis (*Concept*, p. 73ff.).

14. Fitzgerald, *Theory*, p. 52.

15. In a letter to Lady Welby, Peirce, *Letters*, p. 336, writes: "My Immediate Interpretant is implied in the fact that each sign must have its own peculiar Interpretability before it gets any Interpreter." Fitzgerald rightly observes that this immediate interpretant only deserves to be called an interpretant analogously, since there is no question here of any effect on an interpreter. Nonetheless, he also points out that it should be called an interpretant "because of its role as a ground for the relation between the sign and the interpretant" (*Theory*, p. 77).

16. Fitzgerald does not accept the interpretation of Peirce's teaching made, for example, by Apel, *Peirce*, p. 125, and Wartenberg, *Sozialismus*, p. 222 (who rejects Fitzgerald's affirmation explicitly here). The last two both regard the triad of the emotional, the energetic, and the logical interpretant as synonymous with the immediate, the dynamic, and the ultimate interpretant. Fitzgerald, on the other hand, has convincingly pointed out that the distinction between the emotional, the energetic, and the logical as subdivisions of the dynamic interpretant should not be regarded as parallel to the triad immediate–dynamic–ultimate. As a decisive argument, he suggests that there are real effects on the interpreter in the case of the emotional, the energetic, and the logical interpretant and that neither the possibility of (immediate) interpretability nor the

"would be" of the (normatively) correct interpretation are touched by them, as in the case of the ultimate interpretant. Apel has since come to accept this view.

17. See Apel, *Post-Tarskian Truth.*
18. Peirce discusses the methods of "tenacity" and "authority" and the "a priori method"; see 5.377–5.383.
19. Apel, *Peirce*, p. 82, referring to an expression by James.
20. See Fitzgerald, *Theory*, p. 99f.; Apel, *Peirce*, p. 99ff., who, especially on p. 103f., points to the use five times of derivations from the verb "conceive," which Peirce stresses in a footnote added in 1906 (5.402 n3) as proof of the conceptual knowledge to which he was referring in the maxim and which had to be acquired in the experiment of thought, in contrast to "sensation."
21. See Fitzgerald, *Theory*, p. 110.
22. See the renaming of pragmatism as "pragmaticism," 5.424.
23. Fitzgerald correctly extracts three elements from this passage. 1) Concepts, he believes, may be logical interpretants belonging to the category of thirdness, but they cannot be ultimate interpretants. 2) Although it belongs to the category of thirdness, the habit of action is not a sign in the narrow sense of the word, because the effect produced by it is an action and therefore something that is "second." Finally, 3) if the sign is comparable to a verbal definition, then a habit of action can also be compared with a real definition. This means that the basic content of Peirce's pragmatism can be found in "that the meaning of a sign or concept consists in the habit to which it gives rise in the interpreter. This assertation is based on the fact that the pragmatic meaning is the ultimate logical interpretant" (*Theory*, p. 154).
24. See Apel, *Post-Tarskian Truth.*
25. See, for example, 5.9: "In order to ascertain the meaning of an intellectual conception one should consider what practical consequences might conceivably result by necessity from the truth of that conception; and the sum of these consequences will constitute the entire meaning of the conception."
26. Fitzgerald, *Theory*, p. 167ff.
27. Ibid., p. 168.
28. In his debate with Habermas' consensus theory of truth, Apel speaks of the "iconic evidence of the qualitative phenomenon" in the sense of "evidence for a correspondence between proposition and reality" (*Post-Tarskian Problem I*, p. 398).
29. See Apel, *Morris.*
30. Reprinted in James, *Pragmatism* (1975), pp. 257–270, under the title "Philosophical Conceptions and Practical Results."
31. James, *Conceptions*, p. 258. Peirce refuses to accept the term "practicalism," appealing to Kant (see 5.412). For Kant's distinction between "practical" and "pragmatic," see Pieper, *Ethik.*
32. James, *Conceptions*, p. 259. Even in his presentation of Peirce's conception of the pragmatic maxim, James attributes a tendency to Peirce that is directed toward a practical effect which can be perceived by the senses.
33. See James, *Pragmatism* (New York, 1978), p. xi. At the same time, however, he also regards the "pragmatic theory of truth" as an important step in that direction, "making radical empiricism prevail" (James, *Meaning*, p. xii). For this "radical empiricism," see James, *Essays.*
34. James, *Pragmatism*, p. 54.
35. See Perry, *Thought II*, p. 409: "Pragmatism is largely the result of James's misunderstanding of Peirce."

36. See James, *Meaning*; *Pragmatism*.

37. Dewey, "The Pragmatism of Peirce," p. 714, correctly points out that James' appeal to the "will to believe" for Peirce leads to the "method of tenacity," which he rejects (see 5.378), with regard to the ascertainment of a conviction.

38. Peirce makes a very clear contrast between his own theory of meaning and James'. He says: "My point is that the meaning of a concept . . . lies in the manner in which it could conceivably modify purpose action, and for this alone. James, on the contrary, whose natural turn of mind is always from generals . . . in defining pragmatism speaks of it as referring ideas to experiences, meaning evidently the sensational side of experience, while I regard concepts as affairs of habit or disposition, and how we should react" (Ladd-Franklin, *Peirce*, p. 718). Peirce's note about the normative character of truth expressed in the "contrary to facts" conditional, which he added in 1903 to his *The Fixation of Belief*, is directed against the reduction of truth to verification. In the same way, the emphasis that he places on the reality of thirdness in his lectures on pragmatism, which were arranged by James, is also directed against James' two-dimensional pragmatism. What is remarkable is that James takes no notice of Peirce's change of name from "pragmatism" to "pragmaticism," for which he, as one of Peirce's "kidnappers" (*Papers*, 5.414), may have been partly responsible.

39. Dewey, *Philosophy*, p. 39f.

40. Peirce, 5.387.

41. Peirce explicitly rejects a renunciation of ultimate aims: "The only moral evil is not to have an ultimate aim" (5.133).

42. See Dewey, *Logic*.

43. This is legitimately stressed by Moore, *Pragmatism*, p. 194. Dewey insists, in his debate with Morris, on Peirce's category of thirdness and rejects Morris' behavioristic curtailment. See Dewey, "Peirce's Theory of Linguistic Signs."

44. Dewey, *Human Nature*, p. 147.

45. Ibid., p. 120.

46. Dewey, *Reconstruction*, p. 177.

47. See Dewey, *Quest*, p. 166.

48. In his discussion of James' theory of "veri-fication," Dewey is able to affirm: "I have never identified any satisfaction with the truth of an idea, save that satisfaction which arises when the idea as a working hypothesis or tentative method is applied to prior existences in such a way as to fulfil what it intends" ("What Does Pragmatism Mean?" p. 109). For Dewey's debate with the rationalist or intellectualist theory of truth, see Dewey, "Reality"; "Dilemma."

49. See Dewey, *Essays*, pp. 230–249.

50. See Mahowald, *Pragmatism*, especially pp. 25–28, 167–176. This author speaks of "idealistic pragmatism" as a "synthesis of his idealism with the empirical and practical directness of his thought" (p. 176).

51. Humbach, *Verhältnis*, p. 24.

52. Royce, *Problem*, p. 279.

53. Royce, *World I*, p. 425. See also *Problem*, p. 317: "I have to define the truth of my interpretation of you in terms of what the ideal observer of all of us would view as unity which is observed. This truth cannot be defined in merely pragmatic terms." This "ideal observer" is the divine Spirit, who interprets the world as a whole with ultimate validity and omniscience.

54. For Royce's theory of the self, see Smith, "Introduction," p. 24.

55. Apel, *Peirce*, p. 182. Apel thinks that Royce outlined "the transcendental hermeneutic interpretation of semiotics" (ibid.; *Towards a Transformation*, p. 112); in the

English edition the term "semiotics" is incorrectly replaced by "hermeneutics."
56. Royce, *Problem*, p. 286.
57. Ibid., p. 291.
58. Royce, *Problem*, pp. 273–295. For his debate with James' pragmatism, see Smith, *Infinite*, p. 48ff; Humbach, *Verhältnis*, p. 24.
59. Royce, *Problem*, p. 283.
60. Ibid., p. 315.
61. Ibid., p. 324.
62. This is the title of his twenty-third lecture; see *Problem*, pp. 321–342.
63. Ibid., p. 339.
64. Ibid., p. 346.
65. Ibid., p. 361.
66. Peirce, *Papers*, 8.41; see also 8.39–8.54; 5.436. Mahowald comments: "As a matter of fact, it was from this notion of pragmaticism that Royce derived his theory of interpretation as a triadic theory of knowledge" (*Pragmaticism*, p. 24). For the relationship between Peirce and Royce, see Smith, *Infinite*, pp. 19–31, 69–73, 81f. There is also an important passage on the relationship between the two men in Peirce, 5.311.
67. Morris, "Introduction," in Mead, *Mind*, p. xxxv. Morris put Mead first among those who developed the pragmatic movement; see Morris, "Peirce, Mead, and Pragmatism," pp. 109–127; also *Pragmatic Movement*, which also contains many other references to Mead.
68. Murphy uses these words to describe Mead's philosophy in his introduction to the latter's *The Philosophy of the Present*, XIII. Following him, Reck entitles his chapter on Mead, in his *Recent American Philosophy*, pp. 84–122, "The Constructive Pragmatism of George Herbert Mead."
69. See Mead, *Mind*.
70. See Mead, "A Pragmatic Theory of Truth"; Eames, "Mead and the Pragmatic Conception of Truth," in Corti, ed., *Philosophy*, pp. 135–152; Morris, "Introduction," pp. xf., xviif.
71. See Dewey, "The Reflex Arch Concept."
72. See James, *Psychology*, Chap. XII: "The Self," pp. 176–216.
73. Mead, *Mind*, p. 154.
74. Ibid., p. 108.
75. Ibid., p. 46.
76. Ibid., p. 69f.
77. Ibid., p. 69.
78. Ibid., p. 89f.
79. Ibid., p. 158.
80. Tugendhat, *Selbstbewusstsein*, p. 279.
81. See Goffman, *Asylums; Stigma*.
82. Mead, *Mind*, p. 144.
83. Morris describes Mead's position as specifically and unrestrictedly behavioristic; see his "On the Unity of Pragmatic Movement." Like Mead, he assumes a theory of interpretants and is conscious that a disposition to action is brought about by the sign in this interpretant. He also insists that the basis of Mead's analysis of the sign of the gesture is the nature of the interpretant that is orientated toward behavior, and that Peirce's semiotics also tend in this direction. On the other hand, Mead is seen as the founder of symbolic interactionism, which he considers in the perspective of a sociology of action.
84. Tugendhat, *Selbstbewusstsein*, especially pp. 245–263.

85. See Mead, *Philosophy of the Act*; *Philosophy of the Present*.
86. This means that the word should not be addressed to any individualistic voluntarism. Mead correctly emphasizes the aspect of institutions that act to stabilize behavior and are therefore what Gehlen has called "unburdening." Institutionalized expectations of behavior, however, are not in themselves necessarily right when confronted with individual claims. They have to establish their legitimacy in the presence of such claims by means of the criterion of the socially necessary restriction of free communication. Mead himself observes that "universal discourse is then the formal ideal of communication" (*Mind*, p. 327). Institutionalized restrictions of dialogue have to be measured against that "formal ideal."
87. Tugendhat believes that Mead "did not succeed in providing evidence of the modes of behaviour that make a symbolic language in the sense in which he used the term possible." He is of the opinion that Mead "simply named criteria that a behaviouristic theory of symbolic language would have to satisfy" (*Selbstbewusstsein*, p. 258). I cannot agree with Tugendhat here. Although he does not analyze statements, Mead undoubtedly recognizes the differences between signal language and symbolic language, and qualitatively distinguishes the latter as creating meaning. The "evidence" of this is found in his analysis of the process of the formation of symbols via vocal gestures, which are experienced as identical for the ego and alter and which therefore represent both the foundation and the product of mutual agreement.
88. Morris, *Writings*, p. 43.
89. Ibid., p. 43.
90. Morris, "On the Unity," p. 111.
91. Ibid., p. 109.
92. See Morris, "Peirce, Mead, and Pragmatism," pp. 109–127.
93. Morris, *Writings*, p. 103. This quotation from Peirce comes from 5.476.
94. Morris, *Writings*, p. 340.
95. Morris, "Introduction," in Mead, *Mind*, p. xxxv.
96. Morris, "On the Unity," p. 112.
97. Klaus, *Semiotik und Erkenntnistheorie*, p. 53.
98. Morris, *Signification and Significance* (Cambridge, Mass., 1964).
99. Morris, *Writings*, p. 17.
100. If Morris, *Writings*, p. 19, in fact cited the interpretant as the third component of the sign process, then the consequence of this would be the interpreter. I shall go into the change of emphasis that this implies later. See Dewey's criticism in "Peirce's Theory," Morris' reply in Morris, "Letter," and Dewey's answer to this in Dewey, "Letter."
101. Morris, *Writings*, p. 21f.
102. Ibid., p. 36.
103. Ibid., p. 48.
104. Ibid., p. 24.
105. Ibid., p. 45.
106. Ibid., p. 48.
107. Ibid., p. 59.
108. Ibid., p. 64.
109. Apel, *Einführung*, p. 17f.
110. Morris, *Writings*, p. 302.
111. See Morris' arguments against the earlier and too simple theory of behavior

("Peirce, Mead, and Pragmatism"). It is possible for Morris, with his theory of the preparatory stimulus, to regard signs as preparing for action. This means that the question as to whether a sign leads to obvious behavior or not is therefore seen to depend on whether certain conditions regarding motivation and the environment are fulfilled. Those conditions decide whether the disposition can be and is realized in factual behavior. For the difficulty of including the dispositional intermediate stage between sign and behavior within behavioristic categories, see Section 1.3.4 below.

112. Morris, *Writings*, p. 87.
113. For the relationship between the significate and the denotate in Morris, see Müller, *Probleme*, p. 59ff.
114. Morris, *Writings*, p. 113.
115. With the difference that Mead's concept also includes Morris' so-called post-linguistic symbols and the fact that "comsign requires minimum social behaviour does not necessarily mean that this act be reciprocal social behaviour or cooperative social behaviour—it is sufficient that the organisms perform response-sequences of the same behaviour-family" (Morris, *Writings*, p. 121). This passage makes especially clear Morris' reduction of the analysis of intersubjectively constituted and intersubjective action to the observation of similar behavior.
116. Morris, *Writings*, p. 146.
117. The fact that Morris introduces an analogy for truth in the non-designative sphere and relates T- and F-ascriptors to the other three modes of signification is regarded by Apel, *Einführung*, p. 22f., as an advance compared with the earlier form of behaviorism and with the notions of Bühler and Popper, which one-sidedly confine the "distinction of the logos" of human language (see Apel, "Zwei paradigmatische Antworten") to the designative sphere. Morris' extension of the question of truth and reliability to all modes of signification can be seen as anticipating Austin's questioning, from the vantage point of the theory of the speech act, of the primacy of the question of truth and Habermas' four validity claims.
118. For the differences with Carnap's theory of construct languages, see Morris, "Pragmatism and Logical Empricism."
119. Morris, *Writings*, p. 320.
120. Ibid., p. 205.
121. Ibid., p. 206.
122. Ibid., p. 308.
123. According to Morris, humaniora are object signs taken from literature, art, morality, religion, and so on, whereas humanistics form a meta-language about the humaniora.
124. Morris, *Writings*, p. 316.
125. Müller, *Probleme*, p. 3.
126. This takes place if the organism is not asked to what it is disposed. When this happens, of course, the observer abandons his position as an objective observer. This question at the same time means to what behavior the observer's interpretation of the sign may lead him.
127. See Müller, *Probleme*, p. 77ff, who claims that "without a recognition of the concept of rule as a primitive term in semiotics the fundamental data of semiotics cannot be grasped" (p. 85). Wittgenstein, Winch, and Searle have all made it abundantly clear that no conclusions can be drawn from the regularity

of modes of behavior for the regularization that underlies behavior.

128. Müller, *Probleme*, p. 67.
129. Morris, *Writings*, p. 20.
130. Müller, *Probleme*, p. 58ff., asks Morris these questions insistently. He summarizes the problem as follows: "The division of the correlate of the sign into denotate and significate, the distinction made between the object and a certain characteristic and the inability to make a distinction with behaviouristic means constitute the greatest crisis in behaviouristic semiotics" (p. 64).
131. Morris, *Writings*, p. 184.
132. Apel, *Einführung*, p. 56; p. 52ff.

# === 2 ===

# Approaches to a Pragmatically Oriented Materialistic Linguistic Theory

## 2.1 VALENTIN N. VOLOŠINOV

### 2.1.1 THE MAIN ASPECTS OF VOLOŠINOV'S SEMIOTIC THEORY OF LANGUAGE AND IDEOLOGY

"The first extensive Russian prolegomenon to semiotics"[1]—this is what Ladislav Matejka calls the book on Marxism and linguistic philosophy published by Valentin N. Vološinov in 1929. In this book, *Marxism and the Philosophy of Language*,[2] the author engages in creative debate, on the one hand, with "individualistic subjectivism" in linguistic philosophy, following Wilhelm von Humboldt, and, on the other, with the antithesis of this, the "abstract objectivism" of de Saussure especially. His aim is to achieve a dialectical synthesis within the framework of a materialistic linguistic philosophy.

This work has played hardly any part in recent discussion. It is, however, important and has great contemporary value[3] for several reasons. The author anticipates both the essential questions and the results of the present debate on pragmatics. Moreover, Vološinov considers both on the basis of a materialistic conception of language, according to which language is understood as fundamentally sign-mediated social communication in a process of social interaction.

Vološinov is clearly opposed to any mechanistic form of the theory of reflection, in which an illustration of the material basis in the ideological superstructure is regarded as a monocausal effect of the first on the second.[4] He formulates his semiotic theory of ideology accordingly: "Any ideological product is not only itself a part of a reality (natural or social), . . . it also . . . reflects and refracts another reality outside itself. Everything ideological possesses meaning: it represents, depicts or stands for something lying outside itself. In other words, it is a sign. Without signs there is no ideology" (p. 9).

A sign is a phenomenon of the outside world and at the same time also "reflects and refracts another reality" (p. 10). Signs come about in a process of social interaction "on interindividual territory" (p. 12). Insofar as this field is socially organized and is an area in which the individual consciousness represents a social and ideological fact, it "takes shape and being in the material of signs created by an organized group in the process of its social intercourse" (p. 13).

Because he recognizes this, Vološinov is able to say that "the logic of consciousness is the logic of ideological communication, of the semiotic interaction of a social group" (p. 13). It is in signs—and that means principally in words—that social communication is manifested and that social being is also ideologically refracted in understanding or in interpretation. What is attained is a dialectical interplay between psyche and ideology. These dialectically penetrate each other in a unified and objective process of social communication. As Vološinov says: "The psyche effaces itself, or is obliterated, in the process of becoming ideology, and ideology effaces itself in the process of becoming the psyche" (p. 39).

### 2.1.2   THE ANTITHESES "INDIVIDUALISTIC SUBJECTIVISM" AND "ABSTRACT OBJECTIVISM" AND VOLOŠINOV'S SYNTHESIS

Vološinov contrasts his materialistic philosophy of sign-mediated social interaction with the two tendencies in philosophical linguistic thinking that predominated when he was writing, and their assimilation and development by Marxism. These are "individualistic subjectivism" and "abstract objectivism" (p. 48). In the first, the individual creative speech act is regarded as the basis of language; its representatives, Wilhelm Wundt, Karl Vossler, Benedetto Croce, and, on the Russian side, A. A. Potebnja, are oriented toward Wilhelm von Humboldt's energetic conception of language. The most striking expression of "abstract objectivism" lies in its rationalist tendency in which an appeal is made to Leibniz and Descartes. It is found in work of the so-called School of Geneva of Ferdinand de Saussure. This is directed toward language as a permanent and unchanging system of normatively identical linguistic forms, whose laws have to be investigated independently of individual speech acts and without reference to the history of language.

According to Vološinov, this second movement tends toward an "objectivized" conception of language (see p. 67), which assumes that the system only represents an abstraction and that language acts as a system of signals rather than of signs. Both for the one speaking and for the one understanding, however, "what is important for the speaker about a linguistic form is not that it is a stable and always self-equivalent signal, but that it is an always changeable and adaptable sign" (p. 68). Vološinov goes on to say that, unlike a signal, this sign is not only recognized as identical, but is also understood precisely as a sign, that is, in relation to its context and to whatever situation is prevailing at the time.[5] Since abstract objectivism isolates the linguistic form from its ideological content and its meaning, it is both theoretically and practically oriented "on the study of defunct, alien languages preserved in written monuments" (p. 71). It is also similarly directed toward isolated, closed monologues and can, in its deciphering and teaching of the "alien, foreign-language word" (p. 74),[6] be guided by an abstract systematization that is blind to the possibility of historical change and social conditioning. Instead of a vital plurality of meanings, the word has only one meaning as opposed to the "living multiplicity of meaning and accent" (p. 77). Because of this, abstract objectivism overlooks the relationship between meaning and context[7] and wrongly believes, both by isolating the word and by stabilizing its meaning outside the text, that it can guarantee the unity of meaning, which, in fact, can only be guaranteed dialectically as a unity in a plurality of meanings.

The theory of expression is especially characteristic of the point of view of individualistic subjectivism. This theory implies that priority should be given to inner experience, which is changed in objectivization by expression. This can even lead to a radical rejection of expression as "something that deforms the purity of the inner element" (p. 84f). According to Vološinov, this theory of expression and experience is completely wrong. He says that "the experiential, expressible element and its outward objectification are created, as we know, out of one and the same material. After all, there is no such thing as experience outside of embodiment in signs. . . . It is not experience that organizes expression, but the other way around—expression organizes experience. Expression is what first gives experience its form and specificity of direction" (p. 85).[8] To that extent, the orientation of experience is social. The social situation and the social environment determine it, as it were, from within and enter into it. The word, precisely as word, is the product of interaction between the one who speaks and the one who is listening. In a clear parallel with Mead, Vološinov argues: "I give myself verbal shape from another's point of view, ultimately, from the point of view of the community to which I belong" (p. 86).[9]

With regard to the problem of consciousness, Vološinov concludes from his analyses that it is outside objectivization, that is, outside an incarnation in a definite material, a fiction. The concrete incarnation of consciousness in definite social organizations, in which it has a lasting ideological expression in ideological systems (science, art, literature, and so on), is contrasted by Vološinov with the whole complex of everyday experiences that are manifested in the ideology of everyday life. It is in that whole complex that the objectifications of linguistic interaction live and have an effect and are understood and interpreted. In that way, their presence is maintained in the collective consciousness.

According to Vološinov, then, the essential function of language is not to be found in the expression of inner experience but in communication and orientation toward the "sign community" (p. 23). This means that he can say, with both conceptions of language to which he is opposed in mind: "The actual reality of language-speech is not the abstract system of linguistic forms, not the isolated monological utterance, and not the psychophysiological act of its implementation, but the social event of verbal interaction implemented in an utterance or utterances" (p. 94).

Linguistic interaction is therefore seen by Vološinov to be the "true reality" of language. Every expression is consequently no more than a moment in linguistic communication and interaction. It is always accompanied by social acts of a non-linguistic kind (work), and can never be understood outside its relationship with a concrete situation. Even expressions in the form of a monologue have also to be seen as situationally related fragments of dialogue. Vološinov insists, for example, that "a book, i.e., a verbal performance in print, is also an element of verbal communication" (p. 95).

Linguistic interaction and therefore language itself are, however, always involved in a constant process of change that accompanies the linguistic and non-linguistic activity of speaking individuals and groups. The laws of this process of change are not individual psychological laws. They are sociological laws. They do not, as such, determine the development of language in a mechanistic form of necessity. On the contrary, they are consciously understood and directed by the sign community and lead to language developing in "free necessity" (p. 98).

### 2.1.3 THE PROSPECT: VOLOŠINOV'S HERITAGE

Valentin N. Vološinov laid the foundations for a consistently pragmatic materialistic linguistic theory. His work runs parallel to that of Peirce and Mead, especially insofar as he makes the "sign community" of the socially interacting and interpreting people the cornerstone of his conception of language as linguistic interaction. In his view, it is in that process of interaction that the material basis is reflected and refracted in the ideological superstructure. In this way, Vološinov is able to draw far-reaching conclusions, leading to his theory of linguistically mediated social interaction. This theory is, on the one hand, opposed to a mechanistic and materialistic assertion of a monistically conceived primacy of the basis, and insists on the relative autonomy and creativity of ideology. On the other, it rejects an idealistic assertion of the primacy of the spirit and affirms the effects both of the material basis and of the "relations of interaction"[10] that function as an intermediary between the basis and the superstructure on ideology and of all three on each other.

In this way, Vološinov is able to resist both materialistic and idealistic monism and propose a dialectical conception of social being and consciousness. These are, moreover, synthesized in linguistic interaction, both permanently and provisionally, and both in a state of openness to change and in defense against change. Taking this real sphere of collision between being and consciousness and their mutual cancellation as its point of departure, a materialistic theory of signs has to question the mechanism and the substratum of social interaction. A materialistic theory of ideology, on the other hand, confronts the problem of discovering the ideological legacy of social semiosis and the effects of both on each other.

The conclusion for a materialistic linguistic philosophy is that it has to conceive them as a theory of social communication. Finally, a materialistic theory of the text and literature has the task of understanding texts as elements of the social communication and interaction in which they are materialized, given a lasting value, and preserved. They are made and kept available for the collective being and consciousness for as long as they enter into the communication here and now of the community of signs, by means of which they remain in the "arena of the class struggle" (p. 23). Vološinov's greatest achievement is that he outlined the tasks confronting a pragmatically based materialistic theory of signs, ideology, language, text, and literature. In his positive approach to the formulation of such a theory, he placed himself in the front rank of pragmatic theorists. It is consequently a matter of urgency that his fundamental theses should be accepted by pragmatic thinkers and not only by them.

# Notes

1. Matejka, "Prolegomena," p. 163.
2. The English-language edition appeared in 1973; it was republished in 1986. Quotations from the latter edition are indicated in the text. The French edition (Paris, 1977) names Mikhail Bakhtine as the author.
3. See Weber, "Einschnitt."
4. As this is affirmed in the vulgar Marxist and vulgar idealistic reception of the Marxist dictum of being, which determines consciousness. Engels' thesis of the relative independence of the ideological superstructure is directed against this reception.
5. The difference between recognizing signals and understanding signs has a parallel in Mead's distinction between signal and symbol. It should also make a far-reaching contribution to the debate on explanation and understanding, which is already proving unusually fruitful (see p. 68f). For this debate, see von Wright, *Explanation*; Apel, *Understanding*.

6. Vološinov does not use the concept "text." Instead, he speaks of word, expression, or utterance. It is, however, possible to work in this context with the terminology of text theory, and certainly possible to regard Vološinov as the forerunner of that theory. His "discourse" is fundamentally an attempt to formulate a materialistic theory of the text. He does this by answering the question of how a literary text as an ideological phenomenon is constituted as an aspect of linguistic interaction, and how the material basis that is not simply external to the text is recorded within the text in the structure of the text. I am of the opinion that Schmidt's text theory, which has frequently been accused of idealism, could be superseded by Vološinov's theory. Unfortunately, however, Schmidt has so far not accepted it (see 4.1). It is desirable that all text theories should seriously consider and come to terms with Vološinov's systematic pronouncements, including his attempt to apply "the sociological method to problems of syntax" (see *Marxism*, pp. 107–159).

7. Vološinov says emphatically: "The meaning of a word is determined entirely by its context. In fact, there are as many meanings of a word as there are contexts of its usage" (p. 79). This statement is very reminiscent of the radical theory of meaning as use formulated by Alston, *Philosophy*, among others who followed Wittgenstein. Vološinov, whose position is dialectical, succeeds, however, in avoiding the aporias of a breakdown of the unity of meaning into the plurality of meanings and types of the contextual use which are found in the work of Alston and others.

8. Vološinov's claim that there is no experience without an embodiment in signs could have been made by Peirce, who declared, for example, that "all thought, therefore, must necessarily be in signs" (5.251). Vološinov's statement can also be compared with Peirce's comments on firstness. Peirce's idea of "quality of feeling" is perhaps the closest parallel to Vološinov's concept of experience.

9. Even in the terminology used by Vološinov, we are reminded of Mead's "I" and "Me."

10. This term seems to owe its origin to Marx's "relations of production," and points to the area between the basis and the superstructure in which both meet in social interaction.

# 3

# The Late Wittgenstein, Ordinary Language Philosophy, and Speech Act Theory

## 3.1 LUDWIG WITTGENSTEIN'S PRAGMATIC LANGUAGE-GAME THEORY

### 3.1.1 THE BREACH: FROM "IDEAL LANGUAGE" (EARLY WITTGENSTEIN) TO "ORDINARY LANGUAGE" (LATE WITTGENSTEIN)

In his later philosophy, as outlined above all in the *Philosophical Investigations*, Ludwig Wittgenstein makes a radical breach with the philosophy of the ideal language of unity representing the world, for which he laid the foundations in his *Tractatus*. This breach is documented in the implicit and explicit debate with the *Tractatus* that is conducted in the later work. In the early work, Wittgenstein takes his transcendental criticism of language to the paradoxical conclusion of self-cancellation. In the *Philosophical Investigations*, however, he takes the opposite view and insists that "the preconceived ideas of crystalline purity" be removed "by turning our whole examination round" (PI 108). The question is in this way radically changed. It is no longer the world as "everything that is the case" (T 1), as the entirety of facts and situations represented in propositions, which corresponds to the whole complex of all true elementary propositions expressed in the general form of proposition, that is debated. On the contrary, what is discussed now is language, in other words, the way in which language functions in the praxis of its use.

There is a comment in the *Philosophical Investigations* on the statement that appears in the *Tractatus*: "The general form of proposition is: Such and such is the case" (T 4.5). It is that "one thinks that one is tracing the outline of the thing's nature over and over again, and one is merely tracing round the

41

frame through which we look at it" (PI 114). The breach in Wittgenstein's thinking is clearly marked in this statement. The program that he follows in his later philosophy can be summarized as tracing the different forms which are previously given and cannot be reduced to each other, and through which we look at the nature of the world, the inner nature of man, and the nature of society. The transcendental orientation in his work continues, since his investigation "is directed not towards phenomena" (PI 90). Its orientation toward the criticism of language also continues.

To that extent, it is possible to speak of an aspect of continuity in Wittgenstein's thought. There is, however, a clear discontinuity in his method, the material that he considers, his intention, and the results. That discontinuity, in my view, is so critical that I propose to take it as my point of departure,[1] being unable to accept the emphasis placed on continuity by Kenny, Winch, and others.[2] In this, I would appeal to Wittgenstein's interpretation of himself in his foreword to the *Philosophical Investigations*, in which he refers to the connection between his ideas as formulated in the *Tractatus* and those made explicit in the later work. In this statement, he says "that the latter could be seen in the right light only by contrast with and against the background of my old way of thinking" (PI, p. viii).

### 3.1.2 LANGUAGE-GAMES AND FORMS OF LIFE

The "unity of language-game and form of life" represents the highest category of Wittgenstein's linguistic philosophy.[3] Language-games, in which everyday language is used and functions in involvement with forms of life, form the object of the descriptive intentions which do not violate the usage of the late Wittgenstein and provide material for his exemplary linguistic analyses. The construction of the *Tractatus* is replaced, in the *Philosophical Investigations*, by description, a cataloguing of "the multiplicity of language-games" (PI 23) in the "album" (PI, p. 10) of the philosophical observer. In that album is documented "the prodigious diversity of all the everyday language-games of which we remain unconscious because the clothing of our language makes everything alike" (PI, p. 224). The philosopher, then, plays the part of a collector. "The work of the philosopher consists in assembling reminders for a particular purpose" (PI 127).

The aim of the later Wittgenstein's work in the *Philosophical Investigations*, then, can be summarized succinctly in the following way: he wanted to point in an exemplary way to the interweaving of the multiplicity of everyday language-games with the multiplicity of forms of life. He wanted, in other words, to present the "family resemblances" (PI 67) that make language-games "a complicated network of similarities overlapping and criss-crossing" (PI 66), combine them with each other, and bind them to the form of life that are implied in the conventional rules of usage.

The expression "family resemblances" points to the fact that there is no underlying substance common to the many different language-games. They are not forms in which the essence of language appears, but are correlated by many different forms of interdependence in the praxis of linguistic and non-linguistic activity. As Apel has suggested, a language-game can be understood "as a unity, functioning as a form of life, of linguistic usage, corporeal expression, behavioural praxis and disclosure of the world."[4] Language-games and interaction therefore refer to each other, and it is in this sense that Wittgenstein's concept of the language-game as defined in his *Philosophical Investigations* should be understood: "I shall also call the whole, consisting of language and the actions into which it is woven, the 'language-game'"(PI 7).[5]

He does not in any sense use this concept of the language-game in a unified way. Some interpreters are therefore right in distinguishing different meanings in the phrase "language-game."[6] I believe that it has three basic meanings. In the first place, it is a rudimentary linguistic model. Examples of this meaning of "language-game" are Wittgenstein's paradigmatically constructed building workers' language and the training of little children in the mother-tongue by means of naming exercises. In the second place, linguistic functional units that are manifested in typical sequences of speech acts or other actions are described in "language-games." Thirdly, the term points to the whole complex of linguistic activities which are involved with forms of life and to which each individual language-game is related.

It is therefore possible to establish an inner connection between the different meanings of the concept "language-game" that are held together by the previously existing "unity of language game and form of life." That unity is admittedly quite arbitrary. It is based, like language itself, on convention and is expressed in the grammar of the language concerned, which itself consists of agreements. "You must bear in mind that the language-game is so to say something unpredictable. I mean: it is not based on grounds. It is not reasonable (or unreasonable). It is there—like our life" (OC 559).

Wittgenstein's assertion that language-games are conventional has caused many interpreters to overlook the realistic aspect of his later philosophy and to regard it, in sharp contrast to his earlier thinking, which was orientated toward a theory of representation, as the "hitherto most radical presentation of conventionalism known in the history of philosophy."[7] It is, however, possible to agree with Rolf Zimmermann's objection to this understanding of his later work,[8] on the grounds that sharing a form of life at the same time also means sharing facts of experience that transcend doubt (see OC 519), a procedure in which universal propositions about experience refer to facts that are "fused into the foundations of our language-game" (OC 558).

The need for a practical orientation toward judgments about facts that are regarded as beyond doubt because they are verified in practice does not exclude a fundamental fallibility for Wittgenstein. Insofar as he recognizes facts that are "fused into the foundations" of each language-game or each form of life, however—and he points out, in his comments on Frazer's *The Golden Bough*, that it would be wrong to assume that other cultures have fundamentally different conceptions of reality and experiences with nature—discourse about a radical conventionalism is not justified in the case of Wittgenstein. Facts and judgments about facts are, it is true, related to the language-game that is in each case presupposed and to the form of life that is implied in that language-game, but there is such a thing as a "material substratum" that "has always been introduced into the structural form of life of men."[9] The multiplicity of forms of life, which cannot be reduced to each other or transmitted from one to another and are therefore incompatible, the multiplicity of "views" that have the same meaning on the basis of the material substratum of the human form of life—this can be understood and catalogued descriptively. The aporias to which this thesis of incompatibility leads in view of the descriptive understanding of all other language-games, which is both presupposed and practiced in fact by philosophical language or the philosophical language-game, will be considered below.

### 3.1.3  MEANING AND USE

In his *Philosophical Grammar*, Wittgenstein says: "I want to say: the place of a word in grammar is its meaning. But I might also say: the meaning of a word is what the explanation of its meaning explains. . . . The explanation of the meaning explains the use of the word. The use of a word in the language is its meaning. Grammar describes the use of words in language" (PG 23).[10] In his *Philosophical Investigations*, he says: "For a large class of cases—though not for all—in which we employ the word 'meaning' it can be defined thus: the meaning of a word is its use in the language" (PI 43).

Many interpreters have failed to take into account Wittgenstein's restrictive comments on his identification of "meaning" with "use," and have consequently extrapolated from these and similar passages in his work[11] a "use theory of meaning."[12] Wittgenstein did not, however, intend to equate "meaning" and "use." As Stegmüller and J. Zimmermann have shown,[13] such an identification would have been contrary to his conception of philosophy. He was concerned rather with the direction taken by the questions. His instruction for the elucidation of a word, a proposition, or a language-game was that the context within which, the aim toward which, and the manner in which it was used should be investigated. That instruction points to a descriptive understanding of the many different ways in which linguistic elements can be employed, rather than one which seeks to define. Presupposing a multiplicity of meanings that cannot be restricted simply to dictionary definitions and explanations, Wittgenstein can be said to explain "meaning" in terms of "use."

Insofar as it can be said of every sign that "in use it is alive" (PI 432), that is, that signs only become a living reality where they are functioning and playing a part,[14] only two interpreters are capable of experiencing their meaning. First is the one who leaves and analyzes signs within the framework of the language-games in which they are used, instead of taking them out of the context in which they are active and isolating them from the praxis that is bestowed on them by their meaning.

The second kind of interpreter is the one who looks at language at work[15] instead of contemplating its "celebration" (see PI 38). If understanding a word, a proposition, or a language-game means knowing how it is used and being able to use it (PI 10), then understanding language is, as Habermas has so correctly observed, "the virtual recapitulation of the training through which 'native speakers' are socialized into their form of life."[16] The entire process of active and passive use is "one of those games by means of which children learn their native language" (PI 7). A child, however, is introduced to the praxis of use by being trained, on the basis of examples by means of "ostensive teaching" (PI 6), to employ language correctly, in other words, in conformity with the rules (see PG 138; PI 5). In this process, the naming of things has a special function. It is, in other words, "preparatory to the use of a word" (PI 26).

Wittgenstein's explanation of "meaning" in terms of "use" is, in fact, "undetermined."[17] It can be described and summarized as an argument directed against any "objective theory of meaning"[18] that does not aim to violate the multiplicity of linguistic use in which meaning is again and again manifested by seeking to define, but tries rather to look at language at work and let it speak for itself. J. Zimmermann is therefore right to introduce the concept of "showing," familiar from the *Tractatus*, into this context. He says: "What the meaning of an expression is has to be 'shown,' not, it is true, by contemplating language in the light of an ideal, but by reflecting about the concrete use of words and propositions in the context within which they are uttered."[19]

### 3.1.4 RULES AND GRAMMAR

The use of elements of language, which bestows on them their meaning, which is in each case dependent on their context, is governed by rules. Use takes place on the basis of a practiced convention and is recorded in the grammar of the language-game or the language itself. To that extent, Wittgenstein is able to say that grammar consists of conventions (PG 138) and to describe it as the "account books of language," from which the "actual transactions of language" can be learned (PG 44).

The title and contents of his posthumously published *Philosophical Grammar* show clearly that "grammar" has two meanings for Wittgenstein. On the one hand, it means the science of the rules governing the use of language and, on the other, it means those rules themselves.[20] Philosophical grammar as a conceptual investigation therefore discloses the grammatical rules that underlie and precede the use of language. It can consequently be called a reconstructive science, which describes the grammar that is found at the deepest level of linguistic use. Its rules can be seen in philosophical analysis, which, insofar as it does not violate the use of language, does not try to include it within a generative theme as the intersubjectively shared "customs" (PI 199) of a community of interaction.

According to Wittgenstein, grammatical rules are arbitrary, insofar as they can be established purely conventionally, and "cannot be justified by showing that their application makes a representation agree with reality" (PG 134). "Grammar is not accountable to any reality. It is grammatical rules that determine meaning (constitute it), and so they themselves are not answerable to any meaning, and to that extent are arbitrary." They are as arbitrary as the "choice of a unit of measurement" (PG 133), which enables us to measure and to compare only when it has been chosen. Wittgenstein expresses his conventionalism most clearly in his arguments about the arbitrary nature of grammatical rules. Conventionalism regards the rules of grammar as constituted only by conventions, and acknowledges the presence of a connection between them and the needs experienced by men or groups of men.[21] The basis that is common to the following of all rules is "not agreement in opinions but a form of life" (PI 241). It is based on the common praxis of judging with regard to facts of experience (OC 519; cf. OC 358f.) Wittgenstein's analysis of the concept of "obeying a rule" exemplifies the implications of action governed by rules." Rules "rest on a social context of common activity."[23] A rule is fundamentally public. In order to be a rule at all, it must be shared by at least two persons. To that extent, a rule is necessarily intersubjective. The possibility of a private rule or a private language is therefore excluded.[24]

Wittgenstein insists that "it is not possible that there should have been only one occasion on which someone obeyed a rule. It is not possible that there should have been only one occasion on which a report was made, an order given or understood, and so on. — To obey a rule, to make a report, to give an order, to play a game of chess, are customs (uses, institutions)" (PI 199). A little later, he also says: "And hence also 'obeying a rule' is a practice. And to think that one is obeying a rule is not to obey a rule. Hence it is not possible to obey a rule 'privately': otherwise thinking one was obeying a rule would be the same thing as obeying it" (PI 202). We are therefore trained to obey rules just as we are trained to obey an order, and "we react to an order in a particular way" (PI 206).

Wittgenstein's analysis is very compelling. Like action that is governed by rules, rules themselves must be verifiable. They are subject to public criteria against which they can be checked and by means of which we must be able to verify whether we are really obeying a rule or whether we simply think we are obeying it. This question can be answered on the basis of the intersubjective character of the rules themselves. The intersubjectivity of the rules underlying a familiar and practiced language-game is documented in the players' participation in that game. On the basis of the criterion of the intersubjective consensus of those who are acting, deviations can be confirmed as not agreeing with the rule. "'So you are saying that human agreement decides what is true and what is false?'—It is what human beings say that is true and false; and they agree in the language they use. That is not an agreement in opinions but in form of life" (PI 241).

What is the precise meaning of "agreement"? How does it come about? How is it re-established when it has been disturbed? How should action that is governed by rules be verified in the concrete? On what basis do mutual understanding and agreement ultimately rest? Wittgenstein does not discuss these questions as a theme, and to that extent his analysis is incomplete. Not only is it incomplete—it also reveals the fundamental weakness of a concept of "rule" which has not been subjected to a criteriological reflection[25] and within which the levels of habit, custom, and convention as regulative factors have not been distinguished from the constitutive level of that which makes the regulative level possible, guarantees its functioning, and ensures agreement about it. I am therefore bound to concur with Apel in his conclusion that Wittgenstein's later work contains a central problem that he has not solved, that of the "transcendental-pragmatic foundation of the conventions for establishing or interpreting rules."[26]

### 3.1.5 WITTGENSTEIN'S REJECTION OF REFLECTION IN THE NAME OF THERAPY AND DESCRIPTION—HIS CONCEPTION OF PHILOSOPHY AND ITS APORIAS

"But if the general concept of language dissolves in this way, doesn't philosophy dissolve as well? No, for the task of philosophy is not to create a new, ideal language, but to clarify the use of our language, the existing language. Its aim is to remove particular misunderstandings; not to produce or create a real understanding for the first time" (PG 72). Again and again, Wittgenstein points out, with only very slight terminological variations, that philosophy merely describes, and explains nothing (see PG 30; PI 109, 124, 126). "The work of the philosopher consists in assembling reminders for a particular purpose" (PI 127). His activity is therapeutic. He does not provide us with a method but with "different therapies" (PI 133). With those therapies he treats the questions raised by philosophy, "like the treatment of an illness" (PI 255), and curses the "philosophical disease" that has been caused by "a one-sided diet" (PI 593). Seen in this light, philosophy is primarily concerned with itself, and its self-negating results are "the uncovering of one or another piece of plain nonsense and of bumps that the understanding has got by running its head up against the limits of language" (PI 119).

Wittgenstein's definition of the tasks of philosophy, then, clearly has essentially negative aspects. It has to cease to regard itself as a form of teaching. It has to be conscious of its own intentions (see PI 116) as unsuitable for everyday language and ordinary linguistic use. It has also to take up the struggle against the "bewitchment of our intelligence by means of language" (PI 109) that it has practiced itself. As a criticism of ideologies and of philosophical thought in particular, Wittgenstein's philosophy reveals the striving of philosophy to achieve depth, a crystalline purity, and the discovery of the essential being of such things as dogmatism and confusion. It also sets itself the aim of ensuring "that the philosophical problems should completely disappear" (PI 133).

The task of philosophy to eliminate philosophy is fulfilled not by thinking out philosophical problems to their end, but by ceasing to think philosophically. By turning the whole reflection round (PI 108), philosophy is reconstituted as an activity that clarifies meaning. The concepts "therapy" and "description" embrace the two central tasks of this philosophical activity. The first is related to the negative aspect and points to the duty to provide a diagnosis and a therapy for the nonsense that is produced by philosophy as a form of philosophical teaching. The second is concerned with the positive aim of philosophy to describe, to assemble, and to put in order the natural use of language. It can, however, only yield relatively meager returns, since, if philosophy is only able to ascertain "what everyone admits," (PI 599), and therefore leaves everything "as it is" (PI 124), it must in the end be superfluous. And Wittgenstein's proposition, "The real discovery is the one that makes me capable of stopping philosophy when I want to" (PI 133), would then be related not only to that form of philosophy that is subject to the criticism of ideologies as a form of philosophical teaching, but also to the philosophical activity of description. For what "particular purpose" (PI 127), after all, should such a philosophical activity "assemble reminders" if it is bound to recognize in the end that it has to leave everything "as it is"?[27] Wittgenstein's philosophy has, however, another dimension that can be learned from several of his statements. He says, for example, that his investigation is directed "not towards phenomena, but as one might say, towards the 'possibilities' of phenomena" (PI 90), and that he is not interested in "constructing a building" but in having in front of him the "foundations of possible buildings" (CV, p. 7). For this reason, his philosophy has justifiably been called "transcendental conventionalism,"[28] in which language-games acquire a transcendental status each time that they occur. They appear in his work as the condition governing the possibility and validity of communication, understanding, and agreement. However conventionally each individual language-game may be constituted, the network forming the whole complex of language-games that is so closely interwoven with the form of life provides the transcendental foundation for human interaction.

If we intend to reflect about this foundation—as we are doing now and as Wittgenstein himself did—we are bound to speak about all language-games. To do this, we need a language-game in which the whole complex of language-games can be expressed reflectively as a theme. It is precisely at this point that we encounter the aporia in the philosophy of Wittgenstein, since, on the one hand, all language-games form the object of his philosophy, while, on the other, philosophy is no particular language-game itself. It is not enough to say, as Meyer does, that Wittgenstein "leaves out one type of language-game, namely those language-games in which reference is made to other language-games."[29] Nor can I accept what Strawson says as adequate: "Could not the activities we call 'doing philosophy' also form a family?"[30] It is preferable to confirm the obvious presence of the aporia resulting from Wittgenstein's "doing of philosophy," namely, a transcendental conventionalism which, because of his rejection of transcendental reflection, is not able to take its own foundations into account. It is, in other words, not in a position to account for the conditions of the possibility and validity of its own arguments.[31]

The consequences of this aporia in Wittgenstein's conception of philosophy can be seen most clearly in his central themes. They are present, for example, in the assumed impossibility of going beyond the practiced language-games and institutionalized forms of life and transcending them in reflection. They are therefore to be found in the impossibility of recognizing those language-games and forms of life as historically conditioned and open to change and of receiving impulses along this path that will lead to their being changed in praxis.[32] These consequences are also perceptible in the assumed impossibility of transcending the factual use of language reflectively and of verifying it against the criteria of rules and grammar that cannot be immediately taken from it.

How, then, are we to come to an understanding and reach agreement with regard to the way in which we would like to use a word or a form of language or make a proposition, what it ought to mean, what language-games should be played, and what forms of life should be lived? We should clearly have recourse to the consensus of all those who are involved. That consensus can only be obtained by stepping outside the practiced language-games and lived forms of life and by reflecting about the problems raised by the claims to validity made by the process and their meaning.

I hope that in these concluding comments I have indicated the direction we should proceed on the basis of Wittgenstein's initiative. We should at the same time not lose sight of the immense importance of his pragmatic conception of language and language-games for the formation of a pragmatic theory, if that is to make use of the many disparate and fragmentary ideas that Wittgenstein has left us. As Peukert has so rightly observed: "The very same phenomena which Wittgenstein cannot adequately explain and which arise again in a more insidious form through their radicalization in the theory of language games relate to the central themes of the history of modern philosophy."[33]

### 3.2   JOHN L. AUSTIN'S APPROACH TO SPEECH ACT THEORY

Both in his "Performative Utterances"[34] and his "Performative—Constative," and in his William James lectures given at Harvard University in 1955 and posthumously published under the title of *How to Do Things with Words*, John L. Austin makes an important distinction between constative and performative utterances. Constative utterances are those with which something is said, that is, with which a statement that is either true or false is made. Performative utterances, on the other hand, are those with which something is not simply said, but done. They are, in other words, themselves acts, and instead of being able to be true or false, they either succeed or fail. In view of the difficulty of deciding on an unambiguous verbal criterion for distinguishing between performative and constative utterances, and above all with the danger of the possible failure to which constative utterances are as clearly exposed as performative utterances in mind, Austin asks if "stating something is performing an act just as much as is giving an order or giving a warning."[35] This causes him to postulate "a new doctrine about all the forces of utterances"[36] and to assume that the contrast between performative and constative utterances could hardly be preserved in a more universal theory of speech acts of this kind.

It is also possible to distinguish a parallel train of thought in Austin's Harvard lectures, the first seven of which, according to Forguson, "chronicle the rise and fall of the performative-constative distinction."[37] Austin regards the difficulty of providing a criterion for distinguishing between performative and constative utterances as connected with those cases in which performative utterances are able to be true or false,[38] and this causes him to relativize or revise his original distinction and to abandon it in favor of a new position. He claims that, in the case of every speech act, three closely connected "things" are done or actions are performed (HTW, p. 92). In this way, he extends the position—which he has already taken up on the basis of performative utterances and which can be summarized in the statement, "The issuing of the utterance is the performing of an action" (HTW, p. 6)—in the direction of a theory of linguistic action. According to this theory, every linguistic utterance as a speech act represents a series of actions that are connected with each other and dependent on each other. They are partial actions, and it is the task of a theory of speech acts to investigate the ways in which they are interdependent.[39]

According to Austin, if a speaker utters a statement, he performs a locutionary act of saying that can be sub-divided into three parts. The first part is "to perform the act of uttering certain noises" (HTW, p. 92). This is the phonetic act. The second part is the phatic "act of uttering certain vocables or words" (HTW, p. 92). The third, or rhetic act, has "to perform the act of using the pheme or its constituents with a certain more or less definite 'sense' and a more or less definite 'reference'" (HTW, p. 92f.).[40] Together with these partial acts that constitute the totality of the locutionary act, the speaker "is in general also and eo ipso to perform an illocutionary act" (HTW, p. 98) by saying something. He does this, for example, by pronouncing a warning with the utterance of the locution "I warn you . . ." or by making a statement with the utterance of the locution "I state that. . . ."[41]

From the illocutionary act that is performed in speaking, Austin distinguishes the perlocutionary acts that are not necessarily given with the speech act. These "we bring about or achieve by saying something" (HTW, p. 98). They differ from illocutionary acts in that the "consequential effects" that are denoted with them are "really consequences, which do not include such conventional effects" (HTW, p. 102).

Illocutionary acts, however, also have to do with consequences and effects in three different respects, insofar as the utterance has to be understood by the hearer for the illocutionary act itself to succeed,[42] have results, and produce reactions. This led Austin to look for linguistic criteria for making distinctions that he thought he could find in the construction of normalized reports on a speech act. Taking the question as to whether the report can be made either in the form of "In having said A, he has B-ed" (an illocutionary act) or "By having said A, he has B-ed" (a perlocutionary act), he arrived at an approximate differentiation. He was, however, made conscious of the unresolved insufficiency of this differentiation by a series of verbs with more than one meaning.[43] This caused him to leave the problem of perlocution and to take up again his original contrast between performative and constative utterances, to attempt to include this in a relativized form within the theory of speech acts, and to transform his plan to make a list of explicitly performative verbs into listing the illocutionary part played by utterances. He carried out this plan by identifying those verbs "which make explicit the illocutionary force of an utterance, or what illocutionary act it is that we are performing in using that utterance" (HTW, p. 149).[44]

Furberg has summarized the development of Austin's speech act theory by pointing out that he replaced his "Performative Thesis," which was central to his philosophy in 1946, by the "Force Thesis," propounded in his Harvard lectures. According to Furberg, he arrived at his conception of the illocutionary act "by conflating a performatory and a force-showing one."[45] His way out of the resulting dilemma was to make the illocutionary act indistinguishable from the role-showing act at the end of *How to Do Things with Words*, and to drop the performative aspect altogether. In opposition to Furberg's argument, however, I would say that Austin did not in any sense let go of the performative aspect. On the contrary, he included the thesis that is generalized with regard to all speech acts within the role thesis. The result is that, with their change into the first person singular in the present indicative of the active mood, illocutionary verbs become "performative verbs" in that sense, and that the illocutionary act that is denoted by them can therefore be explicitly performed.[46] The special status of perlocutionary verbs in which the situation of perlocution, which goes beyond the speech act in the narrower sense of the term, is expressed is now that it cannot, by definition, assume the explicitly performative form, since the success of the perlocution does not lie within the scope of the speaker's intention, but is dependent on whatever effects the speech act may have on the person addressed in respect of his further activity. Whether the perlocutionary act succeeds or not depends on the consequences of those actions that go beyond an illocutionary understanding of the speaker's intention and are brought about by understanding.

I cannot fully accept either Austin's emphatic tendency or Searle's tendency to relativize the perlocutionary act to such an extent that it is almost eliminated, and I would therefore insist that the perlocutionary act forms a fundamental part of the theory of the speech act. This is above all because the speaker not only wants to be understood but also must at the same time intend his discourse normally to have effects on the person addressed that are relevant to action.[47]

### 3.3   JOHN R. SEARLE'S SYSTEMATIC PLAN
### OF SPEECH ACT THEORY

Austin had a valuable insight regarding such performative verbs as "assert" and "state." It is that "we could distinguish the performative opening part (I state that) which makes it clear how the utterance is to be taken, that it is a statement (as distinct from a prediction, etc.) from the bit in the that-clause which is required to be true or false" (HTW, p. 90). This insight put him on the track of the double structure of language. This was in turn developed by John R. Searle in *Speech Acts*, although he did not in fact call it a double structure.[48] It is implied in the distinction between the two elements of the syntactical structure of the proposition. Searle describes this distinction, which is seen "from a semantical point of view" (SA, p. 30), as the propositional indicator that marks the propositional content of the performed illocutionary act, and the indicator of the illocutionary role, which shows which illocutionary act is performed with the proposition.[49]

Searle takes as his point of departure the hypothesis that speaking is "a (highly complex) rule-governed form of behaviour" (SA, p. 12), which he transforms into the form that "speaking a language is performing speech acts" (SA, p. 16). On the basis of that hypothesis, he elaborates the rules that underlie speaking, supporting this process by his "principle of expressibility."[50] According to this principle, "for any meaning X and any speaker S, whenever S means . . . X then it is possible that there is some expression E such that E is an exact expression of the formulation of X" (SA, p. 20). The principle of expressibility also allows him "to equate rules for performing speech acts with the rules for uttering certain linguistic elements" (SA, p. 20). He then goes on to look for the necessary and adequate conditions governing the performance of individual speech acts. On the basis of these, the task that he sets himself is to "extract from those conditions sets of semantic rules for the use of the linguistic devices which mark the utterances as speech acts of those kinds" (SA, p. 22).

Basing his reasoning and terminology to some extent on Austin,[51] Searle regards the performance of speech acts as composed of three kinds of acts. These are: 1) the performance of utterance acts, 2) the propositional act, and 3) the performance of illocutionary acts. Austin did not clarify the status of perlocutionary acts, and they disappear completely from Searle's field of vision. He in fact mentions them in his work on *Speech Acts*[52] but dissociates himself from them in his debate with Grice, and the latter's concept of meaning,[53] on the basis of an understanding of the speaker's intention as the illocutionary effect, with which Searle is essentially concerned in the speech act.

In his elaboration of the rules underlying speaking, Searle makes a distinction between regulative rules, as those which "regulate a pre-existing activity, an activity whose existence is logically independent of the rules," and constitutive rules, as those which "regulate antecedently or independently existing forms of behaviour" (SA, p. 34) and constitute and therefore at the same time also determine an activity whose existence is logically dependent on the rules. On that basis, he constructs a hypothesis which he summarizes as follows: "That the semantic structure of a language may be regarded as a conventional realization of a series of sets of underlying constitutive rules and that speech acts are acts characteristically performed by uttering expressions in accordance with these sets of constitutive rules" (SA, p. 37).

Searle used the analogy of a game of chess or football to illustrate these constitutive rules. Underlying rules not only make possible the institution of such games as both regular and rule-governed behavior, but also determine it.[54] This leads him to insist that an analysis of illocutionary acts should explain the connection between, on the one hand, the rules for the use of expressions employed by a speaker to achieve an effect on a listener, in the sense of his intention, by means of knowledge of that intention and, on the other, the expression that aims to produce that intention. An analysis of the illocutionary acts has therefore to throw light on the way in which the speaker is able to produce the illocutionary effect that he wants to produce on the hearer by inducing him to recognize that he intends to produce that effect and by making it possible for the hearer to understand the utterance. Understanding the performance of certain speech acts, in the sense of the analogy of a game as institutional facts, Searle is able to investigate the institution of "promise" paradigmatically and, in this way, to explain the performance of that speech act "by stating a set of conditions for the performance." At the same time, he is also able to affirm that, in so doing, "we shall have paved the way for the second step, the formulation of rules" (SA, p. 55).

From his analysis of the "promise," Searle achieves a number of results concerning the determination of the structure of illocutionary acts. They are quite relevant to the speech act theory in general and can be summarized as follows. For a speech act to be performed at all, seven conditions must be fulfilled: 1) normal conditions of entrance and exit, which exclude both obstacles to communication and secondary forms of communication,[55] 2) conditions of the propositional content, 3) introductory conditions that are typical of the speech act and, in the case of the promise, what Stegmüller[56] called the first and second presupposition of the promise, 4) the condition of sincerity, 5) the condition essential above all for the constitution of the type of speech act, 6) a condition not conceptually expressed by Searle but which, when fulfilled, ensures that the speaker intends to make known to the hearer by the speech act that, through the utterance, he has accepted the obligation, into which he entered through the speech act, to carry out that to which he had committed himself in the essential condition, namely, what the hearer ought to know, and 7) a condition that the speech act is uttered correctly and sincerely only when the first six conditions have been fulfilled. It is on this basis that Searle formulates rules for the indicator of the illocutionary role. These, in his opinion, can be regarded as rules for the semantic use of the intentions implied by the speaker for the achievement of the illocutionary effect he intends. They can be subdivided into rules of the propositional content, introductory rules, the rule of sincerity, and the essential rule.

Searle consequently believed that he had confirmed his initial hypothesis, that speech is an intentional form of behavior governed by rules, by defining the rules that constitute that behavior in its performance of the speech act. He was also convinced that, in so doing, he had initiated "a study of a langue" (SA, p. 17), that is, the reconstruction of the semantic structure of language and therefore of the representation that is possible on the basis of his principle of expressibility of its pragmatic dimension at the level of semantics.

This semantically oriented self-understanding of Searle's speech act theory, however, is precisely what prevents him from knowing the fundamental pragmatic status of the constitutive rules which explicate the condition of the possibility and validity of communicative agreement. It also leads to their becoming merged with the ways which are based on them and in which these rules are realized in individual linguistic forms and in the form of conventions. The attempts by both Habermas and Apel to correct this self-understanding of Searle's theory and to subject it to a critical analysis form one of the most important aspects of their approaches to the problem. I shall be discussing the question later in this book.

### 3.4 DIETER WUNDERLICH'S FURTHER DEVELOPMENT OF SPEECH ACT THEORY WITHIN THE FRAMEWORK OF LINGUISTIC PRAGMATICS

What Dieter Wunderlich requires of a speech act theory is that it should "not only generally formulate the conditions of such speech acts . . ., but also investigate the possible forms in which speech acts are realized in a definite language and a definite type of discourse."[57] This means that the speech act theory or the analysis of speech acts become for him the object, on the one hand, of theoretical and, on the other, of empirical linguistics. Empirical linguistics, at the same time, has a universal part and comprises an "investigation of speech acts that is related to individual languages."[58]

In a speech act theory, language is regarded as a specifically human activity. The act-character of human speech, Wunderlich believes, not only allows but also calls for a close connection between a theory of action and a science of language. He is also very conscious of the interdependent elements present in both, which are relevant to a strategy of research. He is aware "that the pragmatic basis of the speech act theory has to be linked with the theory of action and that linguistic analysis can also make a contribution to the development of the theory of action" (Stud 31). This means that the speech act theory is already oriented toward a theory of interaction and that it investigates the function of speech acts within the total context of social processes.

Wunderlich is firmly opposed to a conception of the speech act theory in the sense of a universal philosophical theory that seeks to elaborate what is common to all possible linguistic acts. He is equally opposed to what he regards as the erroneous notion of a speech act theory, which abstracts from concrete linguistic acts and proceeds on the basis of an ideal. He contrasts this with his own conception of the analysis of speech acts, which does not project any ideals but rather reconstructs "the procedures that are in fact employed in linguistic activities" (Stud 10).[59] In this form of analysis, the inclusion of fundamental categories of the theory of action has enabled him, within the framework of an admitted "philosophical orientation" (Stud 22), to develop a speech act theory which avoids the narrowness of Austin's and Searle's theories, is firmly based on linguistic theory, and is practicable in empirical linguistic terms.

Wunderlich believes that actions generally are characterized by three factors: 1) they are "contained within a complex space of action" (Stud 23), 2) they point to "certain systematic stages" through which they have to pass when a scheme of action is applied, and 3) they are "arranged according to certain definite levels" (Stud 24). He goes on to say that a similar situation prevails in the case of linguistic acts, with the result that, in an analysis of such acts, individual speech acts should not be isolated, as they are in Austin's and Searle's procedures,[60] but should be investigated within the context of the events leading up to and following them.

This attempt to give a historical perspective to the analysis of speech acts, Wunderlich believes, should be continued by incorporating quasi-institution-alized sequences of speech acts into a classification of types of discourse,[61] although he has not done this so far. In the meantime, he is trying to "historicize" this analysis by considering the presuppositions and the consequences of speech acts and, in combination with this, analyzing the "sequential nature of speech acts" (Stud 100).

Searle's investigations, in which only the presuppositions formulated in his "conditions" play a part, are described by Wunderlich as unsuitable as a model of pragmatic analysis. He has therefore decided to analyze the consequences that are associated with the performance of initiative speech acts, those in which a sequence is established. In his view, the illocutionary force of an utterance is situated in the way it affects the conditions governing interaction. This means that speech acts can be differentiated according to whether, as in the case of initiative speech acts, they introduce new conditions of interaction or, as in the case of reactive speech acts which conclude sequences, they either withdraw previously established conditions or fulfil existing ones.[62]

Wunderlich claims that many of the suggestions that have been made regarding the speech act theory have only taken the subjective factors of the intentionality of the persons concerned into account. He believes that he has overcome this disadvantage, in which "the objective factor of speech acts, namely that speech acts have consequences that can be expected for the further development of the situation that the persons concerned have in common" (Stud 57) is neglected, by approaching the question from the point of view of the conditions of interaction. In Wunderlich's opinion, light can be thrown on the obligations expressed in those conditions, which are valid for both sides, by a semantic and pragmatic analysis which combines both the subjective and the objective factors. Within semantics, the "distinctive aspects of fundamental speech acts"[63] can be clarified.[64]

Although Wunderlich explicitly includes semantic analysis, he is opposed to Austin's and Searle's attempts to give an emphatically semantic value to the speech act theory, which he detects in the reduction of the problems "that are connected with the carrying out of speech acts . . . to the semantics of verbs designating speech acts."[65] He is therefore in favor of a strongly contrasting analysis which goes beyond the meaning of propositions (semantics) and is concerned with the "meaning of sentences in context" (pragmatics).[66] This analysis, he thinks, would turn its attention especially to the presuppositions and conditions which depend on the context and which govern the success of a speech act, on the one hand, and the carrying out of the intentions that are connected with it and their consequences, on the other.

Searle limits his analysis to the conditions that he formulated for successful locution and illocution on the part of the speaker, which he regards as realized in an understanding of the utterance, in other words, in a grasp of the propositional content that is communicated and the interpersonal relationship that is thereby intended. This means that he is unable to transcend the individual speech act.

Wunderlich, on the other hand, is determined to enlarge Searle's narrow concept of success to include a concept of being successful. He says, for example: "It is only if we take both concepts together that we can envisage the realization of speech acts on the one hand and the consequences of those acts in interaction on the other at the same time and then relate them to one another" (Stud 111).

Being successful, which is related to the consequences in the further development of the situation of interaction, in the opinion of Wunderlich, implies, in cases of speech acts, which introduce new conditions of interaction, three different aspects: 1) understanding, 2) acceptance, and 3) fulfilment. The first, understanding, implies that "the person addressed should know (in accordance with the speaker's intention) that the speaker is expressing a definite attitude." The second condition, acceptance, means that "the person addressed should adopt (in accordance with the speaker's intention) a corresponding attitude." The third, fulfilment, is that "the person addressed or the speaker himself (in both cases in accordance with the nature of the speech act) should fulfil the condition of interaction that has been introduced" (Stud 115f.).[67]

Success of this kind does not come about automatically, and Wunderlich has therefore to go further and consider what might cause the hearer to accept a speech act and consequently fulfil the conditions of interaction established by it. In my opinion, however, it is quite clear from his investigation "into the consequences of speech acts"[68] that he has approached those consequences, in the sense of conditions governing conformity and action,[69] from the side of the speaker. This at once gives rise to two questions. First, from what source does a linguist obtain the right to formulate such firm conditions? And secondly, how is it possible for him to provide a linguistic justification of the consequences on the side of the hearer? Furthermore, I strongly suspect that Wunderlich, in appealing to the principle of cooperation and various conversational postulates,[70] has concealed from himself the fact that he has gone beyond the framework of linguistic research that he has constructed for himself. This would mean that he has confused his hypotheses, which are extraordinarily fruitful in more than the merely linguistic sense, with an ethic of communication, with unfavorable results both for a clear determination of the scope of linguistic analysis and for the point of departure of philosophical reflection.[71]

### 3.5   UTZ MAAS' THESES FOR AN
### ACTION THEORY OF LANGUAGE

Although he has not yet fully systematicized his various theses, Utz Maas has proposed a number which are closely connected with the work of the later Wittgenstein and the speech act theory and which change the latter materialistically in the sense of an action theory of language.[72] He does not accept an approach to a theory of communication that is oriented toward Bühler's sign model,[73] and prefers instead a conception of language based on a theory of action which regards language as the "performance of social labor which creates its own conditions in that labor, that is, in grammatical categories as coagulated labor."[74] The social aspect of language, according to Maas, is expressed in the fact that it is in language that situations are given a symbolic independence, which can then be regarded as socially binding.

Viewed in this perspective, the "social situation, as introduced by the speaker with his speech act and carried out by his partner," according to Maas, can be established "as the meaning of a speech act."[75] Speech acts succeed if there is an agreement between the partners in the interaction with regard to the presuppositions leading to their social situation, if the partner accepts the consequences for the situation resulting from the act, and if he then realizes that act when the occasion arises.

Maas analyzes these presuppositions in the case of elementary speech acts, in particular acts involving demands, questions, and assertions. In his view, commands are "perverted demands"[76] that can be understood as partly doing away with the possibility of calling into question and justification that is assumed in the case of every speech act. He regards demands, questions, and assertions, on the other hand, as coagulated acts in which structures of action are symbolically bound. That is why grammatical analysis, in his opinion, forms no more than a part of the whole meaning that is given with the speech act, insofar as it is an analysis of "aspects of the action that have been made independent"[77] that has been included in the theory of action within the relationship to social situations that have to be reconstructed.

This very broad outline of Maas' thought, as revealed in his essay "Grammar and the Theory of Action," can be made more precise in the light of some of his other writings. In discussing the distinction made by Wunderlich between "understanding" and "acceptance," he explains the former in the light of the theory of action as an "experimental acceptance,"[78] in which the "decisive aspect of the action"[79] corresponds to a definitive acceptance in the theory of action. He also stresses, in opposition to Wunderlich's need to have recourse to intentions as psychologically private, the social binding force of intentional mediation, which he defines as "taking on itself the socially binding consequences of a structure of action; it is not a question of feelings."[80]

Maas is critical of equating the Marxist concept of labor with the bourgeois concept of action, although he himself equates them and has not carried out his criticism.[81] He is also critical of an elaboration of the individualistic definition of that concept of action as "an objective category of bourgeois relationships of communication."[82] In addition to these criticisms, the arguments in his series of lectures on the theme "Can one teach language?" mark a further development in his approach to a theory of action in discussion with speech act theory and in his acceptance of Wittgenstein's conception of grammar.

Maas recognizes the "most advanced tendency at the time in the bourgeois theory of language"[83] in speech act theory, and he uses Grice's work as an example of its limitations. The latter's idea of a contractual relationship, in Maas' opinion, forms the basis of his analytical postulates and in particular his principle of cooperation. Both in Grice and in the speech act theory, the elementary principle is that of rational behavior directed toward a goal. Grice uses this principle in his analysis of conversation to make explicit "definitions of a form of communication that is based on a formal societization." To that extent, he is in a position to analyze strategic situations of argument that are directed toward a goal, but not in a position "to make an argumentation in solidarity explicit in a collective situation."[84]

By taking the idea of the association of free individuals as its point of departure, bourgeois linguistic theory reverts, according to Maas, "to the level of a Robinson Crusoe adventure. In other words, it makes use of the linguistically mediated product of societization in the special form of bourgeois society, the consciousness of the autonomous subject which enters into contractual relationships with other subjects, in order to make explicit its own production or conditions of production, that is, among other things, language."[85] Similar ideas in the work of Austin and Searle[86] had already been proved by Wittgenstein to be meaningless. By regarding grammatical categories as thematic, that is, as categories of experience instead of observation, which have to be reconstructed as historically and socially necessary conditions for the production and appropriation of experiences, Maas is clearly basing his theory on Wittgenstein's conception of grammar. In his opinion, Wittgenstein exposes "the practical basis of linguistic praxis" within the framework of a "praxis of life in which speech fulfils certain definite tasks."[87]

Wittgenstein's deliberations about the concept of rule, which shows that a privacy that appropriates a social element is a fiction, constitute an attack against the "private appropriation of the prevalent linguistic theory"[88] and point in the direction of a reflection about grammar based on a theory of action. Maas regards grammar as that part of language that "is the product of reflection about the form of life."[89] He consequently also believes that "what is radically new in Wittgenstein's approach" is to be found "in his consistently thinking out to the end of grammar as a concept of reflection which only has meaning in the reconstruction of a praxis of life."[90]

Maas further develops this grammatical reconstruction of situations in a participatory perspective by making an initial attempt to reconstruct elementary categories of linguistic acts. In this, he has described the question act as the "fundamental category of speech act."[91] It is the fundamental category insofar as it expresses a situation as a theme by questioning its conditions and opening the way to possible answers and to a further definition of the situation, and therefore includes possible changes. In this process of presenting situations as a theme and questioning them, they are, however, deprived of their natural mode of appearance. The way toward an agreement about their acceptability, correctness, and need for change is therefore opened, and action that can change the situation is also made possible. Maas' practical concern in developing his theory of action is to enable this to take place on the basis of a reconstruction of social situations.[92]

# Notes

1. See Apel, *Transformation I*, p. 172; Peukert, *Science*, p. 87; von Savigny, *Philosophie*, p. 113; Stegmüller, *Hauptströmungen I*, p. 561; Wuchterl, *Struktur*, p. 110; Zimmermann, *Hermeneutik*, p. 10, who also points out that "the continuity is as obvious as the divergence"; what is in the foreground depends on one's point of view: "Divergence with regard to the leading concept of language is . . . opposed to continuity in the conception of philosophy as an activity that throws light on meaning" (*Hermeneutik*, p. 87).

2. Kenny, *Wittgenstein*, emphasizes "the continuity of Wittgenstein's thought" (p. vii) and points out "many connections between the earlier and the later work and many assumptions common to both" (p. 219); he sees "the most striking feature of Wittgenstein's work" in "the permanence of his general conception of philosophy" (p. 229). See also Pears, *Wittgenstein*, p. 16. Schulz, *Negation*, notes an agreement between T and PI in respect of the self-cancellation of every philosophy; Winch, "Unity," p. 19, takes the "unity of Wittgenstein's philosophy" as his point of departure and regards his later work simply as a "rearrangement" of the propositions made in T; Lorenz, *Elemente*, p. 113, sees in PI "the necessary foundation for the carrying out of the programme in the *Tractatus* . . . and the same goal."

3. Meyer, *Sprachbetrachtung*, p. 132.

4. Apel, *Transformation I*, p. 321.

5. The concept "language-game" is central for the first time in PI. The concept does not appear in the PG until PG 26, where it is identified with the concept of calculation. Although "game" is often encountered in this later work (see PG 11f., 68, 73, 124, 140), what is normative for PG is what is formulated by the author in PG 140: "For us language is a calculus; it is characterized by linguistic activities." For the relationship between the concept of language and that of calculation, see Wuchterl, *Struktur*, pp. 107ff., 132ff.

6. Strawson, "Investigations," p. 71, speaks of two uses of the term; Stegmüller, *Wahrheitsproblem*, makes a distinction between three meanings of "language-game," as do Specht, *Grundlagen*, p. 41f., and Wuchterl, *Struktur*, p. 122. Zimmermann, *Hermeneutik*, p. 126, distinguishes four uses of the term. I believe that the concept has three meanings and take this as my point of departure in my argument in this section. I understand "language-game": 1) in the sense of a primitive linguistic model (see the language of the building workers in PI 2 or training in the mother tongue in PI 5ff.); 2) in the sense of a linguistic functional unit, as this is manifested in typically and partly standardized sequences of speech acts and actions (see the examples in PI 23); finally, 3) in the sense of the whole complex of linguistic activities involved with forms of life. What is, I believe, expressed in particular in this third meaning is the fact that each language-game, however primitive it may be, is related to the entire unity of language-game and form of life, and that it cannot be played outside the context of the previously given convention of that unity. Against this background, Wittgenstein is therefore able to say: "Something new (spontaneous, 'specific') is always a language-game" (PI, p. 224).

7. Apel, *Towards a Transformation*, p. 157.

8. See Zimmermann, "Sprache und Praxis."

9. Ibid., p. 323.

10. See PI 560.

11. See PI 20, 79, 120, 138, 197, 421, 432, 532; PG 10, 29; PR 59ff.

12. See, for example, Pitcher, *Philosophy*, p. 249ff.; Kenny, *Wittgenstein*, p. 120ff.; Alston, *Philosophy*, p. 32ff.; von Savigny, *Philosophie*, who implies this (p. 72ff.).

13. See Stegmüller, *Hauptströmungen I*, p. 577; Zimmermann, *Hermeneutik*, p. 112f.

14. See Wittgenstein's comparisons with the functions of machines, for example in PG 58, PI 12; his discourse about language as a tool-box, PG 11, 31; PI 11, 14, 16; and his reference in OC 64: "Compare the meaning of a word with the 'function' of an official. And 'different meanings' with 'different functions.'" He discusses the connection between purpose, role, and meaning in PG 32. In PG 84, he

explains, still using the concept of calculus, "the role of a sentence in the calculus is its sense."

15. A comparison with Humboldt's energeia concept of language comes forcibly to mind here; see Humboldt, *On Language*.

16. Habermas, LSS, p. 146.

17. Von Savigny, *Philosophie*, p. 73, regards Wittgenstein's thesis that use is like meaning as "so hopelessly vague that it is best to avoid it in any attempt to characterize Wittgenstein's linguistic philosophy." He does not, however, fail to recognize Wittgenstein's intention, in accordance with his task of "the preconceived idea of crystalline purity" (PI 108), not to violate by means of vague, undefined concepts "with blurred edges" (PI 71) the multiplicity of uses that seek to define, but instead to let them speak for themselves (PG 2).

18. Wittgenstein's controversy with the "representational theory of meaning" is connected with his criticism of Augustine's theory of meaning in PG 19f.; PI 1, 3f., 32, according to which meaning is the object for which the word stands.

19. Zimmermann, *Hermeneutik*, p. 112. "Reflect" should admittedly be replaced by "description" to preserve Wittgenstein's sense. For the problematical relationship between these two concepts, see 3.1.5 below.

20. See Specht, *Grundlagen*, p. 124ff. Pole, *Philosophy*, p. 31, stresses the second meaning, as do Habermas, LSS, p. 134, and S. Cavell, "Availability," pp. 67–93. Hacker, *Insight*, p. 151, clearly understands the two meanings of Wittgenstein's concept of grammar in regarding it as a structural description of language, on the one hand, and as described structure, on the other. J. Zimmermann has similarly grasped this double meaning in distinguishing between grammar as the "hermeneutics of conventions" (*Hermeneutik*, p. 181) and philosophy as "consciously made grammar" (p. 170).

21. Lorenz, *Elemente*, p. 129, goes so far as to speak of "human needs" as "guidelines" in Wittgenstein's "reflections about linguistic analysis." The connection between "rule" and "need" emerges, in my opinion, most clearly from the examples in the *Lectures*: "You could regard the rules laid down for the measurement of a coat as an expression of what certain people want" (p. 5), and "The rules of harmony, you can say, expressed the way people wanted chords to follow—their wishes crystallized in these rules" (p. 6). It is moreover obvious in the second example that the word "wishes" is not used to denote subjective preferences, but that it is a question here of intersubjectively shared collective orientations and that the word "needs" could be used. Wittgenstein himself adds in brackets: "The word 'wishes' is much too vague." See PI 108: "The axis of reference of our examination must be rotated, but about the fixed point of our real need."

22. See Cavell, "Availability," pp. 69–74; Wuchterl, *Struktur*, p. 132ff.; Zimmermann, *Hermeneutik*, p. 114ff.; Specht, *Grundlagen*, p. 142ff.; Winch, *Idea*, p. 24ff.; Meyer, *Sprachbetrachtung*, p. 124ff.; Kenny, *Wittgenstein*, p. 170ff.

23. Winch, *Idea*, p. 84.

24. For the question of the impossibility of a private language, see the controversy between Strawson and Malcolm in Strawson, "Notice," pp. 70–99, and Malcolm, "Investigations," pp. 120–129. See also Kenny, *Wittgenstein*, p. 178ff.

25. This has to be said, although Wittgenstein gives great emphasis to the concepts of a criterion of understanding (PG 41ff.) and a criterion of obeying rules. Indeed, it is possible to say, with Zimmermann, *Hermeneutik*, p. 173, that the concept of criterion is "at the centre of Wittgenstein's deep grammatical analysis" as the "methodical key to his hermeneutics of the language-game."

26. Apel, *Towards a Transformation*, p. 157.
27. Rossi-Landi's argument that linguistic alienation can be detected in Wittgenstein's ultimately self-sterilizing philosophy, and that the latter reflects the systematic divorce of academic activity from the rest of culture and of philosophy from the rest of intellectual work (Rossi-Landi, *Language*), is correct, but it is not sufficiently specific to provide a satisfactory explanation for the consequences of his philosophy.
28. Apel, *Transformation II*, p. 161, believes that this concept in Wittgenstein's philosophy expresses the closeness of his thought to Kant's transcendental philosophy and the distance from it.
29. Meyer, *Sprachbetrachtung*, p. 152.
30. Strawson, "Notice," p. 78.
31. Peukert, *Science*, p. 90f.
32. In one place at least, a reflection about linguistic change can be seen in Wittgenstein's work; see OC 63.
33. Peukert, *Science*, p. 92.
34. Austin, *Philosophical Papers*, pp. 220–239.
35. Austin, "Performative Utterances," pp. 220–239, especially p. 238.
36. Ibid.
37. Forguson, "Locutionary and Illocutionary Acts," Berlin et al., *Essays*, pp. 160–185, especially p. 160.
38. For example, in cases of what he called "expositives," such as the verb "state"; see How to Do Things with Words, pp. 102, 106.
39. For Austin's philosophical conception of "linguistic phenomenalism," see Furberg, *Saying*; Graham, *Austin*.
40. Austin combines the "reference" and the "sense" under the heading of "meaning." For a criticism of Austin's locutionarily determined concept of meaning and its relationship with the illocutionary force, see Alston, *Philosophy*, p. 36f.; see also Holdcroft, "Meaning," pp. 128–143; Cohen, "Forces," pp. 118–138; Cooper, "Meaning," pp. 69–77; Strawson, "Austin and 'Locutionary Meaning,'" Berlin et al., *Essays*, pp. 46–68, especially p. 53f.; Searle, "Austin," pp. 405–424, who, in connection with the difficulties of Austin's concept of meaning, tries to destroy his distinction between the locutionary and the illocutionary act (p. 40ff.). The opposite view is taken by Forguson, "Locutionary and Illocutionary Acts," p. 173ff; see also Habermas, CES, p. 42ff., who presents "force" and "meaning" as two categories of meaning.
41. For the question as to whether statements are performative, see HTW, p. 133ff.; Holdcroft, "Performatives," p. 13ff.
42. Furberg, *Saying*, p. 269, speaks of the "audience-directed dimension" that is constitutive for all speaking. The illocutionary effect as a conventional effect of the illocutionary act in which the latter comes to a close is achieved if the hearer understands the role intended by the speaker and the meaning of the utterance. If that takes place, the illocutionary act succeeds (see HTW, p. 117). Whether or not it is really successful (see Wunderlich, *Studien*, p. 111) can only be known from its interactional consequences.
43. See Austin, HTW, pp. 123–127.
44. Searle, "Taxonomy," p. 351, says correctly that Austin's list contains a classification not of illocutionary acts but of illocutionary English verbs.
45. Furberg, *Saying*, p. 212.
46. I have taken this distinction between "illocutionary verbs" and "performative verbs," which objectively corresponds with Austin, from Searle, "Taxonomy,"

p. 350, who correctly points out that "not all illocutionary verbs are performative verbs," in other words, not all can be used in the first person singular of the present indicative active.

47. In my view, the relationship between illocution and perlocution ugently requires further elucidation. On the one hand, there is the argument that has been used by Römer, "Dimension," p. 25: "On closer inspection, all linguistic effects disintegrate into nothing." There is also the one-sided and negative selection made by Schlieben-Lange, "Perlokution," p. 323, with which she confirms the impression that "perversions of the speech acts that constitute dialogue are present in the individual perlocutionary acts," and that "a close connection with tabus and hierarchies is urgently necessary for their occurrence." Against these theses, there is a need to consult "persuasive rhetoric." Kopperschmidt, who has unfortunately not made use of Austin's distinction between illocution and perlocution (see *Rhetorik*, pp. 81, 100), has nonetheless defined persuasive communication clearly as a "persuasively functionalized sequence of speech acts in which the partners in communication try to influence each other by means of linguistic arguments with the aim of restoring a consensus by an adequate change of opinion" (*Rhetorik*, p. 99). His rehabilitation of persuasive rhetoric as a "theory of the grammar of rational discourse to be developed within the framework of a theory of action" (*Rhetorik*, p. 21)—a rehabilitation which is directed against an instrumental misunderstanding of persuasive rhetoric and which, among other things, aims to develop a theory of persuasive competence—also, in my opinion, continues the debate about perlocution. Within the framework of a rhetorical theory, which takes as its point of departure the reality of linguistic communication that is oriented toward conviction and consensus, perlocutionary acts can be understood as proleptically intended by the speaker and, to that extent, as mediated via illocutionary acts, that is, via an understanding of the speaker's intention on the part of the person addressed. Those acts are successful if the hearer then makes the speaker's intention his own as far as his further activity is concerned. It is in this sense that we understand perlocutionary acts of convincing, teaching, making clear, and so on. Such perlocutionary verbs as "convince," "teach," and so on can be counted among Ryle's "achievement words"; see his *The Concept of Mind*, p. 130f. If the perlocutionary act is short-circuited with the locutionary act by consciously eliminating the illocutionary act, then the perversions to which Schlieben-Lange so insistently refers will occur, I, however, regard it as quite unjustifiable to see the essence of perlocution in the process of short-circuiting and therefore to place all perlocutionary acts on the list of perversions. A communication that is directed toward convincing the person addressed and toward forming a consensus of wills cannot, after all, be produced without perlocution. Without external linguistic perlocutionary effects, it would remain a communicatively immanent sand-box game.

48. This term occurs for the first time in Habermas, VB, p. 105, but its objective foundation can already be found in the work of Austin and Searle.

49. In accepting Chomsky's distinction between surface and depth structure, Searle frequently sees, in the depth structure of a proposition, the elements that indicate the illocutionary role and those that indicate the propositional content as clearly identifiable from each other. For his attempt to make Chomsky's distinction fruitful for an analysis of the syntactical aspect of the classification of illocutionary acts, see Searle, "Taxonomy," p. 361ff.

50. See Nolte, *Einführung*, p. 23ff.; for a criticism, see Wunderlich, "Zur Konven-

tionalität von Sprechhandlungen," and also his (ed.) *Linguistische Pragmatik*, pp. 11–58, especially p. 51; Apel, "Sprechakttheorie," p. 85ff.

51. Searle admittedly has certain reservations in taking over Austin's terminology of the "illocutionary act," which, in his opinion, served Austin as a name for "complete speech acts" (SA, p. 23) and certainly cannot apply in this case. The illocutionary, like the locutionary act is a part of the whole action of the speech act, and Austin did not introduce a special term for this. For Searle's rejection of the distinction between locutionary and illocutionary acts, see Searle, "Austin."

52. See SA, pp. 25, 43–50.

53. Searle, SA, pp. 43–50, supports Grice in following a concept of meaning that is one-sidedly oriented toward perlocution.

54. For Searle's concept of rule, see Wiggershaus, *Begriff*, p. 66ff.

55. See SA, pp. 57–62.

56. Stegmüller, *Hauptströmungen II*, pp. 77ff.

57. Wunderlich, *Studien*, p. 302.

58. Wunderlich, "Was ist das für ein Sprechakt?," Grewendorf, ed., *Sprechakttheorie*, pp. 275–324, especially p. 321.

59. Wunderlich's conception may be directed in particular against Habermas' universal pragmatics and against Apel's transcendental pragmatics, although he only makes explicit reference to Searle.

60. See Wunderlich, *Grundlagen*, p. 325f.

61. The category of the type of discourse represents for Wunderlich the "linguistic parallel with the sociological category of the institution" (Stud 29).

62. A reactive speech act in which a condition of interaction that has been introduced is then withdrawn is present, for example, when an assertion is revoked. An existing condition of interaction is fulfilled, for example, in the case of an apology.

63. Wunderlich, "Sprechakttheorie und Diskursanalyse," Apel, ed., *Sprachpragmatik*, pp. 463–488, especially p. 467.

64. That is why, within the framework of his distinction between five functionally differentiated levels of interpretation of speech acts at this level, he proposes a distinction between eight illocutionary types or types of speech act (see Stud 77). These semantically given types of speech act are pragmatically analyzed at the level of institutional and situational pragmatics. The first level indicates "what obligations are changed by definite utterances and how they are changed" (Stud 95), whereas at the second level a sense that is relatively modified to the social situation is oriented toward the "institutionalized" sense. See Wunderlich's outline of an integrated theory of grammatical and pragmatical meaning (Stud 51–118).

65. Wunderlich, "Sprechakte," Maas and Wunderlich, *Pragmatik*, pp. 69–188, especially p. 130.

66. Wunderlich, "Sprechakttheorie," Apel, ed., *Sprachpragmatik*, pp. 463–488, especially p. 467.

67. The third condition no longer applies in the case of speech acts that do not introduce a new condition of interaction.

68. In Apel, ed., *Sprachpragmatik*, pp. 441–462.

69. Ibid., pp. 444, 451.

70. For this, see especially, in addition to Grice's works, Gordon and Lakoff, "Conversational Postulates," *Papers*, pp. 63–84.

71. The objections raised by Schnelle, *Sprachphilosophie*, pp. 42–46, to Wunderlich's theory are valid at the linguistic level. As I cannot, however, join him in his

polemics against the "transcendental language-game" and his conception, which quite closely follows Carnap's, I would trace the foundation of Wunderlich's ideas back to "imprecise formulations" (p. 42) and regard these as the result of his failure to make a clear distinction between empirical analysis, theoretical and critical reconstruction, and philosophical reflection. His approach is ambiguous, in the first place, because he alternates between the levels of analysis and reflection. There is also a second reason for ambiguity in his approach: he uses philosophical underpinning in decisive places to support his approaches to a linguistic theory and to various research programs without fully accounting for this, and in so doing he has recourse to fundamental linguistic norms, such as that of interpersonally binding obligation, which can no longer be applicable. The status of these norms cannot be determined by him as a linguist, nor can it be justified by him in its normativity in the case of communication that follows a factually different course.

72. As I have pointed out, Maas follows speech act theory very closely, and his work is oriented toward the later Wittgenstein. He also gives only very cursory consideration to existing plans for a materialistic linguistic theory. For these reasons, I have decided to discuss his theses, which are, as far as their content is concerned, quite close to the materialistic conception of language, within the framework of my treatment of Wittgenstein and speech act theory. Maas' arguments have a fragmentary and programmatic character, but I have called them "theses" and regard them as important and promising for the development of a pragmatic linguistic theory.

73. See Bühler, *Theory of Language* and *Semiotic Foundations*.

74. Maas, "Grammatik und Handlungstheorie," Maas and Wunderlich, *Pragmatik*, pp. 189–276, especially p. 192.

75. Maas and Wunderlich, *Pragmatik*, p. 197.

76. Ibid., p. 210.

77. Ibid., p. 234.

78. Maas, "Notizen zu den Notizen," Maas and Wunderlich, *Pragmatik*, pp. 294–306, especially p. 298.

79. Maas and Wunderlich, *Pragmatik*, p. 302.

80. Ibid., p. 305.

81. See Maas, *Argumente*, pp. 11f., 21.

82. Ibid., p. 13.

83. Maas, *Kann man Sprache lehren?*, p. 121.

84. Ibid., p. 138.

85. Ibid., p. 141f.

86. Maas accuses Austin and Searle of making two mistakes in their thinking. These "represent reversions in philosophical reflection about linguistic theory as it has developed since Wittgenstein" (p. 147). 1) Their first error is that they have misunderstood the analysis of performative utterances as a "system of production and analysis that is independent of the situation," instead of treating it as a reconstruction of speech acts. 2) The second error is Searle's assertion, which is made in connection with the principle of expressibility, that "every utterance can be traced back to or derived from a corresponding form" (p. 148). Maas declares, in opposition to this, that performative utterances are "not fundamental structures of possible language as such, but products of a form of communication that is open to a contractual formalization of acts" (p. 149).

87. Ibid., p. 389.

88. Ibid., p. 388.
89. Ibid., p. 390.
90. Ibid.
91. Ibid., p. 344.
92. Maas' insistence on the fundamental nature of the question act will concern me greatly later on; see Kuhlmann's thesis: "There is no linguistic structure in which performances providing evidence of a knowing subject, so that the latter can acquire knowledge at all can be considered in such a concrete and precise form as in the question. The question is the natural point of departure for a linguistically oriented criticism of knowledge" (*Reflexion*, p. 103). Not only this emphasis, but also his act oriented conception of grammar as a concept of reflection, in contrast to the scientific conception that is latent in speech act theory, is important. In the results of his reconstruction of social situations, he has clearly dissociated himself from the objectivistic tendency in linguistic theory. In my opinion, however, there are, in this dissociation, still certain aspects of linguistic philosophy that have to be considered. It is, for example, wrong, however justified a criticism of Searle's principle of expressibility may be, to represent performative utterances as the product of a definite form of communication. It is true that a whole set of languages may not have grammatical forms of performatives at their disposal in the sense of possessing explicitly performative verbs. I believe, however, that—independently of the form of appearance in each case—the indisputable foundation of all human communication is that men in linguistic activity agree with each other, make promises to each other, exchange gifts, argue, and so on. It is important to distinguish these elementary types of act from linguistic forms that are made present at each moment in history, and Maas does not do this sufficiently. In addition, a criticism of his equation of language and labor and an explanation of their mutual relationship are urgently required. Maas should also clarify his position with regard to the traditions of materialistic linguistic theory and consider the bourgeois tradition in greater detail.

# = 4 =

# The Pragmatic Textual Theory

## 4.1 SIEGFRIED J. SCHMIDT'S PLAN OF A TEXTUAL THEORY WITHIN THE FRAMEWORK OF COMMUNICATIVE ACT GAMES

### 4.1.1 SCHMIDT'S POINT OF DEPARTURE IN THE THEORY OF MEANING

In his study devoted to the theory of meaning, *Bedeutung und Begriff*, Siegfried J. Schmidt's principal intention is to "describe both the intersubjective way in which language has an effect and its informative achievements and its performances related to action and reality in the process of knowledge and communication."[1] He provides a criticism of the weakness of operationalistic theories of meaning, which above all fail to consider the question of the stabilization of use. Then, following Wittgenstein's conception of meaning, he considers "meaning" as a relational concept which is connected with intersubjectivity and operational generality and which is correlated with the concept of language, with which it is placed in a fundamental mutual relationships. He regards language "first and foremost as a form of action that provides information and establishes contact" (BB 52). This means that it is the task of linguistic philosophy in its quest for reality "to determine the process of man's debate with his reality and the role, performance and importance of language in that process" (BB 53). Schmidt believes that there is no reality seen from the point of view of the subject who simply aims to know, and that reality points to a space of possible situations and "histories" with which men are associated and "entangled."[2] This leads him to take as his point of departure the "performance of language as constituting reality" (BB 60). He understands this in the sense that "it is the presupposition of the determinability of elements of history and relations and formally prescribes the (syntactical) accomplishment of predication/relation-forming of symbolically represented correlates" (BB 61).

Schmidt shares the view held by Kamlah and Lorenzen that language is the accomplishment of acts organized in "activity schemata."[3] He also follows Pike's linguistic theory based on the theory of behavior. This enables him to achieve a consistent view of linguistic and non-linguistic activity with regard to the structure and function of language within a perspective of meaning that sees both as intentional activity that is governed by rules and oriented toward success.[4]

The knowledge that questions about meaning are meta-questions prevents us, Schmidt believes, from engaging in a phenomenological and descriptive process in determining "meaning." In any attempt to develop a theory of meaning, a conception of meaning has of necessity to be presupposed as a working hypothesis. Schmidt bases his own conception on Peter Hartmann's statement "that linguistic signs can only occur when bound to a text,"[5] and formulates it as follows: "Meaning is not an entity which transcends language, which is encountered in speech and to which one can be related. It is rather a function of factors of operations that are socially relevant or relevant to action" (BB 78).

Texts have meaning, then, in situations as the framework for meaningful linguistic acts. This implies that an analysis of meaning must determine the relationship between the text as a whole and semantically relevant selections from the text. For the latter, Schmidt introduces the concept of the "semantic situation" (BB 85).[6] By this he means the situation of the construction of meaning and the semantic fixation of the naming elements of a proposition within the framework of a text. In this process, the situation also takes place within a "history." The process of constituting meaning is summarized by Schmidt as "a progressive selection governed by the intention of the discourse and taken from the effective and functional possibilities of the presuppositional elements that are known in their relevance by the speakers, as an individualization of the functions which are already given as norms and options in the system of the langue and which are determined according to class and formally characterized. This process points in the direction of an intentional and situational adequacy of linguistic modes of action that is relevant of communication" (BB 139).

Schmidt, it will have been noted, makes use of Saussure's distinction between "langue" and "parole." He situates the "concept" as a lexem in isolated treatment at the first level, which contains in use in the "parole" a meaning of performance (meaning as a factor in the act). "I therefore call 'meaning,'" Schmidt continues, "a communicative relevance of linguistic acts that is adequate to the intention and the situation. It is also a function of the systematic use of linguistic means. That function is informatively and performatively (or prescriptively) successful, in other words, it fulfils a recurrent expectation and it comes about as the result of an exploitation, which is specific to the situation, of the possibilities of forming sem combinations within the framework of a syntactical matrix that fulfils intentions" (BB 144).

The consequences, for linguistic philosophy, of this analysis of meaning, within the framework of a language as a mechanism for guiding the activity of understanding conception, point—in a dictum that is borrowed from Wittgenstein, "Asking about meaning is giving qualified attention to the results that can be or are in fact aimed at" (BB 147)—to the category of the "communicative act game." I shall deal with this in greater detail in the following section.

### 4.1.2   THE CATEGORY OF THE "COMMUNICATIVE ACT GAME"

Several very different linguistic and ontological tendencies are included in Schmidt's category of the "communicative act game." First, there is the insight of theoreticism,[7] namely, that we always encounter "reality" only as the self-manufactured product of our own knowledge in that reality, in a theoretical construction of models of reality which at the same time guides our praxis. Then there is Blumenberg's definition of the modern concept of reality, which is oriented toward a historical understanding of "concept" and in which reality is conceived as a relative factor that is related to a constitutive performance by subjects, that factor representing a limit concept which is associated with intersubjective experience and can be complemented.[8]

Schmidt has also drawn a number of conclusions, based on the theory of knowledge, from the discussion of the concept of reality that has taken place at the levels of the theory of science and linguistic philosophy. These are that the discourse about "reality" cannot begin with phenomenal reality. Its point of departure must be those human acts which are presupposed in constructions and operations and in which the reality of experience is constituted. "The factually a priori state of every knowing subject is his occurrence as the speaker as in the 'space' of a language, a living person in situations of communication."[9] Via Kamlah and Lorenzen, Wittgenstein and Schapp, Schmidt comes to the conclusion that, if reality is not an objective fact that is independent of theory, and communication has to be seen as a primary phenomenal datum, "one arrives at something that can be called 'reality' only in the context of and via communicative behavior."[10] Following Gebauer's interpretation of Wittgenstein,[11] Schmidt regards language as a system of communication that only occurs in linguistic and non-linguistic forms of work in "communicative act games" that integrate complex communicative processes. Both linguistic contexts and extra-linguistic situations of communication, in which only linguistic forms function and constitute "realities" that are always already images of reality in the accomplishment of "communicative act games," form a necessary and integral part of "communicative act games."

If, however, "reality" must not be regarded as the objective third position

with regard to the speaker and language, the question concerning the connection between language and reality has to be redefined as a question
concerning the status of "'reality' within communicative act games."[12]
Schmidt sees language and reality as related to one another in such a way
that models of reality are designed and interpreted in the language that is
realized in situations of communication. These models are, moreover, stabil-
ized by recurrence in a community of speakers by concepts, as guides to a
definite activity in situations of communication, and are made socially binding and become capable of being made present in situations of experience.

Communicative act games have the ability to act as norms in situations of
experience. In this process, because of this characteristic of communicative act
games and their constituent parts, language acquires the "function of 'constituting reality.'"[13] As Schmidt points out, "The communicative act game, with
its characteristic complex of linguistic and non-linguistic constituent parts, is
seen, within the framework of these considerations, to be the specific place
where concepts are formed (where grammatical meaning is constituted) and
where internalized concepts are applied to the articulation and (realistic)
interpretation of situations of experience according to the criterion of social/
recurrent normative processes of those situations of experience."[14]

In his later works, Schmidt considers in more precise detail his notion of
the communicative act game and includes the arguments put forward by
Niklas Luhmann and Ursula Oomen in the "system theory of texts."[15] In
accordance with these arguments, he sees communicative act games as
simple social systems that can be defined by the following characteristics: 1)
a space of perception that can be clearly delineated; 2) acts of communication that have complementary roles in the case of a potential similarity of
perceptions; 3) a limited variance of partners in communication; 4) a meta-
communicatively verifiable thematic orientation of the acts of communication; 5) an embedding in the social system of society; and 6) the formation of
texts as an ordered sequence of processes of decision and selection.

According to Schmidt, this results in the following "hierarchy of embedding."[16] Linguistic and non-linguistic constituent parts are embedded
in acts of communication, and these are in turn embedded in communicative
act games within types of situations of communication. These are in turn also
embedded in the society of communication, and this again is embedded in
the society of interaction. The whole complex of communicative act games
within a society of speakers therefore constitutes that society as a society of
communication.[17]

## 4.1.3 ASPECTS OF A TEXTUAL THEORY

Schmidt's reflections about a theory of meaning and his deliberations
about the category of the "communicative act game" come together in his

plan of a textual theory. This theory takes into account the fact that textual-ity, according to Schmidt, is "the universal, social way, which is obligatory for everyday linguistic usage, in which communication is accomplished."[18] Linguistics, which are conceived as a textual theory and which aim to construct a theory of verbal social interaction by investigating the production and reception of communicatively functioning texts within the framework of communicative act games as simple social systems, in Schmidt's view have certain clear aspects. These he calls the semantics of instruction, the refer-ence theory, the presupposition theory, textual grammar, the production of the text, and the coherence of the text.

In accordance with the approach that he has adopted in his theory of meaning, he regards lexems as rules or instructions for the production of definite behavior. This means that he sees semantics conceived on this basis as "semantics of instruction." These are investigated by the communicative functioning of lexems in lexematic fields within the framework of com-municative act games. A semantic analysis of texts has to take three fun-damental aspects as its point of departure and, similarly, must describe communication under three headings. These are: a) semantically, as a man-ifestation of a fundamental, coherent logico-semantic depth structure of the text; b) symbolically and technically, as a systematic complex of elements according to rules; c) at the level of efficiency as a symbolic act and as a (successful) informational and communicative operation in communicative act games" (TT 58). The "semantic characteristics" that belong to the "depth structure of the text" are seen by Schmidt to be heuristic hypotheses. In this, he postulates the meaning of the constituent parts of the text as constructed from elements according to rules in contexts for functions. In this process, the construction of a system of semantic characteristics, which has to be measured against the criteria of objective linguistic verifiability, coher-ence, and concrete value for research, has "a technically heuristic value in the field of research that can only be assessed in the context of concrete problems of research" (TT 71).

In the wider framework of the theory of communicative act games, Schmidt believes that reference has to be treated as a category at the level of communication rather than at the level of the proposition or the statement: "'Reference' names the guidance given to the partners in communication with regard to the constituent parts of the text" (TT 77). Within the framework of the semantics of instruction, then, a reference theory has the task of working out the criteria that will restrict the guidelines given to the partners of communication, specifically to the situation, by means of a constituent part of the text.

Schmidt makes use of Frege's distinction between "sense" and "meaning"[19] and reformulates it by describing "sense" as "virtuality of instruction," or "canonical instruction," and "meaning" as "actuality of instruction," or "situative instruction." " 'Canonical instruction,' " Schmidt explains, is "the linguistic hypothesis concerning the content of guidance about an isolated constituent part of the text which is described as an ordered cluster of semantic characteristics (of various types) . . . . 'Situative instruction' points to the factual achievements in instruction of an expression in factual communicative act games" (TT 85). If the canonical instruction of a statement can be denoted by the term "proposition," and that of a lexem by the term "concept," then the situative instruction of texts and the constituent parts of texts, Schmidt suggests, should also be called "socio-communicative relevance." If he has in this way included the concept of the proposition in the textual theory and, what is more, as he himself stresses, following Stalnaker and Searle, "consciously as a theoretical construct" (TT 92),[20] then he is clearly giving the concept of the proposition a very important part to play in the context of a textual theory.

Schmidt has also worked out hypothetically a very adequate classification of presuppositions. In this, he has had recourse to a number of reflections about the theory of presuppositions.[21] In his own classification, his point of departure has been that presuppositions are "all kinds of implicit (co-asserted) prior assumptions that are made by speakers when they want to carry out an act of communication illocutively and successfully . . . . If that act of communication is to be successful, all the partners in the communication process must be able to infer them from the utterance and regard them as true" (TT 102).

Schmidt distinguishes between various categories of presupposition. These are what he calls the lexical-semantic, syntactical-semantic, contextual, situational, pragmasemantic-referential, and act-semantic presuppositions. He regards only the last three, however, as presuppositions in the strict sense of the word, the entire system of which is concerned with the "complex situation of presuppositions" in which the partners in communication are placed. This "complex situation" contains "all the specific conditions, restrictions and provisions to which the partners in communication are subject in processes of communication" (TT 104). These are socioeconomic, socio-cultural, cognitive and intellectual, and, finally, biographical and psychological. The presuppositions, as actualized prior assumptions, are called "situational presuppositions" by Schmidt. They form a partial quantity of the presuppositions operating in the "complex situation of presuppositions" and "can be described as constituents of that 'possible world' that is presupposed in a communicative act game as the obligatory level of interpretation for the uttered text as a quantity of guide-lines" (TT 106).

Schmidt leaves the problem of the grammar of the text within the framework of a textual theory, merely drawing attention to the approaches made by van Dijk, Wunderlich, Lakoff, and Kummer, who have aimed at producing a model for the production of texts via depth structures. He himself proposes a model of orientation for textual production, following a discussion of the problem of a new version based on the textual theory of the concept "text" and the question of textual coherence that is connected with that problem. Because of the presupposition outlined above, that all communication is textual, it is obvious that a purely linguistic definition of a text is not possible. Such a definition must contain both the linguistic and the social aspects. This means that texts have to be seen as texts-in-function and, as such, only within the framework of contexts of communication and interaction. In those contexts, certain institutionalized types of action and communication are manifested, with the result that every text is the realization of a type of communication with an illocutionary potential that is specific to the type of communication.

This conclusion has led Schmidt to define text in the following way: "A text is every uttered linguistic constituent part of an act of communication in a communicative act game which is thematically orientated and fulfils a recognizable communicative function, that is, realizes an illocutionary potential that can be known" (TT 150). If various illocutionary acts are in fact realized within an act of communication, then what is involved is an in-text of a text. The text as a quantity of utterances-in-function, however, has to be distinguished from the formulary of the text, which forms the object of research into the textual grammar at the level of the depth structure of the text. Schmidt attempts to delineate Kummer's "pragmatic concept of the text"[22] and in so doing distinguishes from pragmatic coherence a semantic connection which presupposes this and constitutes the semantic concept of the text. On the basis of this, the degree of textuality of a series of utterances can be described.[23]

Seen in the perspective of a hermeneutically conceived, bidirectionally oriented production and analytical model of the text, the generation of texts, on the one hand, and the reconstruction of the stages of production, on the other, can be represented as a productive process of decision by the speaker within the framework of a communicative act game. They can also be seen as the reconstructive elaboration of the possible elements and stages of a similar process of decision by the hearer or reader.

The following stages may or must be verified in that process. In a complex situation of presuppositions, the speaker is determined by his communicative competence or by the competence that he assumes to be present in his partner in communication. On this basis, he projects an image of the situation in which the communication takes place, taking as his point of departure various hypotheses about the intellectual and social capacity of his partner or partners. Then, in respect of the illocutionary potential intended by him in selecting the type of discourse and text that is suitable for the purpose that he has in mind, he sets up a program of the act of communication based, on the one hand, on his own intention to communicate and, on the other, on the intended effect of his communication. He then sets about the task of carrying out that program via the conception of a textual depth structure that is deciphered in a sequence of connected concepts. This program is realized by means of the utterance of the text that is produced from the concepts in the statements that are oriented toward communication via a formulary of the text that is specific to the situation and the intention and with the help of suprasegmental factors.[24] Schmidt believes that in this model he has defined the elements of a program that has to be elaborated in detail by research into textual theory.

Many aspects of his presentation are postulatory, and his own theory often gives the impression of being a very eclectic association with disparate parts of other theories. What is important in his work, however, is his attempt to integrate very diverse approaches within the framework of a linguistic analysis that is oriented toward the fundamental fact of textual communication as a textual theory. This represents a very big step toward the formation of a pragmatic theory.

# Notes

1. Schmidt, *Bedeutung und Begriff*, p. 3.
2. Schmidt has borrowed this word from Schapp; see Schapp, *In Geschichten verstrickt.* Schmidt is oriented toward Schapp's conception of history, which is mediated with Wittgenstein, but he does not share his phenomenological view; see Schmidt, "'Text' und 'Geschichte.'"
3. See Kamlah, "Handlungsschemata," Kamlah and Lorenzen, *Propaedeutic*, p. 41ff. Schmidt recognizes a number of "instructive parallels" with his own conception in "Kamlah's and Lorenzen's linguistic theory based on the theory of action"; see BB 153.
4. See Pike, *Language*; Schmidt, BB 66–73. Schmidt does not, like Habermas, make a distinction in the orientation toward success in linguistic and non-linguistic action between a communicative and a strategic or an instrumental orientation. This means that there is ambiguity here about the kind of success that is described, or that Schmidt has simply not recognized the fundamental distinction between agreement oriented toward consensus and strategic or instrumental activity.
5. Hartmann, "Begriff," p. 221.
6. Later he replaced the "not particularly happy choice" of this term by the expression "situation of communication"; see "Handlungsspiel," p. 109.
7. Schmidt goes no further here than simply alluding to Popper's theory of science and that of his pupils Albert and Lenk, as well as to Quine's compatible thesis,

according to which speaking about "reality" is only speaking about the factor that makes our discourse about it true or false.

8. See Blumenberg, "Wirklichkeitsbegriff." Here too Schmidt simply makes allusions.

9. Schmidt, "Handlungsspiel," p. 106.

10. Ibid., p. 107.

11. See Gebauer, *wortgebrauch*, in which the author, following the later Wittgenstein, develops a theory of meaning in which he understands language as a social "form of labor" or form of life that consists of the two components, "linguistic" and "non-linguistic" forms of labor. A part of considerable importance for the meaning of "linguistic forms of labor" is played in this by the "non-linguistic forms of labor." The latter can be understood as the "context of the discourse and, vice-versa, the 'linguistic' forms of labor can be seen as an activity through language" (*wortgebrauch*, p. 17).

12. Schmidt, "Handlungsspiel," p. 110.

13. Ibid., p. 113.

14. Ibid., p. 116.

15. Luhmann, "Systemtheoretische Argumentation," Habermas and Luhmann, *Theorie der Gesellschaft*, pp. 138–165; see also Luhmann, *Soziologische Aufklärung I* and *II*, especially "Einfache Sozialsysteme," pp. 21–38; also Oomen, "Systemtheorie der Texte," Kallmeyer et al., eds., *Lektürekolleg II*, pp. 47–70.

16. See the outlines provided by Schmidt, "Texttheorie und Pragmatik," p. 17, and "Texttheorie," p. 49, which I have summarized here.

17. The criticism that Schmidt is guilty of idealism is the result of the view that society has become absorbed in his work in communication. This criticism appeals to the arguments noted in my text and to similar ones. It fails to appreciate, however, that Schmidt does not simply equate society with communication, but regards "society as a communication-society within the framework of society as a society of verbal and non-verbal interaction" ("Texttheorie," p. 45, or "Texttheorie und Pragmatik," p. 15). I would, on the other hand, certainly agree that his arguments fail almost completely to take into account the part played by non-verbal forms of interaction or "forms of labor" (Gebauer), and are not adapted to do adequate justice to the part played by the latter in constituting society and "reality." In my opinion, however, Schmidt is right to insist also on the linguistic mediation of non-verbal forms of interaction, which links the latter to the verbal forms in the form of life.

18. Schmidt, "Texttheorie," p. 145.

19. See Frege, *Logical Investigations*.

20. See Stalnaker, "Pragmatics"; Searle, *Speech Acts*, pp. 29–33.

21. See Schmidt, "Texttheorie," p. 95ff. See also Petöfi and Frank, eds., *Präsuppositionen*.

22. Schmidt, "Texttheorie," p. 158, refers to a manuscript by Kummer: see Kummer, *Grundlagen*.

23. Schmidt's utterances about the semantic concept of the text are far from concrete. Above all there is a lack of particulars regarding the process by which texts are qualified semantically as texts beyond the reference which is constitutive for pragmatic coherence to judgments by the partners in communication. I suspect that Schmidt regards this qualification, regarding the specification of a model for the production of a text, as guaranteed and believes that this model leads in reverse, in other words, in reconstructive application to a semantic concept of the

text via an analysis of the constituent parts and stages of production that can be distinguished in an existing pragmatic type of text. This would also correspond to the "bidirectional" employment of the model for producing a text and for analysis. In this, the problem of the hermeneutical circle has to be taken into account, and Schmidt has not thought about this.

24. See "Texttheori," p. 165.

# 5

## Karl-Otto Apel's Transcendental Pragmatics as a Reflection about the Conditions of the Possibility and Validity of Linguistic Communication

### 5.1 APEL'S TRANSFORMATION OF TRANSCENDENTAL PHILOSOPHY

In his transformation of transcendental philosophy, in the sense of transcendental linguistic pragmatics, Karl-Otto Apel sets himself the task of "renewing the Kantian question of the conditions of the possibility and validity of scientific knowledge as the question concerning the possibility of an intersubjective agreement about the meaning and truth of sentences or systems of sentences." In this way, he also seeks to "transform the Kantian criticism of knowledge as an analysis of consciousness into a criticism of meaning as an analysis of signs."[1]

The connection that he establishes in his work with transcendental reflection clearly contradicts the scientifically oriented philosophy of science and such twentieth-century philosophical movements as positivism, logical empiricism, or critical rationalism. These movements, Habermas and others have pointed out, claim that they are the inheritors of the theory of knowledge, but, in their denial of reflection, they have in fact become absorbed in their work into the philosophy of science.[2] It may have been and may still be possible to draw no more from Kant's *Critique of Pure Reason* than conclusions regarding the philosophy of science in the sense of a scientism that limits the idea of knowledge to the modern natural sciences.[3] This, however, is something that Apel rejects.

Apel has reconstructed Kant's paradigm of philosophy as a philosophy of consciousness to develop his own philosophy within the framework of the paradigm of transcendental semiotics, a paradigm that has been initiated by twentieth-century analytical philosophy and has to be explained with regard to the agreement within the community of philosophers in mind.[4] He uses this reconstruction to oppose, with the help of Kant's argumentation, Kant's limitation of the constitution of the object of possible objectively valid experience to phenomena of natural scientific knowledge. Reflection about the conditions governing the possibility and validity of scientific knowledge, according to Apel, has resulted in Kant's transcendental philosophy being corrected in a number of important aspects. These corrections have been made, above all, in the light of a philosophy that has been at least partly determined by twentieth-century linguistic criticism. This corrective process has led to a transformation, or even to a raising to a higher level and cancellation in the Hegelian sense, of the central concepts and themes of the transcendental theory of knowledge, which in this way has become transmuted into transcendental semiotics. In Kant's philosophy, the transcendental question aimed at prelingual and precommunicative conditions of contemplation and intellect governing a constitution of the object that is of necessity valid for every consciousness as such. That constitution, moreover, regarded the conditions, present in the transcendental synthesis of apperception as the unity of consciousness of the object and consciousness of self, as Kant's "highest point" of transcendental philosophy. Apel, however, has made fundamental changes in his approach, on the basis of the *a priori* of the language-game that was overlooked by Kant, and consequently also on the basis of everyday language, as the inescapable condition of the possibility of agreement.

Kant does not take into account either the linguistic conditions of his theoretical discourse or the linguistic conditions of the possibility of an intersubjectively valid and meaningful constitution of objects as something.[5] This means that his "critique of reason" must be preceded by a "meta-criticism" as a "criticism of language." This takes place as a transcendental semiotic reflection about the conditions of the possibility and validity of knowledge, as argumentative agreement about sign-mediated objects of knowledge. It also encounters the communicative synthesis of interpretation as the "highest point" of a semiotically transformed transcendental philosophy. This is because the synthesis of interpretation, in which the synthesis of data of experience must be found both with regard to the validity as meaning and with regard to the validity as truth of linguistically formulated judgments about knowledge, as a unity of agreement about something in a society of communication, constitutes reality as a reality of intersubjectively shared communicative and instrumental experience.[6]

At the level of transcendental linguistic pragmatics or semiotics, then, the community of interpretation is the analogue for the transcendental subject. Unlike Kant's ahistorical consciousness, that community represents a mediation of a real and an ideal community of communication, in which the ultimate agreement of the postulated ideal communication community functions as a regulating principle for the judgment of agreement factually aimed at. From this point of departure, Apel is also in a position to question the Kantian triad of empirical realism, transcendental idealism, and transcendent realism (of affection), in which he is above all critical of meaning. He does this by using an argument similar to that used by Jacobi, namely, that Kant had to make a presupposition of his system with the discourse about the causal affection of our senses through the thing in itself. That presupposition cannot, however, be combined with the second presupposition of Kant's system, that of the restriction of the sense of causality to possible experience.[7]

This enquiry leads Apel, in the tradition of Peirce's transformation of Kant during his earlier period, to reject the idea (which is ultimately contrary to sense) that there is in principle an unknowable world of things in themselves, situated behind the real world.[8] Apel argues that what is real is defined, instead of as what cannot be known, as what, in contrast to what is unreal, can "in the long run" be known, unlike what is factually known.

Apel in this way reaches the point where he can outline a realism that is critical of meaning. In that realism, the real subjects, with the raising of a claim to universal validity which is implied in every statement (assertion) that is related to truth, assume the function of the transcendental I of knowledge by anticipating a universal intersubjectivity of that validity claim that aims at the ideal communication community. In this way, these real subjects also anticipate the ideal with every real argument in the real communication community.[9]

I have now sketched out the basic outlines of Apel's transformation of Kant's transcendental philosophy. In the following section, I shall indicate systematic points of contact between his transcendental pragmatics and the work of previous philosophers. In my opinion, these can be found: 1) in the pragmatic semiotics of Peirce and Morris, 2) in Wittgenstein's language-game model, 3) in Chomsky's linguistic theory of speech competence, and 4) in Austin's and Searles's speech act theory.

## 5.2 APEL'S POINTS OF CONTACT

### 5.2.1 THE PRAGMATIC SEMIOTICS OF PEIRCE AND MORRIS

Peirce's semiotics of the three-dimensional relationship of signs is Apel's central point of contract in his transformation of transcendental philosophy. This is because Peirce himself had precisely this semiotic transformation very firmly in mind, and his deduction, within the framework of a logic of relations, of the three fundamental categories of firstness, secondness, and thirdness, on the one hand, and his doctrines of categories and interpretation, on the other, enabled him to point the way to three-dimensional transcendental semiotics. With his realism, according to which what is real is knowable, and which is fundamentally critical of meaning, he was able to critically examine the Kantian idea of the thing in itself and supersede it. Similarly, by replacing the "highest point" of Kant's philosophy (the transcendental synthesis of apperception, by which its function in the constitution of the "ultimate opinion" of the "community of investigators" assumes objective validity and can be achieved "in the long run"), Peirce was also able to historicize Kant's transcendental subject as the regulative principle. He was at the same time able to replace the Kantian notion of consciousness by the unlimited process of investigation within the unlimited community of interpretation. By transforming transcendental into a semiotic logic of investigation, Peirce succeeded in providing a basis for his semiotics of the three-dimensional relationship of signs by a logic of relations in his doctrine of categories. At the same time, he also made it fruitful by a logic of research in his doctrine of the three kinds of conclusions, which he applied to the process of research and investigation, and in which the logic of abduction (or logic of guessing), which constitutes pragmatism, is the motivating force for progress in knowledge.

It is on the Kantian foundations on which Peirce built up his philosophy that Apel has based transcendental pragmatics. On the basis of its proof of the three-dimensional aspect of the relationship of signs, according to which each sign is seen to be constituted as meaning something to an interpreter, Apel is able to demonstrate the "reductive fallacy" of every philosophy of science that leaves the sign aspect out of account, and to regard his philosophy, on the one hand, as a means of exposing such fallacies by a criticism of ideologies and, on the other, as a complete presentation of the way to scientific and philosophical knowledge. Peirce believed that the normative basis for the process of achieving knowledge was a search for truth based on consensus and guided by the ultimate goal of the agreement of all involved. This insight has enabled Apel both to detect the scientific restrictions of Peirce's conception and, with Royce, to raise the scientifically limited concept of the "scientific community" as the "community of investigators" that is sustained by the "self-surrender" of scientific subjects to the level of the universal "community of interpretation," that is, of the unlimited communication community of all beings gifted with reason.

According to Apel, Morris developed a conception of three-dimensional semiotics on the basis of Peirce's philosophy and at the same time reduced it behavioristically. He stressed the unity of semiotics, which, he claimed, consisted of syntax, semantics, and pragmatics and provided a pragmatically integrated semiotic program. At the same time, however, his presentation of his semiotic theory as an empirical science of behavior on the basis of methodical behaviorism gave rise to an aporia. Apel believes that the aporia occurs in Morris' conception of semiosis, in which the meaning of signs and the understanding of intentions, in other words, fundamental communicative phenomena, are reduced to observable behavior, as a comprehensive natural process in which Peirce's interpretants are objectivized as fundamental dispositions of behavior that are accessible to experimental verification. Whereas Peirce stressed the normative basic intentions of semiotic pragmatism, Morris emphasized a scientific basic attitude, which, in its program of an objective, value-neutral science of signs gives way to a "naturalistic fallacy" in terms of biologism, in other words, to the "illusion" that "biologically defined normative values can be used as value-neutral empirical and designative concepts."[10]

Morris' semiotics, with their scientific orientation, can be and are, de facto, accepted by the logic of analytical science. For Apel, however, Morris' teaching is important as a unique development, extremely relevant for the history of effects, of a pragmatically integrated three-dimensional form of semiotics, the naturalistic restrictions of which, by going back to Peirce, can be used to explain in an exemplary way the normative foundations of a complete theory of signs. Morris' three-dimensional framework of syntax, semantics, and pragmatics therefore provides Apel with a model for his own conception of transcendental semiotics and for a semiotic reconstruction of the paradigms of first philosophy, including the typology of possible forms of reductionism abstracting from this three-dimensionality.[11]

## 5.2.2  THE LANGUAGE GAME MODEL OF THE LATE WITTGENSTEIN

Apel also has a second important point of contact. This is the later philosophy of Wittgenstein. In the perspective of the latter's pragmatics of possible language-games, Apel introduces his own transcendental linguistic pragmatics on the basis of the transcendental language-game that is presupposed in all other language-games as the condition of the possibility and validity of agreement. He does this with Wittgenstein, in opposition to Wittgenstein, and going beyond Wittgenstein.

With Wittgenstein, Apel insists on the connection between language-game and form of life, regarding the first primarily as "a unity, which functions as a form of life, of linguistic use, corporeal expression, behavioral praxis and disclosure of the world."[12] In this, he obviously shares Wittgenstein's pragmatic criticism of meaning and even more particularly his argument against the possibility of a private language.[13] That argument is also critical of meaning, and Apel uses it as a crucial argument in his conception of the *a priori* of communication, in which he attempts to expose Descartes' dream argument as meaningless, and to overcome the "methodical solipsism" implied in it. With Wittgenstein, too, Apel affirms rules only in the sense of a secondary abstraction from the unity between language-game and form of life that has to be understood in the light of the part that is always primarily played by those taking part.

In opposition to Wittgenstein, Apel has also shown that the latter's relativistic conclusions are of the kind of a "pluralistic, relativistic and finitistic 'pragmatism of the present,'"[14] and he has pointed out that this comes from their phenomenological and descriptive restriction to analyses of exemplary language-games. He therefore challenges Wittgenstein's assumed reflective competence of the philosophical language-game as a transcendental factor, on the basis of which only the rules of language-games as conditions of the possibility and validity of agreement and understanding, presupposed by the conventional realization of those language-games, can be established. In opposition to Wittgenstein's denial that anything could be known about the essence of language itself in the concept of the language-game, Apel emphasizes that the transcendental pragmatic implications of the concept are constitutive for the concept of language as such, and thus breaks radically with Wittgenstein's transcendental conventionalism.

In this, he goes beyond Wittgenstein in the direction of transcendental linguistic pragmatics. These pragmatics are connected with Wittgenstein's central and unsolved problem in his later philosophy, that of the transcendental pragmatic foundation of conventions for the establishment or the interpretation of rules. This problem leads Apel's pragmatics, in its explanation of the "transcendental language-game," to a solution that includes Wittgenstein's criticism of meaning and even continues it, which means, according to Apel, taking it consistently to the end.

### 5.2.3 AUSTIN'S AND SEARLE'S SPEECH ACT THEORY

The speech act theory provides Apel, above all, with two points of contact. The first is established by its demonstration of the double structure of the discourse. The second is found in its concept of the rule, which at the same time also contains the key to the normative implications of speech act theory itself.

I have noted that Searle followed Austin in pointing to the double structure of speech acts, composed of a propositional and an illocutionary component. Apel develops this idea in the direction of his distinction between the linguistic conditions governing the interpretative constitution of the object and the agreement about the meaning and truth of statements that reflects about validity. Apel identifies Searle's propositional acts of reference and predication as linguistic pragmatic conditions of the prereflective synthesis of something as something, a synthesis that constitutes the object. He therefore sees the possibility of reflection about validity in the embedding of propositional acts in illocutionary acts. According to Apel, the performative expression, "I assert by this confronted with every possible partner in discussion . . ." shows paradigmatically that the performative part of constative speech acts discloses a dimension that links the universal claim to truth (made valid in those acts, as a condition of the possibility of being able to make such a claim in communication about anything) with the claim that is made meta-communicatively and met in an agreement that reflects about validity to an intersubjective validity of meaning. According to Apel, this means that the empirical I in the "I assert by this" assumes "the function of the 'transcendental I' of knowledge by anticipating a universal intersubjectivity in its validity claim."[15]

Apel believes that Austin's and Searle's failure to recognize the transcendental philosophical implications of the speech act theory is due to a series of erroneous conclusions, the most important of which being the one formulated in Searle's meta-criticism of the criticism of the "naturalistic fallacy" of the possibility of a derivation of obligation from being.[16] At the same time, however, Apel is also conscious of the possibility of deriving normative conclusions from the speech act theory, something that is also recognized by Searle himself in the concluding statements of *Speech Acts*,[17] which, according to Apel, point to "the possibility and necessity of a transcendental philosophical interpretation of the speech act theory."[18] The point of departure for this is Searle's concept of rule, in which the pragmatic difference between statements and speech acts—which Searle overlooked because of his orientation toward the semantics of statements, on the one hand, as a not yet successful fulfilment of the ideal of the illustration of speech acts in state, formulated in Searle's principle of expressibility, and, on the other, as constitutive in the sense of an innovation that changes conventions and rules—compels us to revise fundamentally our self-understanding of the speech act theory as oriented toward "langue."

Apel has undertaken this revision. In so doing, he makes a distinction between linguistic competence, or "langue" competence, and communicative competence, which is based primarily not on "langue" conventions but "rather on universal norms of human ability in discourse."[19] Accordingly, he contrasts the universal pragmatic rules with the individual linguistic conventions.

Searle did not take this step. By understanding the constitutive rules of language in analogy with the constitutive rules of institutions, he lost sight of their fundamental difference. This is that, in contrast to conventionally established institutions, which are therefore in principle replaceable by others, the constitutive rules of language represent the "normative condition of the possibility for all ways of establishing rules institutionally by conventions."[20] These rules also constitute the meta-institution of communication as the condition of the possibility of constituting, criticizing, justifying, and changing all human institutions. According to Apel, then, the rules of communication have a transcendentally normative, grounding function. This was suggested by Searle in his speech act theory, but not elaborated by him.

Apel also uses Searle's example of the promise to demonstrate that this does not simply represent, as Searle believed, a conventionally regulated institution, but that it also has to be presupposed as a condition of the possibility of valid conventions: "We can therefore claim the normative conditions of the possibility of a valid promise as conditions of the possibility of that argumentative discourse in which we are always engaged if we ask and discuss the question concerning the intersubjective validity of norms. In this way, the normative conditions of the possibility of a promise are indicated as part of that transcendental language-game that is presupposed as inescapable and has to be claimed in the case of every possible discussion."[21]

The argumentative discourse, Apel insists, is not a language-game alongside other language-games: "Its relationship with all conceivable language-games and institutions . . . is that of a meta-institution."[22] In such a discourse, the transcendental language-game reaches the point of "explicit consciousness and institutionalization of its transcendental function."[23] It also becomes conscious of two factors in connection with the universal pragmatic norms of the ethics of communication. The first is that those norms have to be presupposed and recognized as conditions of the possibility of meaningful argumentation in the argumentative discourse. The second is that those same universal pragmatic norms represent the fundamental norms of all communication, in which we contrafactually always anticipate the normative ideal of an ideal speech situation as one of unlimited agreement within an ideal communication community. This anticipation of the ideal takes place in the real communication community of our factual situations of conversation, and we at the same time direct those real situations toward the ideal ones as situations that have to be made real.

### 5.3 APEL'S TRANSCENDENTAL PRAGMATIC PHILOSOPHY OF THE COMMUNICATION COMMUNITY

If the Kantian origins of Apel's philosophy are viewed together with the points of contact between his thought and pragmatics, the language-game model, and the speech act theory, the following picture emerges. Apel's philosophical conception renews Kant's question about the conditions of the possibility and validity of knowledge. Apel sees the original Kantian question, above all, as one concerning the conditions governing the possibility and validity of intersubjective agreement within practices of the language-game and forms of life that are always previously given, practices that can at the same time be made into a problem and can be transcended and institutionalized. He believes this can be done by having recourse to the transcendental language-game that underlies all language-games that are played in fact.

It should be clear from this that, if someone enters into an argument and therefore communicates with others with possible agreement in view—and human life would be unthinkable without entering into communication; Apel has said of the person who fails to do this that "by behaving in this way, he is almost like a plant"[24]—he has implicitly recognized the fundamental ethical norm of communication. He has recognized that, in taking part with others in the real communication community with the aim of agreement, he is anticipating the unlimited agreement that will be achieved in the ideal communication community as the norm and goal of the real community. In this way, by entering into communication in common with others, he has implicitly recognized every other person as a partner in communication, with rights that are in principle equal. Confronted with that partner, he is obliged to justify the validity claims that he has made with his statements, with agreement in mind. That agreement should be shared by all participants and it should be agreement about what they want, what they ought to want, and what they ought to recognize and realize as what is and ought to be wanted.

Apel believes that this reflection, about what subjects are always bound to do and presuppose if they are to be able to communicate at all, provides the ultimate philosophical foundation for ethics of communication that can be discovered in transcendental reflection. Its point of departure is the reflective insight, critical of meaning, into the foundations of the very process of argumentation, which cannot be criticized: "If I cannot dispute something without self-contradiction and at the same time cannot ground it deductively without a formally logical petitio principii, then it must be one of those transcendental pragmatic presuppositions of argumentation that we must always already have recognized whenever the language-game of argumentation is to preserve its meaning. For this reason, the transcendental pragmatic mode of argumentation can be called the form that is critical of meaning of the ultimate foundation."[25]

Popper believed that a resolution has to be made in favor of rationality, in the sense of a decision, and, in the light of this decision, that rationality cannot, for its part, be motivated but has to be seen as being based on faith in rationality.[26] In opposition to this view, Apel insists that an exclusive orientation toward a model of deductive foundation, by the critical rationalists, prevents them from acquiring an insight into the possibility and necessity of reflective foundation on the basis of discovering the transcendental foundations of factual argumentation ("reflective" in this case being "effectively self-reflective").

By reflecting about what has of necessity to be presupposed in order to conduct an argument, a person will arrive at the following foundations. First, there is the communication community, since it is as impossible for him to conduct an argument alone as it is for him to obey a rule alone. Secondly, he is conscious of making validity claims for what he has said in his argumentation. He must be able to make, stand up for, and justify these claims in confrontation with every possible partner in communication, and this procedure can only have a final effect if it involves everyone. For that reason, if he is to establish a criterion in order to distinguish between factually accepted and normatively correct and justified validity claims, he is bound to distinguish the real communication community from a community which is assumed to be effective and is anticipated as ideal in communication, and which provides the ideal norm for the factual community and should be moving toward the real community, mediated by the praxis of its members.

Apel's transcendental pragmatics are based, then, on a number of reflective insights. There are his insights into the dialectics of the real and the ideal communication community, into the *a priori* of communication as the fundamental ethical norm, and into the fundamental recognition that is always presupposed in this of all the others participating in the communication. Each one of these others, in Apel's transcendental pragmatics, is seen as a subject who possesses equal rights, who is able to make his claims valid with regard to me and with whom I have to reach a consensus in respect of the ideal consensus of all participants.

These, then, are the cornerstones of Apel's transcendental pragmatics. His work can therefore be seen as the philosophical foundation for the formation of any pragmatic theory. Even if we take the threefold dimension of the relationship of signs as our point of departure, the subject of the communication that is mediated by signs is still at the center of a pragmatic philosophy, in which that subject is understood with all possible subjects in view. That philosophy, moreover, derives its energy from the synthetic power gained from bringing together important stages in the formation of a pragmatic theory in a renewed transcendental philosophy. What is clearly recognizable in the latter is an attempt to rehabilitate reflection and consequently a theoretical philosophy, which culminates in a practical philosophy (an establishment of ethics), on the basis of the twentieth-century criticism of meaning and language.

The range and significance of Apel's transcendental pragmatics will be considered after an examination of Habermas' universal pragmatics. I will deal with the matter in this order because the crucial question emerges most clearly in a confrontation between the two philosophies, via long passages in both Apel's and Habermas' thinking, in which their conceptions of fundamental pragmatic reflection or theory run parallel. The crucial question is whether universal pragmatics should be understood as a reconstructive science or as philosophical reflection. When this question has been answered, I shall consider another: whether a universal pragmatic theory for its part presupposes transcendental pragmatics or is an alternative to it.

In trying to answer these questions, I shall also, in the light of my intention to reconstruct systematically the history of the formation of a pragmatic theory, have to ask yet another question. This third question is whether there is one single pragmatic conception that integrates the many different approaches, perspectives, and results that are under consideration. In my attempt to answer this question, I shall have in mind whether transcendental or universal pragmatics combined can incorporate or can be extended to incorporate the integrated conception that I am seeking or whether neither of them can do this.

# *Notes*

1. Apel, *Transformation II*, p. 163f.
2. Habermas, KHI, p. vii, has expressed this tendency strikingly in the formula: "That we disavow reflection is positivism."
3. See Apel, *Understanding*.
4. For Apel's paradigms of first philosophy, see "Transcendental Semiotics."
5. In oppositon to this, Apel uses Hamann's insight "that language has already synthesized the world of phenomena before the distinction between sensuousness and intellect is made and that a 'meta-criticism' as a 'criticism of language' has therefore to precede Kant's 'critique of reason'" (*Transformation I*, p. 139).
6. Apel's conception of reality as linguistically mediated and linguistically constituted does not lead to idealism, because he regards its linguistic constitution as mediated with the material constitution, in other words, with labor. In this, he stresses even more clearly than Habermas the primacy of language, which in a certain sense underlies linguistically mediated labor. According to Apel, however, his *priori* of the communication community points to "the principle of a dialectics (on this side) of idealism and materialism" (*Towards a Transformation*, p. 280) in the dialectical interrelationship between the real and the ideal communication community. The postulate of a mediation of idealism and materialism (or realism) in transcendental semiotics is determinative for Apel.
7. See Apel, "Zur Idee," p. 295.
8. Contrary to sense insofar as it represents knowledge about what is presumably unknowable; see "Zur Idee," p. 295f.
9. Whereas Habermas acknowledges four universal validity claims, Apel only recognizes that of truth.
10. Apel, "Morris," p. 56.

11. See Apel, "Transcendental Semiotics," p. 9ff.; "Zur Idee," p. 286ff.
12. Apel, *Transformation I*, p. 321.
13. Ibid., p. 268.
14. Apel, "Sprechakttheorie," p. 33.
15. See Searle, SA, pp. 131–136; see also Apel, "Sprechakttheorie," pp. 56–80. Apel is correct in saying that, in deriving obligation from being, Searle was in practice deriving a value-statement from a descriptive statement. He was thereby making the mistake of overlooking the fact that his assumedly purely descriptive premises were already functioning as value-loaded. This mistake, according to Apel, is connected with the fact that Searle made a strict distinction between the use and the meaning of statements and regarded the logical deducibility of propositions from propositions (the level of meaning) as independent of the illocutionary role of the utterance of statements (the level of use). This, Apel believes, can be falsified if "the real point of Searle's discourse about the deducibility of the validity of conclusions from their description" ("Sprechakttheorie," p. 64) is seen as conditioned by the apparently descriptive surface structure of the descriptive statement, which must have the character of a value-loaded statement in its depth structure.
16. See Searle, SA, p. 198; Apel, "Sprechakttheorie," p. 81.
17. See Searle, SA, p. 198.
18. Apel, "Sprechakttheorie," p. 82.
19. Ibid., p. 87.
20. Ibid., p. 101.
21. Ibid., p. 120.
22. Ibid., p. 123.
23. Ibid., p. 124.
24. Aristotle, *Metaphysics IV*, 1006b, 14. Apel considers Aristotle's statement to be a transcendental pragmatic doctrine in this respect: Everyone who says anything at all, that is, who enters into an argument—and to be able to and to have to do this marks man off from the plants—has in this way clearly recognized the fundamental ethical norm of argumentation.
25. Apel, "Problem," p. 72f. For the ultimate foundation of the ethics of communication, see Apel, *Towards a Transformation*, pp. 225–300. In opposition to this, Albert, *Träumereien*; see Albert, *Treatise*, which repeats his objection that every attempt to provide an ultimate philosophical foundation is confronted with "Baron von Münchhausen's trilemma."
26. See Popper, *Open Society I*, p. 188ff. In opposition to this, see Apel, *Towards a Transformation*, p. 267ff.

# 6

# Jürgen Habermas' Universal Pragmatics within the Framework of the Theory of Communicative Action

## 6.1 THE STATUS OF UNIVERSAL PRAGMATICS WITHIN THE FRAMEWORK OF A THEORY OF COMMUNICATIVE ACTION

As I noted in the preceding chapter, Apel has accepted many different philosophical approaches but, again and again, has concentrated, in his transcendental pragmatics, on the question of the conditions of the possibility and validity of communicative agreement. As a result, his thinking has acquired in this respect a "pyramidical" outline, in which everything tends to move from every part of the base up toward the apex.

Unlike Apel, Habermas gives the immediate impression of taking an extremely broad approach. Habermas includes the most widely different areas of philosophical reflection and seems to be trying to integrate a whole series of partial theories. Apel directs every philosophical tendency that he is considering to the royal highway of transcendental reflection. Habermas, on the other hand, works hard at the most divergent theoretical approaches, whose immanent movement he pursues to a suitable connecting point, where they can be integrated as complementary theoretical parts of an all-embracing postulated theory of communicative action.

Habermas' inclusion of so many different traditions of thought and research in his so-called universal pragmatics has two immediate consequences here. In the first place, it is necessary to go further than I have so far done in this book, in considering his points of departure. In the second place, however, those points of departure enable us to look into his philosophy for a systematic central point, around which the various partial theories are clustered. The search is made all the more urgent because of the very multiplicity of Habermas' points of departure. I have no hesitation in saying straightaway that, in my opinion, the central core of Habermas' universal pragmatics is his theory of communicative competence. In that theory, he aims to identify and subsequently reconstruct the universal conditions of possible agreement, in order to analyze "the infrastructure of our action" (ThdG 208). This communicative competence is expressed in the sense of a theory oriented toward the model of the reconstructive sciences via an analysis of elementary speech acts. Following Chomsky's concept of (linguistic) competence as the "ability of an ideal speaker to master an abstract system of linguistically generative rules" (VB 101), Habermas calls for a concept of communicative competence that is pre-switched into linguistic competence and has to be developed in a theory of communicative competence. The theory has the task of investigating the "universal structures of possible situations of discourse," which are themselves produced linguistically (VB 102).

In analogy with Chomsky's linguistic theory of grammatical transformation, the theory of communicative competence also represents a theory of communicative ability on the part of speakers or hearers. It certainly goes very much further than Chomsky's theory, and is opposed to his giving an absolute value to the syntactical and semantic approach, with its claim to "reconstruct the ability of adult speakers to embed sentences in relations to reality in such a way that they can take on the general pragmatic functions of representation, expression and establishing legitimate interpersonal relations" (CES 32).

Later in this chapter, I develop this very brief outline of the foundation and methodology of, and the claims made by, Habermas' universal pragmatics. In the meantime, however, I would affirm that it forms the systematic central core and pivot of a far-reaching network of theories, which, within the framework of the concept of a "theory of communicative action," includes the dimensions in which such communicative action takes place at the level of the subject, society, and history.[1] There is still a great need for an integrative theory of the subject, society, and history, on the basis of universal pragmatics and within the framework of a theory of communicative action, as a development of all its aspects. This intention undoubtedly plays a decisive part in Habermas' approach to the question. While I hold in mind the explicative and integrative performance that is expected of universal pragmatics in this network of theories, I want to outline at least the range and significance of the theory of communicative action at which Habermas is aiming.

At the level of a theory of society, Habermas has a basic theory of the social sciences in mind, as a reflection about their logic, on the basis of the philosophy of science. The foundations of a theory of society result from the universal pragmatic reconstruction of the constituent parts of society. The reconstruction provides the basis for a plan of a theory of society that dialectically integrates the Marxist approaches as well as those based on system and the interaction theories already in existence.[2]

Habermas intends also to formulate a theory of the subject. Presenting the constitution of the subject as derived from intersubjectivity, his theory contains a further theory of the development of the subject's cognitive, linguistic, and interactive competences. Habermas is concerned here chiefly with elaborating the interactive competence that enables a responsible participation in communication and with demonstrating its gradual formation within the context of the acquisition of other competences. His theory of the subject also contains his elaboration of symbolic interactionism, the cognitivistic psychology of development and the analytical psychology of the ego, his theses on the theory of socialization, and his work on the problem of the identity of roles and the ego.[3]

At the same time, he also follows, within the framework of a reconstruction of historical materialism and a critical acceptance of certain elements of Luhmann's system theory, a number of ways leading to an all-embracing theory of history as a theory of social evolution. He does this by taking as his point of departure the hypothesis of the possibility of seeing phylogenesis and ontogenesis in parallel, and then, in analogy with the discovery of individual competences, attempting to reconstruct the formation of "competences of the human race" in their sequence, following a logic of development.[4]

On the basis of the partial theories and approaches outlined above, it is possible to claim that a theory of communicative action can be expected to furnish three analyses: 1) of both the constituent parts and the process of man's becoming and being a subject; 2) of the constituent parts of society together with an elaboration of a suitable apparatus for research into existing and past societies; 3) of history. The theory of evolution has to be borne particularly in mind in this third analysis, as well as the need to define the "dynamic forces" and the "direction" of history, with special emphasis on the formation and preservation, on the one hand, of communicative structures, in other words, fundamentally human structures, and, on the other, on their suppression and the dangers to which they are exposed.

Within this total framework of the theory of communicative action that Habermas aims to formulate, universal pragmatics form the systematic central core. They have this status because they reconstruct the elementary concepts and categories of human action and therefore provide, with the total conception in view, the analytical apparatus and the criteria against which the interrelationships of both micro- and macro-actions can be measured. Both the scope and the systematic priority of universal pragmatics can be seen in the fact that these criteria, which have evolved on the basis of elementary actions, are able to function as normative standards of evaluation for successful interaction.

In this presentation of universal pragmatics, it is not only heuristically suitable and appropriate, in respect of Habermas' own way of proceeding, but also important, from the systematic point of view, to look carefully at Habermas' concept of action.

This concept, after all, is today one of the most debated and disputed in sociological and philosophical reflections about foundations. Since the time of Max Weber, it has played a central part in all attempts to define the area and the object of research into the social sciences and the approach to the so-called action sciences and the practical philosophy of continental imprint. It has also become increasingly important in the sphere of analytical philosophy. Finally, in pursuing my presentation here of the development of the formation of a pragmatic theory, I must state that all pragmatics are a theory of human action as man's sign-mediated association with the natural outside world, with his own environment, and with himself. This makes a consideration of the concept of action all the more urgent in the case of the formation of a pragmatic theory.

## 6.2  HABERMAS' CONCEPT OF ACTION

Underlying Habermas' concept of action is his distinction between social and non-social action. The first is always related to other people, either individuals or groups, and is oriented toward their expectations of behavior. In the second, the relationship with the subject is replaced by a relationship with an object that is subjected to one's own control. Habermas speaks in this case of intrumental action, which belongs to the type of "purposively rational action"[5] and is directed toward technical rules based on empirical knowledge, and he equates it with "labor."[6] Instrumental action is essentially technique and the exercise of an effective control over natural processes, and it can be seen, at least according to its intention, as "social technology," concerned with social processes and people. In the last case, experiences acquired in the functional sphere of instrumental action, and constituted in that sphere by the interest of knowledge in the technical control of the objectivized processes, are transferred to the analysis of society and the guidance of social processes.[7] An orientation toward the exercise of control over the object through controlled observation and the making of prognostic statements about its future behavior is done by instrumental and experimental action,[8] so that the object can be manipulated and governed according to rules acquired subject to certain empirical conditions. On the basis of empirically acquired and experimentally controllable data, techniques have to be developed which enable the knowledge stored in the data and hypotheses to be effectively applied in the "purposeful transformation of material" (CES 132) in the process of production. This process has the task of safeguarding our technical power to control the natural outside world and to extend this so that it will continue to be controlled with the purpose of ensuring our material lives and our survival. The process of production, which takes place according to rules of instrumental, as non-social, action, is socially coordinated with the purpose of production, according to rules of strategic action that Habermas has deduced from those of communicative action.

Communicative and strategic actions form the dimensions of social action. Weber saw in this a "subjectively meaningful" action, which he explained as "oriented to a subjectively intended meaning, and thus also motivated" (LSS 53).[9] He also believed that this action could be seen as intentional and explained with reference to the aims and values of the one acting. It can similarly be regarded, according to a behavioristic understanding of this question, as adaptive behavior by an organism toward its environment. Habermas recognizes in social action "the combined result of reactive compulsions and meaningful interactions" (LSS 88). Despite his criticism of a theory of action that takes as its point of departure an autonomous subject who is responsible for himself, he begins with communicative action, saying that the community is constituted in the form of communicative action (ThdG 214), and he tends toward a theory of communicative action that integrates a theory, above all, of social action. This gives us cause to ask how Habermas justifies his assertion of the fundamental nature of communicative action for human interaction, for every theory of human interaction, and for every theory of society, and from where he obtains it.

The fundamental character of communicative action can be justified by demonstrating the non-reducibility of communicative action to instrumental action and, in connection with this, by explaining the rules of communicative action. It can also be motivated by providing evidence, on the one hand, of the interrelationship between communicative and strategic action in a historical analysis of the restrictions and distortions of the first and, on the other, of the development of the resultant mentioned above.

According to Habermas, communicative action cannot be reduced to the framework of instrumental action, because it functions in a different way, has a different structure, and obeys different rules. Whereas in principle instrumental action is in the form of a monologue, communicative action is always a dialogue and rests on the foundation of the intersubjectivity of subjects interacting with each other. This is why he calls communicative action "symbolical interaction" governed by "binding consensual valid norms, which define reciprocal expectations about behavior and must be understood and recognized by at least two acting subjects" (TRS 92).[10] Interaction is symbolically mediated because its coming about depends on the speaking of an intersubjectively shared language. It obeys norms that are valid, at least for the partners, in that interaction, and those norms define reciprocal expectations of behavior because interaction takes place according to rules, and a recognition of those rules is the necessary presupposition for the coming about of the process of interaction.[11] In the observance of these rules there is an intersubjectively binding distribution of roles in the dialogue, on the basis of a mutual recognition of the opportunities and limitations that these roles contain. On the one hand, then, communicative action presupposes an understanding that does not necessarily have to be consciously established, but can be based on an agreement, which is unreflectedly shared, about the expectations of behavior that are mutually directed toward each other. On the other hand, it is oriented toward the bringing about of understanding.

Following Wittgenstein's language-game model, Habermas clarifies the connection between language and praxis, which he sees as realized in everyday language. There is in that form of language a mutual process of interpretation of language and action, which, because of its distinctively reflective character, acts as a guarantee for the possibility, in principle, of its self-interpretation. It owes this self-interpretation to "its complementary relation to the non-verbal forms of expression found in action and expression, which it can in turn express in the medium of language itself" (KHI 169).

Communicative action takes place in these three "classes of utterances," which are integrated in the everyday praxis of life. This proceeds according to definite rules and is subject either to norms that are valid by being recognized or to norms that call for recognition by being valid. In the first case, it is the genesis of the norms that we have to examine. Norms come about as obligatory mutual expectations of behavior by those expectations being mutually accepted as justified. In the second case, it is the consequences resulting from the normalization of interaction that have to be considered. Those consequences have been deposited, like the sediment of countless interactions that have taken place in the past, in the social norms mediated by everyday language.

Social norms that are confirmed by sanctions form the institutional framework for a society, which Habermas regards as representing "a relation of social force," that is, "a form of life that has been rigidified to the point of abstraction" (KHI 52). With a clear orientation toward Freud, he sees this social framework, constituted by compelling norms, in connection with the repression of dynamic drives, which have to be imposed generally in the system of self-preservation, and which can be gradually overcome to the extent that a shortage of goods can be overcome by new social forms of production and organization, resulting in a loosening up or a "rationalization" of the institutional framework. This can only take place "in the medium of symbolic interaction itself, that is, through removing restrictions on communication" (TRS 118).

A memory of the social and historical contexts,[12] which are, on the one hand, partly detemined by communicative action and in which that action is, on the other hand, embedded, means, for that process of determination, not only that it cannot be understood simply insofar as it constitutes interaction, but also that it depends on the objective possibilities of its own expression.

There are, as I have demonstrated, two aspects of communicative action. It is the foundation of all intersubjective understanding and agreement, and its structure, development, and restriction with regard to the interests of the self-preservation of the social system take on certain historical and social forms. Both of these aspects together can be explained in a theory of communicative action.

Habermas contrasts another form of social action with communicative action. This is what he calls strategic action, which represents the social aspect of purposively rational action and as such is oriented toward the realization of "defined goals under given conditions" (TRS 92). Directed toward "labor,"[13] strategic action implies an attitude of rational choice and, therefore, a correct assessment of possible alternative attitudes, in which use is made of values and maxims. Insofar as it is related to the social organization of the process of labor, it also implies a coordination of activities with the goal of production. In both cases, there is a need to elaborate and apply strategies that will point to the best way to reach the intended goal via the most effective possible organization of means.

With "interaction" in mind, Habermas also makes a distinction between strategic action and communicative action that is oriented toward reciprocal expectations of behavior. He does this by abandoning the orientation toward values that are recognized by both in strategic action, and replacing it by an orientation toward interests. "Interests" should be understood in this context as "desires that have once again assumed the form of a monologue" (ThdG 252).[14] Viewed within the framework of interaction, strategic action can therefore be seen as the degenerate form of communicative action in which the orientation toward value, common to both on the basis of a fundamental consensus regarding social norms and institutionalized values, is abandoned and replaced by a type of behavior, whose model is "competition for goods in short supply" (ThdG 251).

According to Habermas, the reason for this abandonment can be found in the dissent that comes about as the result of making institutionalized values problematical. This is done by questioning the distribution, which is normalized by those values, of opportunities for a legitimate satisfaction of needs by socialized subjects, and by depriving those values in that way of their basis for legitimation, which for its part rests on the motivation of those concerned.[15] If these institutionalized values suffer from a crisis of legitimation because there is a lack of motivation by those concerned to accept them, value-orientated communicative action is bound to give way to interest-governed strategic action.

Because it is directed toward the individual satisfaction of subjective needs that have been dissociated from universally binding values, strategic action will inevitably attempt to define these needs in the form of a monologue, and to satisfy them as fully as possible in the interest of obtaining the greatest possible individual share in the competition for the distribution of opportunities. In this way, the interacting individuals cease to be partners in dialogue and become participants in a competition. The conclusion that Habermas draws from these reflections is quite consistent: "Strategic action is a limit case of communicative action" (ThdG 252).

Bearing in mind what I said earlier about "labor," it is possible to state that strategic action occupies the position of a hybrid between "labor" and "interaction." The social aspect of labor is expressed in it, as it is a form of interaction that is restricted to quasi-instrumental action. Strategic action, as it were, realizes labor as a process of communication in the form of communication that is threatened by instrumentalization. I would therefore define strategic action as related, on the basis of its application, to society, that is, social, and in its form of organization instrumental, that is, non-social.

## 6.3 THE SPECIFIC ASPECTS OF COMMUNICATIVE ACTION

### 6.3.1 CONSENSUS AND COMPETENCE—THE CONDITIONS OF COMMUNICATIVE ACTION

Unlike strategic action, communicative action is oriented toward mutually recognized values and norms. The recognition of norms of action is, however, connected with the conviction of those who recognize them that they are legitimate and can be legitimated, in other words, "that I can be convinced discursively in cases of doubt" (ThdG 264).[16] The acceptance of discourse as the basis of legitimation therefore points to conviction regarding the ability and the need to reach consensus in the case of valid norms. A norm is valid, in other words, if it is intersubjectively recognized and followed for so long—and only for so long—as a consensus about it is assumed.

Habermas calls this consensus "background consensus." As action that is subject to intersubjectively valid norms, communicative action is based, then, on a background consensus. This means that it can only be maintained while its continued existence and the possibility of making sure of it in discourse are assumed by those taking part in the action. In order to be able to act communicatively at all, I must take as my point of departure the conviction, on the one hand, that it is possible to reach agreement with my partners in communication and, on the other, that this agreement already exists in respect of what Habermas calls "the presupposed basis of validity claims that can be mutually recognized" (CES 3). To that extent, then, communicative action is clearly oriented toward and dependent on consensus. Its intention is to establish agreement between the partners in communication, and the achievement of that intention also presupposes fundamental agreement as a basis.

Apart from this intersubjective consensus, a presupposition of participation in communicative action on the part of the subject is also a communicative or interactive competence.[17] By this is meant the specific ability to take part in communicative acts. This is established, in the first place, by acquiring primitive patterns of interaction through a selective identification, along the way to an increasingly deep interiorization of motives to action (a process which is analogous to an increasing interiorization of the schemes of action). In the second place, it is also gained by the formation of increasingly general and abstract structures (in a process of universalization and generalization). This continues until the state is reached where the individual is able to participate fully in interactions.

Habermas has evolved a scheme of stages in interactive competence.[18] To do this, he has taken over the theoretical framework provided by Mead, Parsons, and Goffman and has considered the sequence, according to the logic of development, of the acquisition of general qualifications, in role action, in its connection with the general structures of communicative action. In this process, the first aspect of interactive competence is concerned with "the perception of the cognitive components of role qualifications" (CES 86), in which the degree of reflectiveness of expectations of behaviour is conditioned by Piaget's three cognitive levels (pre-operational, concrete operational, and formally operational thought).[19]

The second aspect of interactive competence refers to "the perception of the motivational components of general role qualifications" (CES 86). This can be distinguished according to the degree of abstraction and generalization, as well as differentiation "from the mere facticity of an expression of will" (CES 87), and represents adequate normative expectations of behavior.

The third dimension of interactive competence has to do with "the perception of a component of general role qualifications which . . . presupposes the other two and has both cognitive and motivational sides" (CES 87). This proceeds, in the course of a progressive generalization, from perception of concrete acts and actors, via a differentiation of acts and norms, actors, and role-players, to a distinction between particular and general norms. In this process, the actors can no longer be seen as a combination of role attributes but are valid rather as individuals who, by the application of principles, organize a biography, which is in each case not exchangeable.

Another concept of competence can be distinguished from the genetically oriented concept I discussed above. In this second concept, Habermas has included the presuppositions and conditions governing the possibility of communicative action. It is characteristic that he should maintain, as the program for a theory of communicative competence, that it should "explain the performances that speakers or listeners undertake with the help of universal pragmatic structures when they transform sentences into utterances" (VB 103). A reconstruction of the abilities of competent speakers and listeners results from explanations of their performances. In an understanding of competence as rule-governed competence, the emphasis is on a mastery of the rules, that is, on an ability to apply them correctly. In the same way, what is prominent in the concept "performance" is a factual application or carrying out of the rules themselves and the result of that procedure. In the case of competence understood in this sense, the speakers' performances have to be explained by means of a "subsequent reconstruction of the system of rules, according to which we produce or generate situations of possible discourse" (VB 102).

Habermas follows Searle in his definition of speech acts as "elementary units of discourse" (VB 103). He also understands them as the basis for the structures of the situation of discourse. Because they also occur as linguistic expressions in the discourse itself, he calls these structures, alongside a number of classes of words and their applications within grammatical forms which also structure discourse, "universal pragmatic structures" (VB 103). He also takes the same point of departure as Austin and Searle. That is the double structure of the speech act, which is composed of "a performative statement and a statement of propositional content that is dependent on it" (VB 104). From this vantage point, he is able to see the "double structure of communication in everyday language" (VB 105), represented in the concept.

This means that agreement is only possible if two subjects speak at the same time with each other, at the level of intersubjectivity and at the level of objects and experiences about the latter, in such a way that communication only comes about in simultaneous meta-communication.

Habermas divides speech acts, considered as universal pragmatic structures, into four classes: 1) the communicatives, referring to the "pragmatic sense of the discourse as such" (VB 111); 2) the constatives, which express the "sense of the cognitive application of statements" (VB 111); 3) the representatives, referring to the "pragmatic sense of the speaker's representation of himself in the presence of a listener" (VB 112); and finally 4) the regulatives, expressing the "sense of the practical application of statements" (VB 112).

He relates the four classes of speech acts to the fundamental distinctions between "being and semblance," "essence and appearance," and "being and obligation" (VB 113). As Peukert has correctly pointed out,[20] these can also be related to the individual competences on the basis of which the distinction between them can be motivated. In the same way, communicative speech acts are related to linguistic competence (and a claim to "intelligibility" of what is uttered is made in them); constative speech acts, which make the claim to "truth" explicit, to cognitive competence; and finally, representative and regulative speech acts each to one aspect of interactive competence. This goes together, in the first case, with a claim to "correctness" in the acts or in their underlying norms and, in the second case, a claim to "truthfulness" in the utterances.

A radical question arises about whether these claims are or can be met. It is that of competence in the sense of ability to judge. It can only be answered on the basis of a distinction between action and discourse, in the context of reflections about the validity claims implied in communicative action and the manner in which those claims are met.

## 6.3.2  FORMS OF EVERYDAY COMMUNICATION:
### COMMUNICATIVE ACTION AND DISCOURSE

Habermas makes a distinction between two forms of everyday communication, according to the degree of their integration into other contexts of life. These two forms are communicative action and discourse. The first is usually associated with non-verbal acts and expressions and is therefore inserted into a context of extra-linguistic utterances that forms a total context of interaction. This is not found in the case of discourse. Although the context is given as an epiphenomenon, it is not given as a component part of the discourse, in which only linguistic utterances are admitted. In communicative action, communication and interaction belong closely together. In discourse, on the other hand, interaction plays no part. As Habermas has said, it "removes from contexts of experience and action" (LC 107).[21]

Communicative action is dependent on consensus or background consensus between the participants. So long as this exists, the "language-game" functions, and understanding is reached on the basis of a presupposed agreement. The validity claims of the truth of the statement and the correctness of the action or its underlying norms are, however, sometimes made problematical,[22] in other words, they are no longer accepted "naively" and without question, as given and fulfilled, and this may result in the agreement becoming problematical. When this happens, the discourse has to restore the agreement by motivating it.

According to Habermas, a "virtualization" of "compulsions to action" and of "validity claims" is the essential presupposition for this (VB 117). This virtualization means that an existential reservation has to be expressed about the objects under discussion. The participants in a discourse have to resist the compulsion to act with the speaker by keeping to the rules of the game of "pure" communication. An essential aspect of this is that "no force except that of the better argument is exercised; and that, as a result, all motives except that of the cooperative search for truth are excluded" (LC 108).

The purpose of the discourse may be to motivate or justify validity claims that have become problematical, and to go beyond those claims and aim at a consensus. To this end, Habermas has distinguished between two forms of discourse in which consensus is brought about, according to rules that may be different in each case. These he calls simply practical and theoretical discourse. The second refers to the motivation of the claim of statements to truth, whereas the first refers to the justification of the claim of norms to correctness. Both are concerned with reaching agreement by argument. In the case of theoretical discourse, the arguments are explanations. In the case of practical discourse, they are justifications. The "logic of discourse" as a pragmatic logic of argumentation[23] is different in each form of discourse, in that it operates, in the first case, according to the principle of induction and, in the second, according to that of universalization. Fundamentally, however, because of the "rationally motivated recognition of the validity claim" (LC 107) and the "force of the better argument" (Wth 240) that is characteristic of discourse, both are in harmony with each other. The aim of both is to reach consensus by argument.

The central question in Habermas' consensus theory of truth is how the attainment of this goal is safeguarded and what proves the consensus to be intersubjectively guaranteed.[24] It is important to discuss this theory in the same context as the theme of the discourse. In striking contrast to all those who have evolved ontological theories of truth, Habermas understands truth as essentially related to linguistic systems, as well as to statements and to the potential consent of all to those statements. It is not possible to make a reproduction or an illustration of reality the norm of truth. That norm can only be the consent of all. If a statement is said to be true when the predicate attributed to the object in question is applied to it, "then and only then" can I "attribute a predicate to an object so long as everyone else who may enter into dialogue with me attributes the same predicate to the same object" (Wth 219).

How is the attainment of a consensus safeguarded, and what proves that consensus to be intersubjectively guaranteed? Habermas' answer to this is that it occurs by means of the formal structures of the discourse, which are those of the ideal speech situation. Several factors play a part in this. No restriction is imposed, for example, on the participants in the discourse. Communication between them is free of compulsion and the burden of action. They can change the form of the discourse. They have freedom to move between action and discourse. Finally, Habermas stresses that they all have potentially "the same opportunity to provide interpretations, explanations and justifications, to make assertions and recommendations and to make problematical, motivate or refute, with the result that no previously held opinion is withheld for the duration of the discussion and criticism" (Wth 255).[25]

According to Habermas, the attainment of the goal of the discourse, that is, the gaining of a rationally motivated recognition of the validity claims, is safeguarded by the formal qualities and the logic of the discourse itself. In accordance with the distinctive character of discourse, this guarantee does not, however, remain valid for all time. The validity claims can potentially be made problematical at any time by anyone and can therefore be once again discursively debated and met.

In the following section I situate these validity claims that are inserted into communicative action, differentiate them, and clarify their relationship with one another.

### 6.3.3   VALIDITY CLAIMS AND THE MODE BY WHICH THEY ARE MET

In his essay "Universal Pragmatics," Habermas develops the thesis "that anyone acting communicatively must, in performing any speech action, raise universal validity claims and suppose that they can be vindicated." These claims, he continues, are "a. uttering something understandably; b. giving (the hearer) something to understand; c. making himself thereby understandable; and d. coming to an understanding with another person" (CES 2). He comes to this thesis by assigning to each of the four classes of speech act one of the validity claims discussed in them. In other words, he attributes the claim of the intelligibility of the utterance to the communicatives; the truth of the statement to the constatives; the truthfulness of the utterance to the representatives; and the correctness of the action (or the norm of the action) to the regulatives. It is the task of universal pragmatics to reveal these validity claims, which are assumed in communicative action as universal conditions of possible understanding, and to reconstruct them.

In this, Habermas' thesis is clearly very close to Austin's and Searle's speech act theory, which expresses ideas on which the "fundamental assumptions of universal pragmatic can be beared" (CES 26).[26] In his analysis of speech acts that are propositionally differentiated and institutionally not bound,[27] he acknowledges the double structure of discourse. He also notes with Austin the "speech-act-invariance of the propositional content" (CES 41) as the presupposed disconnection, for the purpose of differentiating the double structure, of propositional and illocutionary component parts. He also refers to the necessity that is motivated, in the double structure of discourse, for partners in the interaction to come simultaneously to an understanding (a predicative and an illocutionary understanding) about something at the level of experiences and situations, and to do something at the level of intersubjectivity. In the case of the second, it is to accept an interpersonal relationship.

On the basis of a differentiation and a correction of Austin's speech act theory, Habermas deals with the validity claims made in communicative action by relating them to the possible modes of communication and, from that point of departure, demonstrating their universality. The conclusion that he draws from Austin's discovery, that all speech acts have both a locutionary and an illocutionary component, is that the validity claim expressed in constative speech acts represents no more than a special case among those claims that the speaker makes and offers to meet with regard to the hearer. The claim to truth that is unmistakably implied in constative speech acts is also presupposed, Habermas insists, in all other speech acts: "Truth claims are thus a type of validity claim built into the structure of possible speech in general. Truth is a universal validity claim; its universality is reflected in the double structure of speech" (CES 52).

In the cognitive use of language, then, in other words, in constative speech acts, this validity claim, in Habermas' opinion, is stressed thematically. In the interactive use of language, on the other hand, that is, in regulative speech acts, which serve to thematize interpersonal relationships and their normative background, this claim is merely mentioned. The universal validity claim, which is recognized explicitly here and which Austin did not recognize because of his restriction to the single universal validity claim interpreted in the correspondence theory, namely, the claim of propositional truth, is, according to Habermas, the claim of normative correctness.

Habermas also believes that there is a third universal validity claim. This is the claim of truthfulness that is emphasized in the expressive use of language and presented as a theme in intentional statements as paradigmatic for representative speech acts.

A fourth universal validity claim, which cannot be stressed because it represents a presupposition for every speech act, is the claim of intelligibility. Habermas concludes his discussion, about the theme of validity claims and the modes by which they can be communicated, with an affirmation which—provisionally at least—imposes a limitation on whether these distinctions can be put into operation, although it does not restrict their validity: "I am not claiming that every sequence of speech action can be unequivocally classified under these viewpoints. I am claiming only that every competent speaker has in principle the possibility of unequivocally selecting one mode because he must with every speech act raise three universal validity claims, so that he can single out one of them to thematize a component of speech" (CES 58f.).

With regard to the basis of the illocutionary force of an utterance, which

Austin and Searle wanted to reveal in their search for conditions governing the success or failure of speech acts, Habermas is of the opinion that the illocutionary force of an acceptable speech act, which is a tendency on the part of the listener to "rely on the speech-act-typical commitments of the speaker" (CES 62), is based on the connection between this obligation and cognitively verifiable validity claims. If the speaker offers a speech-act-immanent "obligation to provide grounds" (CES 63) in the cognitive use of language, then there is also a speech-act-immanent "obligation to provide justification" in the interactive use of language, and an "obligation to prove trustworthy" that is also immanent in the speech act (CES 64). These obligations, on the one hand, may be fulfilled directly within the context of interaction at the level of communicative action, by having recourse to experiences, by referring to the normative background, or by making sure of one's own evidence. On the other hand, if these offers are not accepted or if they continue to be treated as problematical, they can also be fulfilled indirectly at the level of theoretical or practical discourses. This certainly applies in the case of constative or regulative speech acts, and it takes place through the sequence of consistent actions in the case of representative speech acts. Finally, Habermas stresses that, if the validity claims are expressed differently in the modes of communication and given prominence in the various types of speech act, they must be made simultaneously by the speaker and the listener in all utterances, as universal claims, and recognized by both as legitimate for communication to succeed at all and be maintained as communicative action.[28]

### 6.3.4   THE CONCEPT AND STATUS OF THE
IDEAL SPEECH SITUATION

An important question arises in connection with this treatment of the background consensus that is presupposed in communicative action and the discovery of the truth aimed at in the discourse, as the free and unforced consensus of all participants with the potential consent of everyone else in view. It is this: Under what conditions can a consensus, which is in fact always one involving a few participants in the discourse, be regarded as true, and how can it be distinguished from a false consensus? Habermas replies to this question, concerning a criterion that is capable of distinguishing between a true and a false consensus, by asserting that we "have to assume an ideal speech situation in every discourse, in other words, we have to anticipate contrafactually in the same way as our ability to attribute to the subjects acting in contexts of interaction" (VB 122).

It is possible to suggest a conceptual elucidation of the term "ideal speech situation," on the basis of the contrast between "real" and "ideal." A real speech situation is characterized by the interweaving of language, labor, and mastery, that is, the integration of language into different contexts of life, by which it is co-determined and through which communication is "distorted." In the first place, there is an abstraction in the concept of the ideal speech situation from the conditions and dependencies of real processes of communication, according to the model of pure communication. There is, in other words, an idealization in the sense of a subtraction of all the external conditions and internal insufficiencies that disturb or act as a burden on communication and their establishment at the level of perfection and examplarity.[29]

Another factor is involved, however, which takes us away from the area in which we seek simply to elucidate the concept "ideal speech situation," and into the sphere where we reflect about its role. The concept of the ideal speech situation fulfils a specific function, that of explaining why we can act communicatively at all, what our presuppositions are when we act in that way, what assumptions we make, and to what end we orient ourselves in that action. In our attempt to define the concept, then, we have also to take into consideration, in addition to the aspect of the idealization of factual communication, the normalization of real communication, which goes in the opposite direction and which at the same time provides the yardstick for assessing that communication. "Ideal speech situation" therefore means not only an idealization of the situation that abstracts from concrete insufficiencies of real speech situations, but also the presuppositions of real communication and—although I would add this with some reservation—the "transcendental" question[30] about the conditions of its possibility and validity, the question, in other words, of its normative foundation.

If Habermas' reflections about this ideal speech situation are traced, we find that the matter is first discussed within the framework of a consideration of the conditions governing discourse and as a suggested explanation of the circle that cannot be broken through within the framework of the consensus theory of the truth. According to this explanation, we have no external criterion for judging whether actions are correct or not. We can only judge them internally in our participation in interaction. Despite this, however, in every dialogue we are able to take the possibility of understanding and agreement for granted and the ability to distinguish a true consensus from a false one as our point of departure.

Habermas' suggested explanation is as follows: "We have to mutually presuppose an ideal speech situation in every discourse" (VB 136). He regards this assumption as an "anticipation," providing both a guarantee that a factual consensus will be considered true and a critical norm by which every factual consensus may be questioned and verified with a view to real agreement. Habermas calls a speech situation ideal if "communication is not impeded not only by external contingent effects, but also by compulsions resulting from the structure of the communication itself" (VB 137). This precludes not only systematic distortions of the communication but also all compulsion. It also implies, as Habermas himself suggests on the basis of his four classes of speech act, an equality of opportunities with regard to the choice and application of communicatives and constatives. Finally, it depends on the presupposition that the speaker, as the one who acts, has a guarantee of equal opportunities in his employment of representatives and regulatives.

"The contrafactual conditions of the ideal speech situation are seen to be conditions of an ideal form of life," Habermas points out (VB 139), because and insofar as they do not simply represent conditions of success in discourses but also define a model of pure communicative action which is related to interaction and which is anticipated in the ideal situation or the model. The status of this anticipation of an ideal speech situation or of a model of pure communicative action, neither of which can be identified with the conditions governing empirical discourse and factual interaction, is described by Habermas as a contrafactual assumption. "The structure of possible discourse," he insists, "means that, in carrying out speech acts (and actions), we act contrafactually in such a way that the ideal speech situation (or the model of pure communicative action) is not simply fictitious, but real . . . The normative foundation of interaction is therefore both anticipated and also effective as the anticipated foundation" (VB 140).

Habermas contrasts this concept of the ideal speech situation, as an assumption that is always present in every understanding and agreement, with the regulative principles in the Kantian sense and, as not coinciding with factual historical forms of life, with Hegel's "existing concept." He regards it as most closely comparable with "a transcendental semblance . . . if this semblance . . . were not at the same time the constitutive condition of possible discourse" (VB 141).

The two poles of this concept, closely related to each other, are characterized by a tension between the "already" and the "not yet." These are the normative and the historical poles. In the normative aspect, what is expressed is that communication is simply not possible without a basis of the norm of an association with each other, free of compulsion and deception and toward which factual communication has to be oriented. What is made clear in the historical aspect is that, even if this normative basis of communication is present, it has, as yet, hardly ever been realized in history and is still not encountered as a historical reality but is nonetheless the norm toward which we ought to, and indeed must, interact. The real point of the concept of the "ideal speech situation" is that it is concerned in the "ought to and indeed must," not with heteronomous ethical claims or demands, but with the fact that these are already given to us and are immanent in the structure of communication itself and can, moreover, be justified on the basis of that structure. As a result of this, we do not have first to invent or construct an ethic. All that we need to do is to find it in an analysis of communication. Habermas used a very striking sentence in his inaugural lecture to describe language: "Through its structure, autonomy and responsibility are posited for us. Our first sentence expresses unequivocally the intention of universal and unconstrained consensus" (KHI 314). He thus precisely defines this situation with a term taken from the philosophical tradition: there is a normative foundation of interaction which is expressed in the basic structure of communication, which can be reconstructed and which contains an imperative to realize it.

## 6.4 THE NORMATIVE FOUNDATION OF INTERACTION AND THE FACTUAL NORMS OF INTERACTION

It is clear, then, that there is a difference between real communication and the ideal speech situation, in the form of a distinction between reality and ideal. There is, however, also a difference between the normative foundation of interaction and concrete norms of interaction. This is something that I now have to consider, on the basis of the question concerning the genesis and the legitimation of norms of interaction in the context of evolution. In considering this, I shall also deal with the relationship between norms of interaction, the formation of identity, and evolution (the evolution of world views). I have observed that Habermas' universal pragmatics form the central systematic core of a theory of communicative action, concerned with the reconstruction of elementary structures of human action, that is based on a normative foundation. In the following sections, then, I will show how Habermas has developed a comprehensive conception of a theory of communicative action from the vantage point of its historical aspect and in the light of the elementary structures of interaction discovered in universal pragmatics.

### 6.4.1 THE GENESIS AND LEGITIMATION OF NORMS OF INTERACTION

How do norms come about? They are always already given in any interaction. Interaction is simply not possible without them, because the association of two subjects with each other is regulated by mutual expectations and expectations of expectations. These define the concrete situation and give it its structure. Shared communicative action results from a reciprocal understanding and a reciprocal recognition of these expectations. If they are transferred to larger contexts of interaction, institutionalized, and tied down to roles, then norms arise which a child who is born and grows into those contexts will learn, in the course of his socialization, to understand and, in the course of his deepening initiation into increasingly complex systems of interaction, to master by internalizing them. Norms arise by expectations of behavior being given a lasting value. They also come about when they are tied down to positions and roles and can therefore be expected with some certainty, the latter resulting, on the one hand, from the possibility, which is given with the relatively unambiguous definition of the concept of expectation, that they will be fulfilled and, on the other, from the sanctions that are threatened if they are contravened.

In his investigation of the meaning of validity claims and norms, Habermas has discovered two fundamental and contrafactual expectations, which form the basis for expectations, and claims that are specific to the situation and which confront those who act with each other and assume that their claims will be met. These are the expectations of intentionality and of legitimacy. The first means that we expect "acting subjects to follow intentionally all the norms that they follow" (VB 118) and the second that they "only follow norms which seem to them to be justified" (VB 119). These expectations are connected with the assumption that the subjects are able at any time to leave an action context or structure that has become problematical and take up a discourse.

In the case of the two expectations of intentionality and legitimacy, the coming about of norms as the establishment of definite expectations and the stabilization of complementary expectations of behavior is crucially affected by the fact that, if the expectations are to have a normative character at all, they must appear to be capable of being united with one's own intentions and to be capable of legitimation. This leads to the question of legitimacy and the closely related question of the legitimation of norms of action—questions of central importance, especially with regard to the way in which they arise if the point of departure is that norms cannot become valid without the claim that they are capable of being legitimized.[31]

According to Habermas, "the validity of a norm is based on the claim of discursive foundation. We suppose that subjects can say what norm they follow and why they accept that norm as justified" (VB 119). Since this claim is not or cannot be met in the case of many norms that are in fact valid, it is important to question the mechanism that obtains validity for them either by assuming that the claim can be met or by absorbing and therefore eliminating it. In Habermas' opinion, this is what world views fundamentally must and can do.

### 6.4.2  THE PART PLAYED BY WORLD VIEWS IN THE LEGITIMATION OF NORMS OF INTERACTION

According to Habermas and Döbert, world views are systems of interpretation that function both to integrate society and to secure identity. They "fulfil this function of constituting and maintaining networks of social interaction insofar as they are capable of defining all elements of social action and thus securing an all-embracing complementarity of the expectations of societized subjects."[32] World views fulfil their function in accordance with the stage of social evolution, which is determined by the level of integration of systems and society, by providing an all-embracing system of interpretation that overcomes contingency.

At the level of archaic societies that exist before the state and are structured by relationships of affinity, the integration of social relationships into families and tribes is secured by a "construction of a complex of analogies," which is proposed with the help of myths, "in which all natural and social phenomena were interwoven and could be transformed into one another" (CES 104). At this level, it is not possible to question the part played by world views in the legitimation of norms of interaction.[33] When societies became organized into states and reached the stage of early developed cultures, however, a mythical world view that had become dissociated from tradition in the course of a differentiated time-scale, and contrasted with the system of actions, was able in a narrative manner to justify the ruling families with the help of myths of origin and therefore to legitimate the orders of government. At the same time, myth also became the figure for legitimating social norms. What was dictated by the representatives of the cosmic order who were legitimated by this myth came to be recognized as socially valid.[34] The legitimate power of the myth was no longer accepted as soon as belief in it disappeared, and the myth as a figure of legitimation ceased to exist when it was no longer thought to be worthy of recognition, because, when it was measured against another instance, it did not reach its level of justification. The way in which a new level of justification comes about, however, can be explained in connection with the "social-evolutionary transitions to new learning levels" (CES 185).

Because the mythical and narrative potential for legitimation is not sufficient for an order of government which is no longer firmly tied to individual persons and families, the mythical way of thinking eventually ceased to operate in the developed cultures. Its place was taken by cosmological world views, philosophies, and developed religions, in which narrative explanations were replaced by an argumentative motivation in the form of "dogmatizable knowledge." This was characterized, above all, by an almost unbroken rationality, which only reached its limit when "ultimate grounds" and "unifying principles" (CES 184), which were themselves exempted from argumentation and immunized against all possible objections, were used to explain the world as a whole. It was in principle only possible, on the basis of the universal orientation and structure of world views at this stage, to justify universal norms of action that were valid for all men. The class-structured societies, which were formed in the developed cultures and were characterized by an extreme imbalance in the division of wealth and power, and particular states, which were not able to fulfil the potential for universal justification, are in striking contrast to this.

Habermas believes that it is the task of ideologies to try to redress the balance in this incongruent situation. This task, which has to be undertaken by ideologies with reference to the legitimation of norms of interaction, can be defined as the formation of a connection between, on the one hand, those norms which, seen at the level of their justification, are in principle universalistic and, on the other, those which are particular, and associated with interest and are required by the system of the state and society. In this process, ideologies function as a replacement of world views. They occupy the place previously occupied by the earlier world views and restrict the normative potential that was released in those early world views. They do this as the earlier world views did it before them—and with reference to the indisputable nature of the ultimate principles. They also still do it subject to the conditions imposed by developed cultures. In other words, they act by systematically restricting communication, which forms men's wills. This also only excludes the initial discursive formation of wills, in which the "barriers to communication, which make a fiction of the reciprocal imputation of an ability to attribute . . . at the same time (support) our faith in legitimation, which maintains that fiction as something that is not seen through" (VB 120).

The fourth stage in social evolution is the modern era. When this period was reached, several mechanisms of mediation became, in Habermas' opinion, ineffectual. The conflict, up till that time, had been kept latent or men had not been conscious of it because of these mechanisms. The highest principles were also, for the first time, called into question, and the universalistic potential that was already contained in the rationalized world views could be released. As Habermas says, "The unity of the world could no longer be secured objectively, through hypostatizing unifying principles (God, Being, or Nature); henceforth it could be asserted only reflectively, through the unity of reason. . . . The unity of theoretical and practical reason then became the key problem for modern interpretations, which have lost their character as world views" (CES 105).

In practical questions, that is, in questions concerned with the justification of norms and actions, principles with a specific content have been replaced in the modern era by the formal conditions of justification. "Since ultimate reasons can no longer be made plausible, the formal conditions of justification themselves obtained legitimating force. The procedures and presuppositions of rational agreement themselves become principles" (CES 184). This means that the level of justification has also become reflective, and we have what Habermas calls a "procedural type of legitimacy" (CES 185). Within the framework of this type of legitimation, norms can only be legitimated if they come from the rational will of all, as expressed in a consensus, and if they are the result of a discourse conducted among free and equal partners. In this way, they will be universal and egalitarian, and, as a reciprocal expectation of behavior that has been raised to the level of a norm, they give validity to "a common interest ascertained without deception" (LC 108). Habermas believes that this interest is generalizable, and he uses the term to denote communicatively shared needs that are ascertained in a discursive consensus.

According to Habermas, a level of justification has been reached in the modern era at which norms are bound to coincide with the normative foundation of interaction. This, in other words, is a level at which concrete norms of action are able to build upon that foundation and historically realize in their own development the potentials that are based on and invested in that foundation. These reflections, however, do not in any sense agree with the historically intelligible reality of the modern era. If, however, world views have lost their legitimate power, and this authority for the foundation and justification of norms of action has ceased to exist, we are bound to ask what has replaced it that is able to take over the task of acting as the "rational will of all." The answer to this question is the ideologies that I have already mentioned above. They no longer restrict normative potential as they did in the developed cultures and societies of the past. On the contrary, their legitimating function, replacing that of the earlier world views, is extended, because they affirm the private interests of the ruling classes as capable of generalization. They have therefore taken over the double function of showing "that the validity claim of norm systems are legitimate and of avoiding thematization and testing of discursive validity claims" (LC 112f.) by an unobstrusive and systematic restriction of communication.[35] Habermas is convinced that a criticism of ideologies has the task of going counter to this by contributing to a restriction of communication. This is accomplished by drawing attention to that systematic restriction, reconstructing it in its development, and, playing the advocatory role by means of a simulated discourse conducted in a representative capacity, affirming, reconstructing, and taking care of interests that are capable of generalization and yet suppressed. To that extent, then, this criticism of ideologies is bound to contribute to the formation of the collective will of all those concerned and all participants, taking as its point of departure the following question: "How would the members of a social system, at a given stage in the development of productive forces, have collectively and bindingly interpreted that needs (and which norms would they have accepted as justified) if they could and would have decided on organization of social intercourse through discursive will-formation, with adequate knowledge of the limiting conditions and functional imperatives of their society?" (LC 113).

This question, which reflects the empirical conditions governing the establishment of norms, brings the matter of the social conditioning of norms once again to our attention. This goes beyond dependence on the stages in the evolution of world views. It can only be understood as a state of being conditioned by the degree of mastery over external nature and by the differentiation of inner nature, by the cognitive and motivational potential and the degree of the development of productive power, by the capacity for control, and by the structures of interaction in a given society. In Habermas' view, these questions have to be considered within the framework of a general theory of social evolution.

### 6.4.3   EVOLUTION, THE FORMATION OF IDENTITY, AND NORMS OF INTERACTION

I shall begin with two excursuses that outline Habermas' approach to a theory of evolution and his concept of identity. Next, I shall consider the connection between these two questions and the norms of interaction. I shall do this on the basis of their formation in the history of the human race. I shall then relate the statements implied in the context of these three concepts to questions of the structure and the conditions of communicative action.

*Excursus 1: Habermas' Approach to a Theory of Social Evolution*

Although I cannot go into Habermas' theory of evolution in detail here, it is important to outline its basic structure. He understands social evolution as the evolution of a system of society and a system of personality, which together form a system that is capable of evolution, because the learning process of society is mediated via that of individual subjects.

Habermas distinguishes three aspects of evolutionary learning: 1) cumulative learning processes in the mastery of external nature, in the sense of technical and scientific progress (the development of productive forces); 2) an intensification of the capacity for control, which is present in social systems (within the framework of strategic action and socio-technical planning, the learning processes are at the basis of this); 3) the development of structures of interaction. If the general system theory is in a position to grasp this increase in the capacity for control, then developments in the other two aspects will take place within systems of rules, to which the cognitive or the interactive competence corresponds at the ontogenetic level.

Habermas' point of departure is that the evolutionary process of learning is, in the first place, expressed in ontogenetical learning processes, with the result that individual and collective capacities for learning are formed. These have an effect on the system of society as a whole, in the case of an excessive demand made on the capacity for control by problems that cannot be solved within the framework of that system of society. This leads either to a differentiation being made within that system, at the same level of learning, or to a reorganization of the system by institutionalizing a new level of learning.

Habermas has taken, from the theory of ontogenetic development evolved by Piaget and Kohlberg, the concept of the logic of evolution, in the sense of an invariant, hierarchically structured sequence of different stages of evolution which have to be passed through, each cancelling out in itself the elements of earlier stages, raising it to a higher level, and reintegrating it. In this evolutionary process, an unambiguous direction can be detected in the whole sequence.

Habermas has applied this model to phylogenesis and has pointed to a number of homologies or structural analogies between ontogenesis and phylogenesis. In order to clarify the connection between the development of the productive forces, the intensification of the capacity for control, and the growth of structures of interaction, he has introduced the concept of the principle of organization. This lays down the dominant form of social integration in each situation as an institutionalization of a definite level of learning in society, and at the same time defines the field within which changes can take place in the three aspects outlined above.

On this basis, Habermas differentiates between the stages of evolution at four levels, which he calls the archaic, neolithic or pre-state societies, the early cultures, the developed cultures, and finally the modern era. He replies to the question about the evolutionary learning mechanism and process by pointing to the formation of individual capacities for learning, which, after they have been admitted to the system of interpretation in society, as empirical knowledge (or moral and practical insights in the case of evolutionary challenges), enable society to learn in an evolutionary manner by making use of the cognitive potentials contained in world views for the reorganization of systems of actions.

The institutionalization of the learning processes results in a new level of social integration. The evolution itself takes place in two stages, through processes of learning and adaptation at the given level of learning and in evolutionary thrusts leading to new levels of learning. Habermas regards it as the task of his theory of evolution to reconstruct the logic of the development of these thrusts.

Of central importance in the theory of evolution that Habermas has developed within the framework of his theory of communicative action are his demonstration that the development of normative structures has the function of a pacemaker in social evolution and his attempt to reconstruct the logic of their development. This attempt has resulted in a phylogenetic set of stages that is parallel to Kohlberg's set of stages in the development of individual moral consciousness and that in turn results in the realization of a morality governed by principles and corresponding to universal linguistic ethics.

*Excursus 2: Habermas' Concept of Identity*

Habermas considers the question of identity both at the level of the system of personality, as a question of personal or ego identity, understood as a competence of the subject, who is capable both linguistically and in action of satisfying certain demands of consistency, and at the level of the system of society, as a question of collective or group identity.

Habermas sees a fundamental connection between these two levels and has pointed to homologies between the structures of group identity and ego identity. These can be traced back to the fact that the members of a system of society assert their own ego identity via the group identity by identifying each other as belonging to the same group. Habermas has also looked for socializing conditions in the development of the ego identity, which he understands as an ability that is dependent on the basic qualifications of role action to "solve crises in the 'I' structure by restructuring" (KK 129). Related to this is the ability to "bear ambivalences in role action, to find a suitable representation of the self and to apply interiorized norms flexibly to new situations" (KK 131). With Goffman, Habermas sees the identity of the "I" as a performance by the subject, in interaction that maintains social and personal identity in a state of balance. This is produced by the socialization of the subject and sustained and secured by his individualization.

Habermas traces the stages in the development of ego identity within the framework of the formation of general structures of communicative action, as conditioned by the growth of linguistic, cognitive, and interactive competence by the subject. This has led him to outline a set of stages into which these aspects are integrated. It progresses from natural identity via role identity to personal or ego identity.

The formation of the identity of the subject at the level of intersubjectivity, in the interplay of identification by other subjects and self-identification, has led Habermas to refer back to the connection between the identity of the "I" and membership in a group. The use of the term "I" means that an "I" identifies himself (he points to himself in the referential sense) with all other "I's" (in the performative sense), as a person, and at the same time also distinguishes himself (in the pronominal sense) as a definite and unexchangeable person from all others. This "I" attributes to himself "an unexchangeable place in the symbolic context of a world of persons living together" (KK 221); in other words, he assigns a "we" to himself. The identity of the person produced by self-identification is therefore based "on membership of the symbolic reality of a group and on the possibility of localization within that group" (KK 222).

Taking as his point of departure the thesis that the operation of self-identification varies with the structure of the system of norms, resulting in different forms that can be verified both phylogenetically and ontogenetically, Habermas has established certain interdependences between the system of norms and the formation of identity, and he believes that these are related to the formation of society at each period. They are also related to the connection between "I," "we," and "you," and proceed in the direction of an increasingly abstract distinction between "own" and alien groups. They also culminate in the stage of universalistic systems of norms, where it is no longer possible to distinguish a definite group that might have the power to secure identity by being marked off from alien groups.

The problem that arises at this point, and can only be resolved in a political universal morality, is how to assert the identity of the "I" in relation to all the others with whom that "I" is both identical and non-identical. At this stage of identity, the distinctive characteristic of identity is "still the unchangeable nature of the biographical organization of role play as a whole" (KK 226). The subject, who, in the course of the process of development, has acquired the ability to resolve crises of identity by restoring the balance between himself and others by raising it each time to a higher level, identifies himself at the level of ego identity by representing himself in interaction as integrating the different stages into the continuity of the history of his life and into the unique character of his biography. It is important, in this process, for the stage of identity that can be reached to be traced out socially in advance by a system of norms that is given in each case. At the stage of a universalistic morality that has been reached (privately) now, identity can only be established in an identification of oneself with all others with regard to the identity of the person, the result of this being a dependence on unconditional and reciprocal recognition. It has, at the same time, also to be established by distinguishing oneself from all others, a process in which each is identical with oneself.

The formation of collective or group identity, according to Habermas, is analogous with that of individual identity, in that the "identity projections become more and more general and abstract, until finally the projection mechanism as such becomes conscious, and identity formation takes on a reflective form, in the knowledge that to a certain extent individuals and societies themselves establish their identities" (CES 116). In the case of the possible identity of a world society, this means that this cannot be established in advance as far as its content is concerned, and that it is only conceivable in a reflective form. Habermas himself maintains that it is founded on a consciousness of universal and equal opportunities in processes of communication, in which the formation of identity takes place as a continuous learning process.

It is now possible to consider the question of the connection between evolution, the formation of identity, and norms of interaction against the background of Habermas' theory of evolution and his concept of identity, which I have briefly outlined in these two excursuses. Norms of interaction are always obligatorily defined and sanctioned in the system of norms of each society. This system is the product of the society concerned, and at the same time it also partly produces that society, insofar as it depends on the degree of social differentiation, the capacity for control that is present, the development of productive forces, and the growth of structures of interaction. These are also conditioned by the system of norms.

If Habermas' reflections are correct, there is an interdependence between the system of society and the system of norms. In relation to the process of social learning that is of fundamental importance to evolution, this means that, just as a cognitive level of learning that is equipped with a certain capacity for learning on the part of society is expressed in the system of control and the productive forces, a certain level of learning in the sphere of moral and practical knowledge and consciousness is also similarly invested in the system of norms. It also means that the capacity for moral and practical learning, through making present the superfluous potential that is latent in the world views and systems of interpretation, can be transformed by exemplary processes of learning and manifested at a new level of learning, whenever it is exhausted at the given level. It is precisely because, together with a new level of social integration, learning processes are made possible in this way, in these other spheres, that Habermas is able to say that the development of normative structures has the function of a pacemaker in social evolution.

With regard to the question of the social conditioning of the norms of interaction, I can now say, on the one hand, that it depends on the development of productive forces, the complexity of the social system of control, and the degree of development of the interpretation of needs. On the other hand, I can also say that the norms of interaction, which are invested in the structures of interaction, both condition and constitute society, insofar as they form the foundation of the institutional framework of that society. If they change, they can also change that society.

The connection between evolution, the formation of identity, and norms of interaction can be seen in the reconstruction of the phylogenetic stages of the collective moral consciousness. Habermas attributes to the four levels of society noted above, in the first excursus,[36] the three forms of identity mentioned in the second excursus,[37] and he elaborates, together with the three stages of moral consciousness,[38] the systems of norms that are relevant in each case with the corresponding cognitive and interactive levels. At the same time, he also analyzes the connection that is specific to each phase, between the stage of social evolution and the form of identity that is possible and necessary for that stage, as well as the norms of interaction that are required, favored, and made possible by each stage. He does this in order to draw attention to the normative implications of the logic of development of this connection, which is related to the logic of development of normative structures.

The normative implications that are revealed in a reconstruction point in the direction of a realization of the normative central core of interaction that is possible on the basis of the creation of cognitive, interactive, and linguistic presuppositions. The normative implications of social evolution, in its connection with formations and norms of interaction, amount to a reduction of the distance between the real and the ideal communication community. The aim is eventually to do away completely with that distance, in an ideal and universal communication community, and to bring the concrete norms of interaction closer to the normative foundation of interaction.

There is an obvious connection here with the structure and conditions of communicative action. Interacting at various levels and achieving consensual unity in the case of controversial questions, the individuals possessing ego identity agree—on the basis of the formation of cognitive, linguistic, and interactive competence and therefore also of ability and readiness—with unconditional mutual recognition about what they want and ought to want in the interest of all. In this, they have recourse to what they always already do by acting communicatively, namely, recognizing one another unconditionally and, on that basis, making the assumed reciprocity, equality, and universality the principles of their action. The concrete norms of action, which have to be called into question again and again on the basis of those principles, result from those assumptions.

The systematic, central core of Habermas' theory of communicative action is his universal pragmatics, and this has been related to the three-dimensional framework of the theory of the subject, society, and history. Seen in this perspective, the "procedure" may sound very utopian and illusionary in view of factual, political, and social realities. It is, however, no more than a putting into practice, based on an insight into the structures of communicative action, the conditions of man's being, and the stage of social evolution that has in fact been attained, of what is necessary, insofar as we want to live and survive as men. And what is necessary is fundamentally what we are already doing and what we have to do, even though we may do it to a far lesser (or "private") degree.

# Notes

1. My own priority in this book led me to attempt in this chapter to define as precisely as possible the relationship between the theory of communicative action, the theory of communicative competence, and universal pragmatics.

Habermas himself has never defined this unambiguously. They occasionally appear as synonyms in his approach to a theory of communication (see CES 15). According to CES, the theory of communicative action aims at a systematic understanding and analysis of the following elements at least. These elements are for the most part subsumed (in CES) under the heading of universal pragmatics as "meaning," pragmatic universal structures, validity claims, modes of experience, aspects of action, stages in communication, levels of normative reality, and media of communication. On the other hand, Habermas informs us (again in CES) that "the third aspect of utterances, namely the establishment of interpersonal relations, is central" for a theory of communicative action (CES 34). This is one of the aspects of the analysis made by universal pragmatics and is one of the themes in the theory of illocutionary acts. Seen from this point of view, the theory of communicative action might appear to form part of universal pragmatics. Quite apart from Habermas' inconsistent use of language (for his theory of communicative competence, see VB 103, for his universal pragmatics, see VB 107; ThdG 208; LC 107ff.), I think there are systematic reasons which justify my attempt to define the relationship between his theory of communicative action and his universal pragmatics. This is because the former must include the three dimensions of subject, society, and history, and must derive the normative criteria, and therefore also the guidelines for its analysis of the constitution of subject, society, and history, from universal pragmatics as a systematic reconstruction of elementary actions. I agree with McCarthy's statement: "Universal pragmatics, or the theory of communicative competence, is above all a concerted effort to rework the normative-theoretical foundations of critical theory" (*The Critical Theory*, p. xii), but disagree with what he says later: "A theory of communicative competence . . . would thus provide a unifying framework for a variety of theoretical endeavours, ranging from the theories of knowledge and action to the theories of socialization and ideology" (p. 282). I would say rather that the theory of communicative competence, or universal pragmatics, does not provide a "unifying framework" but forms the systematic central core, as the normative foundation, for this theoretical undertaking that is summarized under the theory of communicative action. When McCarthy says, then, that "the theory of communication is the foundational study for the human sciences, it discloses the universal infrastructure of socio-cultural life" (p. 282), he is wrong. Universal pragmatics fulfil this function of providing a foundation.

2. Habermas has attempted to develop the conception of a critical theory of society by integrating different theoretical statements and a theory of action, for example, in LC and CES, which include aspects of his earlier works, TRS and KHI. He has, since *Structural Transformation* and his early essays, "remained true to his fundamental conceptions" (Kunstmann, *Gesellschaft*, p. 14). I do not agree with Kunstmann in his claim that those ideas are to be found in the anthropologically motivated "dualism of technique and life, of the technique of purpose and self-purpose, which can only be defined from the standpoint of the subject and his circle of action" (p. 14). In my opinion, they are contained in Habermas' concern for a pragmatic theory of action with a practical and emancipatory intention, which is therefore at the same time critical of society. The material taken into account and the methodology and the apparatus used by Habermas have changed with the passage of time, but the intention has remained the same. To that extent, then, I regard his theory of the discourse as a continuation of the historical analyses for public reasoning undertaken in his early *Structural Transformation*.

3. See KK 188–194, 195–231; CES 69–94.
4. See CES; also the works of Eder, ed., *Entstehung von Klassengesellschaften* and *Die Entstehung staatlich organisierter Gesellschaften*; Döbert, *Systemtheorie* and "Zur Logik des Übergangs."
5. Habermas has taken this concept from Max Weber: see Weber, *Economy*, p. 24ff.
6. Habermas also subsumes "rational choice," or strategic action, under this heading in TRS 62 and in CES 132, where he defines the rules of strategic action as "a necessary component part of the labor process." The fact that he also regards strategic action as a limit case of communicative action gives rise to ambivalence (ThdG 250ff.).
7. For the motivation of the thesis of the three interests of knowledge outlined in Habermas' inaugural lecture at Frankfurt in 1965, see KHI 301–317. There the author defines the technical, the practical, and the emancipatory interests of knowledge as anthropologically deeply rooted and as fundamental orientations resulting from "imperatives of the socio-cultural life-form dependent on labor and language" (TP 9) and constituting knowledge and science. In his view, they also form the *a priori* framework of human experience and the foundation of our approach to the sciences of empirical analysis, historical hermeneutics, and criticism.
8. This distinction is made by Habermas in his epilogue to *Erkenntnis*, p. 397, following Schnädelbach, *Über den Realismus*.
9. See Weber, *Economy*, p. 24ff. Weber also regards this action as purposively rational.
10. This definiton is connected with the sociological and socio-psychological analyses and theories of the fundamental structures of human interaction, as expressed in the role theories of Mead, Parsons, and Goffman.
11. Instrumental action is of course also mediated linguistically in the sense that it takes place in connection with language, but it is fundamentally distinguished from communicative action by its symbolic organization. On the one hand, symbolic mediation takes place in this process within the framework of historically formed everyday language, as the expression of interactions of generations of subjects communicating with each other. On the other, in the use, in the form of a monologue and in accordance with instrumental action, of a "pure" language, that is, a formalized language or one that can be formalized, symbolic connections are constituted and mediated of a kind that can be established "by means of rules of inference" (KHI 192).
12. I cannot go further into this question here. For the acceptance of Freud with reference to the "institutional framework," see KHI 246ff., and, for an explanation within the framework of historical materialism reconstructed according to the theory of evolution, see CES 130–177.
13. Habermas does this in CES 132. He ascribes strategic action, in ThdG 250ff., to interaction, thus placing it on the side of communicative action. See above, note 6.
14. This "interest" should not be confused with the anthropologically deeply rooted interests of knowledge, which constitute the objects of our experience.
15. For the connection between foundation, legitimation, and norms of interaction, see LC and 6.4.1 below.
16. An "acceptance of binding decisions that is almost without a motive and is taken for granted" (Luhmann, *Legitimation durch Verfahren*, quoted from ThdG 261) of the political system has so far not been realized and is, within the mode of socialization that is both valid and practiced today, not even conceivable. For a questioning of this mode of socialization, see LC 117–130.

17. Habermas uses the concepts role competence, communicative competence, and interactive competence almost as synonyms. The third concept is the one that he usually employs in his attempt to systematize and interrelate the development of cognitive, linguistic, and interactive competences. It is also the one that he uses to characterize, in the most striking way, the aspect of competence that he is aiming at. H. Peukert assumes that "communicative competence" points to the sphere within which cognitive, linguistic, and interactive competence can be distinguished as "three dimensions of communicative competence" (*Science*, p. 174). For the primacy of interactive competence see U. Peukert, *Interaktive Kompetenz*.

18. As Piaget did before him with regard to cognitive competence and Kohlberg also did, although only descriptively and without discussing the connection with the logic of development, so too for the stages in moral judgment.

19. This extends from an understanding and a following of simple expectations of behavior to an understanding of reflective expectations as norms, and beyond this to an understanding of reflective norms as principles.

20. Peukert, *Science*, p. 181. Habermas does not, however, establish this relationship explicitly. He relates classes of speech acts to different linguistic uses or modes of communication, it is true, but not to the competences that make these possible; see CES 52ff.

21. Schnädelbach, *Reflexion*, p. 148, is rightly opposed to Habermas' apodeictic separation of communicative action from discourse, and prefers to regard this distinction "simply as a difference of sphere." I also agree with his statement, "It is not true that we do not exchange information in discourses" (p. 185).

22. Only these two validity claims are discursive (see Wth 221f.). Claims to truthfulness can only be met in contexts of actions. Intelligibility is one of the conditions of communication and is not one of the validity claims made in communication.

23. See Alexy, *Theory* and "Eine Theorie des praktischen Diskurses," Oelmüller, *Normenbegründung*, pp. 22–58.

24. Habermas has outlined this theory in VB, taking the question of the competence of a critic who is able to distinguish between true and false statements as his point of departure. He did this within the framework of a dialogue with the school of Erlangen and its theory of consensus; see Kamlah and Lorenzen, *Propaedeutic*. He develops his own theory of consensus in Wth 211–265. For a criticism of the consensus theory, see, apart from the already mentioned continuation by Apel, "Post-Tarskian Problem," the criticism of Puntel, *Wahrheitstheorien*, pp. 144–164, which the author has written from the standpoint of the coherence theory; Mans, *Intersubjektivitätstheorien*, pp. 172–283; Beckermann, "Voraussetzungen"; Höffe, "Überlegungen."

25. With regard to the unlimited number of participants and the equality of opportunities in the use of communicative speech acts, Habermas says, with an apparent contradiction, that only speakers are admitted to discourse "who as active participants have equal opportunities to use representative speech acts" and "who as active participants have an equal opportunity to use regulative speech acts" (Wth 256). These "active participants" are people who have "discursive" competence at their disposal, in the sense that they are, on the basis of their abilities to act, in the position to make use of a formal equality of opportunities. This apparent contradiction refers to the connection between interactive and "discursive" competence. It also points to the fact that, for the conducting of a discourse, competence in action represents the decisive foundation and that discourses can consequently only be conducted—and institutionalized—where

there are competent active participants. On the other hand, it is also an indication that the conditions of the discourse are connected with those of the action, in that they represent the "ideal" conditions that have been acquired on the basis of the model of pure communicative action.

26. This fundamental intention is to be found, Habermas believes, in the fact that it postulates a communicative rule competence that is analogous to a linguistic competence with a universal central core, and consequently aims at a description of the fundamental system of rules "that adult subjects master to the extent that they can fulfill the conditions for a happy employment of sentences in utterances" (CES 26).

27. Here Habermas follows Austin's analysis of the standard forms of the speech act as consisting of an illocutionary and a propositional component, in which the propositional component, formed of a statement of propositional content, expresses the content of the speech act, and the illocutionary component, as an illocutionary act performed with the help of a performative statement, carries out the communicative function of the uttered content by establishing a definite interpersonal relationship. In opposition to Austin's restriction of the term "meaning" (as distinct from "force") to the propositional components accessible to linguistic analysis, Habermas suggests that "force" and "meaning" should be distinguished as two categories of meaning. He says that these categories have in view the universal pragmatic functions of communication, on the one hand, and representation, on the other (see CES 44ff.). These functions are appropriated in each case in a different situation of learning, in the performative attitude of participants toward speech acts or in the non-performative attitude of observers.

28. I draw attention here to Habermas' reflections in CES, in which he throws light on the universal nature of the validity claims that form part of the structure of speech, by referring to the "systematic place of language" (CES 66) as the medium by which the speaker and the listener engage in "performances of demarcation." These take place: 1) with regard to an environment (external nature) objectified in the propositional attitude of an observer; 2) in an environment (of society) experienced in the performative attitude of a participant; 3) in one's own subjectivity (inner nature); and 4) in language itself.

29. This idealizing abstraction is entirely in accordance with that of the school of Erlangen. Just as we idealize objects of possible observation from the point of view of physical measurement, so too we idealize assertions about subjects who are linguistically capable and able to act in accordance with a model of pure communicative action.

30. For Habermas' reservation with regard to the term "transcendental," see CES 21 and the controversy between him and Apel in Oelmüller, ed., *Normenbegründung*. See also 7.1 below and Schrader and Klebert, "Begriff." For a criticism of Habermas, in addition to a number of different works in Dallmayr, ed., *Materialien*, see Bittner, "Transzendental," p. 1526, who regards Habermas' (and Apel's) concept as a "trivialized concept of 'transcendental.'" See also Peukert, *Science*, p. 190: "What is transcendental in the realm of practical reason is shown as a transcendental necessity only in free practice and as the necessary reference to this free practice," but is not identical with the term "transcendental necessity" in the classical sense.

31. It is difficult to understand why Habermas restricts the application of the concept of legitimacy to political orders and describes the mythical world views of pre-state societies as constituting rather than as legitimating social norms.

According to the ideas developed in VB, mythical world views are figures of legitimation for social norms (see VB 120). To that extent, in the light of what Habermas himself says, his restricted use of the concept of legitimacy, which is to some degree justified in the context of his controversy with Hennis, cannot be maintained.

32. Döbert, "Logik," p. 335; *Systemtheorie.*
33. This questioning, according to Habermas, is not possible because there is no difference between the system of acts and the world view and because the region of normative reality of a society and objectivized nature are not separated in the consciousness of members of a tribe. See above, note 31.
34. A remarkable circle can be found in the emergence of the recognition of this order and its accompanying norms, because they are seen as "divine" norms mediated by the representatives of the "divine" order. On the other hand, a divine legitimation of those handing on the tradition is the condition for their being recognized as such and being granted, together with the competence to mediate norms, the right to supervise and judge the way they are put into practice.
35. Habermas elaborates the "bourgeois ideology" of "liberty, equality and fraternity" on the basis of detailed analyses in LC, TRS, and *Structural Transformation,* and, in his systematic analyses of performance and function in KHI, arrives at a concept of ideology and a criticism of ideologies from the vantage point of a theory of systematically distorted communication that is close to psychoanalysis. See his "On Systematically Distorted Communication."
36. Neolithic societies, early developed cultures, developed cultures, and the modern era.
37. "Natural" identity, role identity, and ego identity.
38. The pre-conventional, the conventional, and the post-conventional stages.

# === 7 ===

# *The Search for an Integrative Pragmatic Theory*

## 7.1 TRANSCENDENTAL PRAGMATICS VERSUS UNIVERSAL PRAGMATICS

I have tried to reconstruct the history of the formation of pragmatic theory from the standpoint of a theory of communicative action, the foundations of which have been carefully elaborated, or on the basis of the systematic central core of that theory in universal pragmatics. For the purposes of the task of reconstruction, I have regarded universal pragmatics, in its general tendency, as in unity with transcendental pragmatics. So far, in my discussion of the theories and approaches to which they refer and from which I hope, in my treatment of them, to develop a common approach to pragmatics, the differences between them have remained very much in the background. In considering various stages in the formation of pragmatic theory, I have regarded it as sufficient to identify both transcendental and universal pragmatics as developments of a single program centered in the normative core of interaction that is united in its intention.

In this chapter, I shall look for an integrative pragmatic theory. In that search and especially in the search for the foundations of that integration, it is essential to make a distinction between them. This means that the claim made by each has to be taken seriously. At the same time, it is also important to present their common basis, since this will reveal their differences all the more clearly. Transcendental and universal pragmatics have a common point of departure in that both recognize the double structure of discourse and the status of validity claims. Both also differentiate between linguistic and communicative competence and between communicative action and discourse. Both assume contrafactually an ideal speech situation within the framework of an unlimited communication community in the carrying out of communicative action. Finally, both take as their starting point a mediation between the real and the ideal speech situation or communication community, in the sense of a necessary anticipation, taking place within the communicative action, of the ideal that is to be achieved.

It is not difficult to point to clear differences between Habermas and Apel in the question of the distinction between linguistic and communicative competence and of the status of validity claims. By placing linguistic and communicative competence in parallel, Habermas exposes himself, in Apel's opinion, to the risk of failing to observe the differences between the two. The main difference is that communicative competence cannot, like linguistic competence, be transcended in reflection in order that it may, like the latter, become, as a contingent anthropological fact, the theme of an explanative theory. As Apel himself says, "Understanding the 'rules of communicative competence' exclusively in the sense of an extrapolative extension of Chomsky's competence theory as a powerful empirical theory of universal structures or values that can be explained anthropo-biologically . . . fails to do justice to the fact that they must be presupposed in any conception of empirically falsifiable theories as the normative condition of their possibility."[1]

This means that, if a reconstructive theory that has empirical meaning and content is to be elaborated, an unprocurable criterion of reconstruction has to be presupposed within the framework of that theory. This is something that Apel has tried to demonstrate in the case of the conditions of the possibility governing communicative agreement aimed at in universal pragmatics in the self-reflection of the argumentative discourse. Habermas, on the other hand, seems to believe that the criteria of reconstruction can be found in the reconstruction itself, and, in my opinion at least, he also seems to think that this can be achieved by an elaboration of the universal structures of human communication, which he distinguishes from empirical generalities.[2] What may be inferred from his assertion that, "if it were possible to consider transcendental predicates from the natural historical reverse side, they would be anthropological predicates"[3] is Habermas' intention to reach that natural historical reverse aspect[4] by deciphering transcendental as anthropological predicates.

This, in turn, in the case of the theme of claims to validity, which Apel regards as representing "transcendental pragmatic doctrines,"[5] means that it is possible, in Habermas' opinion, to reconstruct such validity claims from the empirical experience of factual linguistic usage. In this sense, he is able to regard his four fundamental classes of speech acts as indications of the fact that validity claims can be empirically reconstructed. However, I do not think it is possible to make it clear or even to justify, by means of empirical reconstruction, that these four classes of speech acts in fact represent the necessary and adequate conditions of construction for the ideal speech situation. What is more, Habermas himself does not reconstruct that ideal speech situation on the basis of empirical conditions. Rather, he reflects, in Peirce's sense of the "contrary-to-fact-conditionalis," about the kind of conditions that might be provided in an ideal speech situation and the kind of communication structures that would have to be established.

Habermas now affirms that he goes a step further than Apel, "and, what is more, behind the practical discourse into contexts of communicative action with the argument that we already have implicitly to presuppose the possibility of practical argumentation in consensual action. The fact that we have always already accepted an implicit normative content of general presuppositions of communication does not depend on the fact we have decided on one or other form of argumentation, but on the fact that we have been born into a communicative form of life."[6]

What we have here is clearly a reappearance, in a concealed form, of a suspicion that he had already expressed in *Legitimation Crisis*, that Apel is guilty of decisionism.[7] Apel defended himself against this criticism with his formula "decision for what is already decided," which has to be understood in the sense of an intentional confirmation of "what can be proved to have been inevitably presupposed in the sense of a foundation."[8] At the same time, Habermas is also showing that this criticism of decisionism can be countered by having recourse to the communicative form of life that is always already given to us. This is not simply an empirical fact, which may be expressed either in that way or in a different way, but a normative factor, which makes the reconstruction of empirical forms of life possible and provides a criterion for their assessment. This cannot, however, be simply deduced from a reconstruction of this particular form of life that is not already empirically present and cannot be identified with anything factual. On the contrary, it calls for a reflection about the constitutive aspects of the communicative form of life, which, since we cannot leave it or go behind it, must have the form of a reflection about what we always and of necessity already presuppose whenever we communicate.

Apel carries out this reflection in the limit case of the argumentative discourse concerned with reflection about validity, to which he attributes the primacy of ultimate foundation, because it "represents an inescapable situation for those engaged in the argument."[9] Apel also emphasizes that the methodical primacy of the argumentative discourse does not in any way exclude the fact "that the material primacy should be conceived in the sense in which it was intended by Habermas." He believes, rather, that the "formal" part of foundation has to be achieved by transcendental pragmatics and that the "material" part of foundation, for which universal pragmatics are responsible—parts "which have a mutual need of each other"—mark "the decisive place where transcendental and universal pragmatics are mediated."[10] In his view, there is a "phase of coincidence" in which universal pragmatics can be localized as the "transitional stage between ultimate foundation in the transcendental and reflective sense and empirical experience."[11]

Habermas nevertheless refuses to take the step that would lead him to transcendental reflection, even though, according to Apel, he has already taken it in what he says about validity claims. By rejecting foundation, according to Apel, he has deprived himself of the possibility of providing conclusive proof of his principle of contrafactual anticipation. He could in this way have attributed "no more than the status of a theoretical axiom"[12] to that principle, thus making it impossible to derive ethical norms from it.[13] It is not without foundation that he has refused to take the step required by Apel and has at the same time also rejected the hierarchy of values given by Apel to the reconstructive science and universal and transcendental pragmatics.

He gives the reasons for his rejection, and, in my view, they are not to be found exclusively in the sphere of the use of language.[14] He has terminological reasons for regarding the concept "transcendental pragmatics" as unsuitable because "the word 'transcendental,' with which we associate an antithesis to empirical science . . . is not suitable for providing a description that cannot be misunderstood of such an orientation in research as universal pragmatics." Despite this, however, the central core of this argument can be found in the fact that "a peculiar connection between formal and empirical analysis"[15] has replaced the separation between the empirical and the transcendental found in the classical form of transcendental philosophy. This, Habermas believes, is because the model of the constitution of experience used for the analysis of general presuppositions of communication, based on transcendental philosophy and the theory of knowledge, is unsuitable, since that analysis generatively thematizes the structures of discourse under the heading of agreement rather than of experience. Habermas is himself aware that what is found behind the terminological question recognized by him— transcendental or universal pragmatics—is the "systematic question concerning the as-yet insufficiently clarified status of non-nomological empirical sciences of the reconstructive type."[16]

I agree with Apel's objection to an understanding of universal pragmatics in the sense of an empirical and reconstructive science, in relation to the "naturalistic fallacy" of the attempt to establish empirical norms. I also think that universal pragmatics validly express a reflection about the foundations of the communicative form of life. At the same time, however, as I have noted, Apel also gives a hierarchy of values to the empirical and reconstructive science and universal and transcendental pragmatics. In addition, he subsumes parts of universal pragmatics, as "transcendental pragmatic doctrines," under the heading of transcendental pragmatics. He does this because of Habermas' objections and, even more importantly, because of his own transcendental pragmatic replacement of these doctrines, and has nowhere demonstrated this. I regard these two actions as quite unjustified.

On the one hand, I recognize and accept the scientific and reconstructive self-understanding that is certainly very vigorously expressed in Habermas' work, and, on the other, I would not want to associate his approach with the very denial of reflection which he himself deplores.[17] For these reasons, I would suggest that the systematic central core of his universal pragmatics should be understood within the framework of his scientific and reconstructive program of a theory of communicative action as a philosophical reflection about the foundations of a communicative form of life, within which Apel's transcendental question about the conditions of the possibility and validity of communicative agreement is included.

Habermas' universal pragmatics, as I have shown, include reflection about the foundations of communicative action and the conditions of its maintenance. Also involved are the validity claims made in communicative action and the possibility of reaching a consensus as soon as those claims become problematic. The discourse required for the purpose and the distinction between this and communicative action also forms part of that universal pragmatic reflection. Finally and of fundamental importance, there is the reflection about the normative core of interaction. All these aspects of reflection constitute the systematic central core of his theory of communicative action, which he calls universal pragmatics.

The name that I would give to this reflective central core of a theory of action and communication, which at the same time is also the instance of foundation for the formation of a pragmatic theory as such, is fundamental pragmatics. I have several reasons for preferring the concept of fundamental pragmatics to universal pragmatics. The first is that it establishes a terminological distance from empirical generalities, whereas the concept "universal" implies a closeness, "empirical generalities" being understood in this context as what factually occurs universally and can also as such be empirically reconstructed. My second reason is that the concept expresses more clearly than that of transcendental pragmatics the dimension of reflection, which is not limited to the transcendental. Third and most importantly of all, I choose to introduce the concept of fundamental pragmatics because I believe that it is a suitable term for designating that factor of foundation which is not identical with universal pragmatics, although it is closely related to and goes beyond Habermas' pragmatics with the integration of the stages in the formation of pragmatic theory that I have described in view.

These fundamental pragmatics have so far been explicated most fully in Habermas' universal pragmatics. In my opinion, they can also make use of the apparatus that his pragmatics provide for the theory of action, and can assimilate the reconstructive analyses of the constitution of subject, society, and history that Habermas has made with a theory of communicative action in view. With this in mind, it is possible to formulate the task of fundamental pragmatics very concisely as that of reconstructing the fundamental structures of human interaction through reflection.

To carry out that task, fundamental pragmatics will inevitably make use of the methods and resources not of the empirical sciences but of philosophical analysis. This would include Peirce's thought experiment and his "contrary-to-fact-conditionalis," Apel's transcendental question, phenomenological analysis, the description provided by linguistic analysis, and self-reflection based on a criticism of ideologies. The use of such philosophical methods and approaches would produce a model that would form the basic structure of interaction, and this could be developed in its various dimensions from the pragmatic partial aspects that are centered around fundamental pragmatics as the normative core in an integrative pragmatic theory. This is still only a far-reaching postulate, of course, but it is nonetheless possible to name the dimensions and aspects of fundamental pragmatics that should be pursued with integration in mind from a reconstruction of the history of the formation of pragmatic theory.

## 7.2   FUNDAMENTAL PRAGMATICS AS THE
## INSTANCE OF FOUNDATION

The point of departure for fundamental pragmatics, as the philosophical foundation of pragmatics in the form of a reflection about the fundamental structure of interaction and indeed for all pragmatic approaches, is the irreducibility of the subject of the process of signs, communication, and action. The constitutive function of that process can be seen, by fundamental pragmatics, to be present both in the foundation, on the basis of the logic of relations of three-dimensional semiotics, and in the discovery of the double structure of language. The central philosophical core of both is to be found, in the case of fundamental pragmatics, in the fact that subjects reach agreement about something by means of a system of signs of communication, in other words, by communicating with each other within the framework of a linguistic system that is regarded as suitable. Communication and interaction are essentially oriented toward agreement. In the light of fundamental pragmatics, this is clear from hypothetical reflection (the thought experiment) about disturbed communication. There would never be any communication of any kind if we had to take certain situations as our point of departure. It would not take place, for example, if the partners in interaction were systematically deluded in their intentions or if they did not assume that they could in fact reach agreement. There would be no communication if one partner could not rely either on the other's telling the truth, that is, only asserting what he regards as true, or on his only doing what is thought to be correct and legitimate. In this sense, communication is only made possible by an assumption of the truth of what is said, the correctness of the norms of action followed, and the truthfulness of utterances made by the communicating individuals. Reflection about the conditions of success in reaching agreement, on the other hand, means that the partners in communication must be ready to make their claims valid for each other, on the assumption that those claims are legitimate and justified. This implies that they are verifiable. There is, however, no "objective" instance for verification that exists independently of the interacting partners. No such objective instance can exist unless other subjects had decided about truth and correctness, the justification of which would also have to have been legitimated by an objective instance, and this would have led to a *regressus ad infinitum*. Since, then, there can be no such objective instance, we have to look for another instance by including the subjects involved in interaction.

The ultimate instance that can be described, and to which we can appeal, and that, I believe, is the climax of Habermas' consensus theory of truth, is agreement with all others. By definition, this cannot be a contingent fact, since there is nothing against which it can be measured. Consensus among all subjects, as discovered in reflection, is therefore in itself normative. Reflection, then, about the triadic relation of signs, on the one hand, and the double structure of language, on the other, results in that this consensus, as a consensus among all subjects about definite situations in a linguistic system, at the same time has to measure itself against those situations, in the case of the factual existence of situations, that are being considered as a theme. This is, of course, the aspect of the evidence of correspondence that Apel takes into account, or what Beckermann calls the realistic presuppositions of the consensus theory.[18]

There must at the same time also be reflection about the fact that the consensus is articulated within a definite linguistic system, the possible inadequacy of which must be included within the framework of transformation into a more adequate system. One point is very clearly expressed from the perspective of fundamental pragmatics in Apel's definition of truth as consensus about the coherence of the evidence of correspondence.[19] That is that consensus has to be measured against the evident insight, which is always already linguistically interpreted and is therefore once again oriented toward consensus, into the application of statements to situations, which are, as formulated in the context of other statements within a coherent linguistic system, once again dependent on consensus about this.

The extension and correction of Habermas' consensus theory, which has been suggested by Apel and which I have adapted, may be validly applied to theoretical discourse. A further problem, however, arises in the case of practical discourse, in which the consensus, as formulated within a particular

linguistic system, cannot be measured against any instance that is "objective" with regard to agreement, since the aspect of the evidence of correspondence ceases in this case to exist. Its place is taken by the internal
criterion that Habermas considered in the concept of the ideal speech situation. According to that criterion, a situation of agreement that is oriented
toward agreement about modes and norms of action is itself a normatively
relevant example of norm-governed action, which possesses in itself a power
that acts as a norm and an example for other forms of interaction.

Certain norms must apply, in this process of the "ultimate instance,"
whenever agreement is reached. This is equally so in the case of theoretical
discourse, although it can be more strongly emphasized in practical discourse. The norms must ensure, first, that no one is excluded; second, that
each subject is able to express his needs, claims, values, and objections; and
third, that a consensus is characterized as a non-contingent normative fact.
These conditions of the discursive situation of agreement, according to
Habermas' reflections, can be seen to be those of an ideal form of life in which
the conditions considered in the limit case of the discourse become the rule
(Peirce's normative "would-be"). The fact that at the same time they also
represent conditions of all communicative action is a reflective insight into
that toward which communicative action is always, of necessity, already
oriented. It is a reflective insight, which comes about on the basis of the
thought experiment of a communication that seeks systematically to exclude
these ideal conditions and therefore also seeks to destroy its own foundations.
The discovery of a normative foundation of interaction is consequently the
result of reflection about the guarantee, which is found in the agreement
itself, of an agreement which in fact fails again and again.

If the normative central core of interaction, as the condition of the possibility of communicative agreement, can only be seen in reflection, then it can be
made the normative criterion for all relationships of communication and
interaction, with the result that it will have a critical function with regard to
the analysis of factual interactions. This implies that it will also have the task
of criticizing ideologies, especially in the case of illusory legitimations of
factual repressive relationships. The innovatory aspect of the ideological
superstructure that not only reflects but also breaks those relationships—an
aspect which transcends the real relationships of interaction—can also be
approached from the standpoint of a semiotic theory of ideology (Vološinov)
as anticipatory.

It is in carrying out this function that the creative role of reflection is
expressed, and for the following reasons. When the existing relationships of
interaction or the units of language-game and forms of life are traced back to
their normative central core, and questioned from the standpoint of that core
in fundamental pragmatics, fundamental pragmatics can judge the institu-

tionalized, experienced, and practiced elements in the sphere of the communication both of the reason that makes this possible and of the telos that is always aimed at in communication. This results in the break-up of the factual relationships of interaction that are ideological, in the sense in which the term was used by Vološinov. Peukert[20] has drawn attention to the fact that the innovatory aspect—which is attributed to fundamental pragmatics as reflection (which has the effect of breaking)—of linguistically established world images and ideologies that are constitutive of reality must be made clear to those pragmatics in fundamental pragmatic reflection about the foundations of the change in the structures of communication and action, which is clearly what he is aiming at in his deliberations about the status of innovatory linguistic acts.

The problem of innovatory linguistic acts, as formulated by Peukert, therefore occupies a central position within fundamental pragmatics. This is because, taking a criticism of the speech act theory as its point of departure, it represents an intensification, which at the same time also delineates more clearly the frontiers of universal pragmatics, of the question of the relationship between rules and conventions. This is precisely what concerns Peukert in his reflections about the performance of innovatory acts that are constitutive for interaction. The fundamental problem of a speech act theory that takes conventions and the constitutive rules that form their basis as its point of departure is, for Peukert, the fact that "speech acts directed at the transformation of conventions cannot at all be understood"[21] by this theory. The intentions of a speaker can, however, be aimed at changing conventions, which, if they are analyzed on the basis of an extended symbolic interactionism and therefore understood in models at different levels of expectations, expectations of expectations, and so on, can be characterized as an intention to change at the level of reciprocal expectations.[22] The "paradoxical status" of innovatory acts is described in the following way by Peukert: "They must be thought of as acts which can themselves break or change the system of rules on the basis of which they can be generated."[23] Peukert has correctly observed that the same problem of innovatory linguistic acts also concerns Habermas, in his presentation of the logic of discourses, in his essay on theories of truth.

In connection with the question of the conditions governing the reaching of a consensus when validity claims continue to be problematical, Habermas names as a formal property of discourses if the occasion arises—that is, if it is not possible to reach an agreement within an existing linguistic system and that system is therefore known to be inadequate—the need to modify it or revise it as a whole. In this context, he also says that "progress in knowledge is achieved in the form of a substantial criticism of language" (Wth 250). What he sees as that criticism in the case of theoretical discourse is the making possible of a gradual radicalization of that discourse, that is, a reflection by the knowing subject, and similarly, in practical discourse, the making possible of self-reflection by the acting subject. Both imply innovatory acts insofar as they aim at a new understanding and indeed a rediscovery of oneself in one's possibilities and intentions. At the same time, the conception that innovatory actions are not only possible and necessary, but are also "constitutive performances,"[24] is also implied in this process. Finally, an emancipatory dimension is also implied in those constitutive performances.

Before leaving Peukert, I must point out another aspect connected with the question of the possibilities and performances of innovatory acts, which he introduces as a test case for a textual theory in respect of poetic texts. It is, moreover, an aspect that follows closely on Vološinov's deliberations about a semiotic theory of ideology. Peukert's key statement is: "Speaking poetically or figuratively, in other words, speaking in metaphors or narrating parables clearly has something to do both with changing constellations of meaning and with changing conventions in an innovatory way."[25] In Peukert's view, "a theory of art, and above all a poetics would have to clarify how creative action opens new dimensions and how metaphorical speech can become the medium of a substantive critique of language, without which a transformation of concrete situations and a coming to agreement about new orientations would not be possible."[26]

At least three conclusions which are directly relevant to fundamental pragmatics can be drawn from this presentation of the idea of innovatory action. The first is that a clear distinction must be made between conventions, which can be realized in interaction and institutionally and transcended and broken through in principle, their underlying constitutive rules, and the rules which make the breakthrough possible and guarantee it. These rules are the basic, elementary, fundamental pragmatic rules of human interaction, in respect of which all other rules and conventions can be relativized or changed and within which they have their normative criterion. Second, fundamental pragmatics must obviously approach innovatory action triadically, that is, in the sense of three-dimensional semiotics. This is necessary with regard to innovation within the systems of signs that are used and thematized in poetry, and those norms, acts, and interaction that form above all the object of ethics. It is also required with regard to the world of situations and facts, with which both theoretical research into foundations and praxis are concerned. Fundamental pragmatics must, in the third place, also reflect about the conditions of the possibility and the scope and implications of innovatory action as something that calls for the most extreme possibilities of human action.

In the following section, I conclude this chapter by going through the various stages involved in the formation of pragmatic theory, in an attempt to consider the partial aspects of and the different areas of research covered in it. I include only those aspects and areas that can be linked together on the basis of fundamental pragmatics.

I would describe this basis in the following way. Fundamental pragmatic reflection about the basic structure of interaction regards that basis as manifesting itself in institutionalized relationships of interaction (units of language game and forms of life). The basis is restricted by them and at the same time determined by the normative central core of an ideal communication. Fundamental pragmatics also discovers this basis in the anticipation experienced by an ideal community of interaction of that continuous interaction, in the form of rule-governed action, which is realized in conventions that can be transcended and innovatorily cancelled out in the triadic mediation of subjects, who are interacting about something and with some purpose in mind by means of sign systems in the reality that is socially constituted by these elements.

## 7.3 PARTIAL ASPECTS OF A PRAGMATIC THEORY AND AREAS OF RESEARCH

In this book I have reconstructed the history of the formation of pragmatic theory. In this concluding section, I throw some light on the sign and textual theories, and theories of action and communication, that I have presented in their relationship with each other and with the fundamental pragmatic basis for the formation of the pragmatic theory, that following Habermas, Apel, and Peukert, I have tried to elaborate. I shall also integrate these approaches within a single coherent framework.

I begin by affirming that these sign and textual theories and theories of action and communication can in fact be integrated on the basis of reflective fundamental pragmatics, which is able to ground them, and that this can be done either as their individual scientific explications or as developments of their various dimensions. In this task, I am also bound to include within my considerations the claim, made implicitly or explicitly by individual pragmatic approaches, that these have prepared the way for or have aimed at precisely such an integration.

There are, in my opinion, three positions to be taken into account here. The first is the claim made by Morris, within the framework of his program of the "unified science," that pragmatically integrated semiotics form the foundation and are the organon for unifying the sciences. The second is the attempt made by Schmidt to use his category of the communicative act game to integrate and explain the approaches and the results of the formation of pragmatic theory within the context of a textual theory. I have to point out here, however, that this does not explicitly constitute a claim to be a basis theory for pragmatics, even though Schmidt allows that claim to be discerned in his insistence on textuality as the universal mode of manifestation for the achievement of communication. The third position is that occupied by Habermas, who has attempted to integrate the theory of action and communication within the framework of a normatively based theory of communicative action that at the same time includes a theory of the subject, society, and history.

I have tried to understand the systematic and normative central core of Habermas' theory of communicative action, in the form of universal pragmatics, in the sense of reflective fundamental pragmatics. This means that an attempt to grasp those dimensions of his theory of communicative action which, in my opinion, he has himself centered around that universal pragmatic core, as partial aspects of the same theory on a fundamental pragmatic basis, should not confront us with any real difficulties. This is because the normative central core of interaction that is discovered in reflection is manifested at the level of the subject, society, and history in the dialectic interplay of the possibility of its development in its relationship with the stage which is conditioned by that possibility and reached subjectively, socially, and historically, and which at the same time reveals the need for a restriction of its normative potential. As I have already dealt in detail with that relationship, there is no need for me to consider it here. It should have been made clear in my discussion of this matter that, in a certain sense, action that constitutes the subject, society, and history has these three dimensions, which have to be reconstructed in accordance with a theory of action.

What, then, is the situation with regard to Schmidt's textual theory as a possible basis for integrating the formation of pragmatic theory? In my view, a distinction has to be made in Schmidt's work between a reflection based on linguistic philosophy about the performances of linguistically mediated action in the constitution of "reality," that is, of models of reality as the foundation for his theory of communicative act games, on the one hand, and the development of that theory by means of arguments based on the theory of action and systems within the framework of a linguistic theory as a textual theory, on the other. Schmidt's reflections about communication as a primary phenomenal datum and about the constitution of reality in the context of and via communicative behavior, in my opinion, clearly have a fundamental pragmatic status and can therefore be included without further ado within the framework of my deliberations about fundamental pragmatics. If this is the case, then his theory of communicative act games as a simple social system is a socio-linguistic theory, which is conceived on a fundamental pragmatic basis and forms the foundation for an explanation of the concept of communicative act games based on the theory of the text.

This explanation is provided in the dimensions of that textual theory initiated or postulated by Schmidt, and at the same time in partial aspects of the semantics of instruction, reference theory, presupposition theory, textual grammar, and the theory of the production and coherence of the text. It is precisely these partial aspects of research into the theory of the text that can be included within my conception as partial aspects of the formation of pragmatic theory, on the basis of fundamental pragmatics. In carrying out this process, however, it is essential to discuss the relationship between this dimension of the theory of the text and the dimensions of semiotics.

It is valuable to go back to Peirce's placing of pragmatism in his construction of a system of sciences, if we are to understand this relationship between the fundamental character of semiotics and the formation of pragmatic theory. According to Peirce, pragmatism is the object of logic, and he identifies logic with semiotics and sees the latter as representing an area of philosophy that he regards as a normative science. I will not try to apply Peirce's entire construction to my conception, but I would claim that his logic (or semiotics), which he regards as a normative science and bases on ethics, can be seen as the result of fundamental pragmatic reflection and localized, in their center, as the normative semiotics of the three-dimensional relationship of signs. It was with good reason that I chose two points of departure in my attempt to discover the fundamental pragmatic central core of the formation of pragmatic theory. The first was Peirce's reflection about the three-dimensional character of the relationship of signs and its foundation in the logic of relations. The second was the normative implications of his conception of semiosis, or the process of signs, in which interpretation which is mediated by signs, related to the object, and forms habits can be normatively understood in the sphere of ultimately valid interpretation, within the unlimited community of interpretation that functions as a regulative principle.

In his fundamental pragmatic reflection about the foundations of the process of signs, about which he reflects as an action which is mediated by signs and related to the object and which results in interpretation, Peirce can legitimately be regarded as the founder not only of the formation of pragmatic theory but also of fundamental pragmatic reflection about the foundations of pragmatic theory. Morris' conception of signs, which is oriented toward Peirce's understanding of the sign process, on the other hand, represents an attempt to dispute its fundamental pragmatic foundations by elaborating semiotics that are oriented toward the behavioral sciences and pragmatically integrated. In Morris' work, pure semiotics as logic have the task of understanding, both terminologically and methodologically, the foundations of the theory of signs, which are of value to the descriptive semiotics of scientific language in the postulated elaboration of their sphere of action, within the framework of the unified science of a natural science of human behavior.

I have already pointed to the aporias in Morris' semiotics of behavior and, in so doing, have at the same time also disputed their universal claim. With the clear distinction that it makes between syntax, semantics, and pragmatics as a formal analysis of the sign process, however, his theory of signs continues to be valid. At the level of individual sciences, these partial aspects of syntax, semantics, and pragmatics can be developed and empirically validated within the framework of theories of syntax, semantics, and pragmatics, which, insofar as they refer to fundamental pragmatic foundations, develop these in each case in a specific sphere of human sign action.

This can take place at the level of a combination of signs, while abstracting actually, and therefore consciously, from their meaning and from their relationship between the speaker and the listener or their syntax. It can also take place at the level of the meaning of signs. Wittgenstein, Wunderlich, Vološinov, and Schmidt, I believe, have all made important contributions of an empirical and scientific nature, and in the question of reflection about foundations, to our understanding of this level. It can also occur at the level of semantics and finally at that of sign-mediated interaction, or pragmatics. No one particular individual science can be ascribed to this last level, the explication of which is shared between a number of widely different sciences. The explication of the three fundamental pragmatic dimensions of linguistically mediated action to which I have referred—a process in which Habermas has gone further than anyone else with his theory of communicative action—calls for interdisciplinary cooperation between the psychological, educational, and sociological approaches to a theory of the subject, and between those to a theory of society and a theory of history. Certain aspects of these and the ways in which they are interdependent can hardly be overlooked, since they are important areas of individual scientific research into pragmatics based on the reconstructive method.

In the same way, the development of modes of communicative action can also take place on the basis of fundamental pragmatic reflection. This development is achieved on the basis of textuality, which is correctly regarded by Schmidt as the all-embracing mode of manifestation, in which communication takes place, and primarily in a theory of the text from which a theory of literature and a theory of the means of communication are produced and, at the same time, represent individual or interdisciplinary scientific approaches.

My search for an integrative pragmatic theory has led to a construction that has the following characteristics. In the first place, it points the way to an integration of the many different pragmatic approaches that have already been elaborated: on the one hand, because it establishes their common basis of reflection and, on the other, because it draws attention to their interrelationship and interdependence on that common basis.

Secondly, that common foundation of fundamental pragmatics, including several extensions, correlates with what is expressed as a theme in Habermas' universal pragmatics, Apel's transcendental pragmatics, Peirce's normative semiotics, and Schmidt's reflection about communication as a primary phenomenal datum and about the constitution of reality in the context of and via communicative behavior.

Thirdly, on the basis of this reflective foundation, communicative action can be related to three areas. 1) Habermas has divided the sphere within which communicative action operates into the three dimensions of a theory of the subject, society, and history. 2) Schmidt has elaborated the modes of communicative action by expanding his theory of the text to include a theory of literature and a theory of the means of communication. 3) Sign theory, which, in Morris' triadic semiotics, analyzes the three aspects of syntax, semantics, and pragmatics of sign-mediated communicative action, is concerned with the apparatus of communicative action.

There are still many aspects of the interdependence of the three dimensions of the formation of pragmatic theory which have to be clarified and further elaborated. Despite this, however, I think that I have demonstrated the unity of that theory on the basis of reflective fundamental pragmatics. At the same time, in my presentation of the three elementary areas of pragmatic research as the sphere, the modes, and the apparatus of communicative action, I have also tried to point toward an integration of the formation of pragmatic theory into a single coherent theoretical framework.

# Notes

1. Apel, "Warum transzendentale Sprachpragmatik?," p. 22.
2. See Habermas, Oelmüller, ed., *Normenbegründungen*, p. 146.
3. Ibid.
4. The sentence, "It is difficult to know how that can be arranged" (ibid.), shows that it is not in principle impossible to reach the reverse aspect.
5. Apel, Oelmüller, ed., *Normenbegründungen*, p. 162, against which Apel "does not regard the classes of speech acts, for example, or the attempt to classify them as reflective transcendental pragmatics."
6. Habermas, Oelmüller, ed., *Normenbegründungen*, p. 127.
7. See LC 158f. n16.
8. Apel, Oelmüller, ed., *Normenbegründungen*, p. 199.
9. Ibid., p. 166.
10. Ibid., p. 197.

11. Ibid., p. 152f. Elsewhere, Apel speaks of the "transitional character of universal linguistic pragmatics," which he recognizes in the fact that they represent "the discipline that mediates between the ultimate transcendental pragmatic foundation and the so-called critical and reconstructive social sciences" (p. 162).

12. Apel, "Sprechakttheorie," p. 121.

13. In contrast to Habermas, Apel quite emphatically combines the relationship between philosophical construction and scientific reconstruction with the foundation of ethics in the formula: "Ethics cannot be grounded by a universal theory of reconstructive social sciences . . . but a transcendental pragmatic foundation of ethics refers to its substantial concretization with the help of the critical and reconstructive social sciences and in this way grounds their interest in knowledge that constitutes the object" ("Sprechakttheorie," p. 121).

14. Even though he gives the reasons "for hesitating to adopt this usage of language" (CES 23).

15. Habermas, CES 25.

16. Ibid.

17. The epilogue to *Erkenntnis*, which appeared in print two years after VB, can be regarded as philosophically superseding the approach made in the latter work to a reconstructive theory of competence. Habermas says: "A criticism of scientism is therefore confronted with the task of making us conscious of . . . the denial of reflection as such (although philosophically it is always already used)." He adds: "A history of philosophy which chooses to follow the figure of self-reflection is bound to present itself to those who do not take self-reflection seriously as a movement of thought as a curiosity" (*Erkenntnis* 369). Habermas clearly does not regard himself as one of those people. His criticism of scientism is rather sustained by philosophical reflection. It is, however, not always apparent that his theory of communicative action is sustained by reflection. Sometimes he regards it explicitly as a reconstructive science, and this, in my opinion, is a serious misunderstanding of his own purpose.

18. See Apel, "Post-Tarskian Problem"; Beckermann, "Voraussetzungen."

19. Apel, "Post-Tarskian Problem."

20. Peukert, *Science*.

21. Ibid., p. 107.

22. See Peukert, "Bemerkungen," p. 308ff.

23. Peukert, Oelmüller, ed., *Normenbegründungen*, p. 157.

24. Peukert, *Science*, p. 202.

25. Peukert, "Bemerkungen," p. 308.

26. Peukert, *Science*, p. 199.

# Afterword

Since I wrote *Kommunikative Handlungen*, of which this book is an abridged English version, some time has passed. In the meanwhile, pragmatic thinking has been developed further in at least three significant aspects. First, a number of studies of individual representatives of the pragmatic tradition, as well as examinations of the history and relevance of American pragmatism, have been published.[1] Second, Karl-Otto Apel's transcendental pragmatics and Jürgen Habermas' universal pragmatics have been differentiated and unfolded, especially by reflecting on the ethical dimension of argumentation or communicative action, which, in both cases, has been done in their common and yet distinctive work toward a discourse ethics.[2] Third, pragmatic thinking has been pushed to the center of philosophical debates with the emergence of American neo-pragmatism, which is represented most outspokenly by Richard Rorty but can also be traced in different modes in the writings of Richard Bernstein and Cornel West.[3] All of these contributions show that the discussion about the logic, reach, and basis of pragmatic thinking is in full swing.

I shall deal with the current state of the discussion by first summarizing significant insights arrived at by pragmatic thinking. Then in a second step I shall sketch a few further developments, referring especially to Apel's and Habermas' approaches. In a third, final section, I shall point to neo-pragmatism's challenges to transcendental or universal pragmatics.

## 1. ACHIEVEMENTS OF PRAGMATIC THINKING

If one intends to summarize some basic insights that pragmatic thinking has arrived at during the history of the formation of pragmatic theory, first and foremost it has to be pointed out that human beings are "lingual or semiotic animals." They approach reality by means of triadically mediated signs, that is, by means of language and communication. Reality is not only socially constructed but linguistically as well. Our reality does not exist as such, independently of communication, and that is why there is no access to it irrespective of language. Reality is always already linguistically constituted; it is both disclosed and interpreted by language. Language is constitutive for human existence, which is bound to communication communities. On this anthropological basis I shall summarize some insights which pragmatic thinking has arrived at in view of the structure of language, action, or communication.

Reality is experienced, known, and changed by making use of all kinds of verbal communication. From such a pragmatic point of view, there are five dimensions of communication or communicative action, which are interconnected and together represent a pragmatic model of language, action, and communication.

First, language has a constitutive intersubjective character. Every individual acquires a language that he cannot choose and always already shares with others. By acquiring a particular language, the individual is integrated into a communication community in which basic suppositions about and approaches to reality are shared. The individual in the process of his socialization has to adopt these views in such a way that he both learns to identify with all others and becomes able to differentiate himself from them. Thereby he acquires an identity which enables him to say "I."

A second fundamental insight of pragmatic thinking relates to the propositional-performative character of language. On the one hand, language deals with something; on the other hand, people do things in using it. This becomes clear if one looks at the basic unit of human communication, the usage of sentences in utterances. The utterance has a double structure: it consists of a propositional element, which indicates the subject matter, and the illocutionary element, which indicates what is done if anybody says something. Whereas the propositional element is performed by a propositional act, the illocutionary element is performed by an illocutionary act. A third component of speech acts refers to the factual effects of what is said, and thereby done, on the hearer. If such an effect is reached, a perlocutionary act occurs. Verbal communication thus has to be analyzed as an intersubjective performance of speech acts, which consist of propositional, illocutionary, and (intentionally) perlocutionary acts.

By speech acts, social relations are established, maintained, and changed. Acts of assertion, request, promise, and the like intervene in reality. Thereby, the inner, the social, and even the outer "world" are constituted as such, disclosed, questioned, and altered. The propositional-performative dimension at the same time implies the questions of what constitutes the truth of the content, what are the right or just intersubjective relations, and how the truthfulness of the communication partners relates to truth and rightness.

Thirdly, language has a textual character. Communication happens by means of texts. This fact points to the textuality or mediality of language. Texts are media of communication, which is encoded, articulated, and mediated in a variety of forms. Texts occur in oral, written, or audiovisual forms. Such an understanding does not identify texts and writing, but recognizes them as an element of every communication.[4] In communication processes, things are done by means of texts. Texts are produced, reproduced, used, and received. Embedded in interaction and linked with nonlinguistic actions, they express the intentions of agents and fulfil certain functions for the communication partners, who use them in order to reach an understanding with others about a subject matter.

Fourthly, communication always occurs in concrete situations. It is always located in a particular context of language and action, which predetermines the meaning and the relevance of the texts employed. The context encompasses both the immediate situation of action and the wider socio-political and cultural surroundings in which it takes place. The contextual character of communication makes it necessary not to restrict one's attention to the particular utterance, act, or text but to keep in mind their interwovenness with and their predetermination by the language-games, institutions, and cultures to which they belong.

Finally, communication has a plurality of ends. By communicating, people intend to influence each other; they want to establish, maintain, or change patterns of interaction and to reach their personal or collective goals. Communication is directed at the creation, maintenance, and transformation of communities. Universal and transcendental pragmatics has pointed out that understanding and agreement are the basic aims of communication. Communication originally is directed toward understanding. Understanding is the specific mark of communication, which is highlighted by universal and transcendental pragmatic reflection on the conditions of the possibility of verbal communication. Agreement is shown as both the original goal and the presupposition of communicative action. Thus the most relevant achievements of pragmatic thinking are sketched. Communication or communicative action appears to be five-dimensional. It is intersubjective, propositional-performative, textual, contextual, and intentional, while its basic intention is its direction toward understanding.

## 2. FURTHER DEVELOPMENTS

I have presented a conception of pragmatic thinking that focuses on the normative dimension of pragmatics and unfolds this dimension via philosophical reflection on the constitutive elements of human language, communication, and action. I have developed the thesis that the normative dimension of pragmatics is made most explicit in Apel's transcendental pragmatics and in Habermas' universal pragmatics. Since I wrote this book, Apel and Habermas have continued their approaches and have made most important contributions to the normative implications of pragmatics, which they unfolded in their discourse ethics.[5]

Discourse ethics aims at a clarification of the normative basis of human action, of human communication and interaction. It does so by employing either a reconstructive or a reflective method. Within discourse ethics, there are two different lines of thought. Karl-Otto Apel's transcendental pragmatics has led him to a transcendental pragmatic discourse ethics. On the other hand, Jürgen Habermas considers his universal or formal pragmatic discourse ethics to be part of his theory of communicative action. Whereas Apel claims to reach at an ultimate philosophical foundation of ethics via transcendental reflection, Habermas refuses any claim to an ultimate foundation of discourse ethics. For him, discourse ethics is woven into a far-reaching web of theories for which the reconstructive sciences serve as a model. The whole web will lead to a comprehensive theory of communicative action. As I tried to demonstrate above, the systematic core of that web is Habermas's universal or formal pragmatics. Habermas's reflections about a foundation of discourse ethics are located within universal pragmatics.

Discourse ethics, whether in its Habermasian or Apelian version, stands in the Kantian tradition. It is characterized by four marks which are peculiar for any Kantian ethics. Discourse ethics, as Habermas points out, has a deontological, a cognitivistic, a formalistic, and a universalistic character.

First of all, discourse ethics is deontological, as it is concerned with the validity of norms, with the "ought to be" of these norms, which determine any action as right or just. The validity of the norms has to be justified, as Habermas says, "in terms of principles worthy of recognition."[6]

The second feature of discourse ethics is its cognitivistic claim. Discourse ethics considers normative rightness as a validity claim, which has analogies with the truth claim of assertions, in that it, like the claim to truth, can be founded rationally as well.

Discourse ethics, thirdly, has a formalistic character. It does not distinguish certain normative contents but constitutes a formal criterion as the principle of justification of any norm of action. Thus it resembles Kant's categorical imperative, but in discourse ethics the position which the categorical imperative takes in Kant's ethics is occupied by the procedure of moral argumentation.

The fourth characteristic of discourse ethics is its claim to universality. Discourse ethics asserts that its principle of morality does not refer to any special epoch, culture, or context, but that it is universally valid. This principle of morality is called the principle of universalizability, and, according to Habermas, it reads: "Only those norms may claim to be valid that could meet with the consent of all affected in their role as participants in a practical discourse."[7]

On the Kantian basis determined by the four marks—deontological, cognitivistic, formalistic, and universalistic—both Apel and Habermas work at a transformation of Kantian philosophy in terms of pragmatics or communication theory. According to Apel, this transformation aims to "renew the Kantian question for the conditions of the possibility and validity of scientific knowledge as the question concerning the possibility of an intersubjective agreement about the meaning and truth of sentences or systems of sentences."[8] Apel's concern is to transform the Kantian critique of knowledge, in terms of a philosophy of mind that implies the notion of a subject conceived of as solipsistic, into an intersubjective philosophy of the conditions of the possibility and validity of an understanding that is mediated by language. In the center of Apel's interest is the argumentative discourse and the one universal validity claim of the truth of the proposition, a claim which is necessarily made in every argumentation. Starting from that, Apel reflects on the conditions of the possibility and validity of communicative understanding, from which he unfolds the norms of an ideal community of argumentation.

Whereas Apel's approach concentrates on the argumentative discourse and on the one universal validity claim of truth, Habermas intends to reconstruct all the dimensions of communicative understanding. In his analysis of the constituents and fundamental orientations of language use oriented toward understanding, he distinguishes four dimensions and accordingly four universal validity claims, which are made simultaneously in every communicative act. What he calls universal pragmatics is designed to demonstrate and reconstruct the four validity claims as universal conditions for the occurrence of communicative action.

For Habermas, the truth-claim and the rightness-claim are discursive. The partners in a communication have the option of leaving the context of communicative action and entering into discourse if they cannot reach agreement about the truth of an utterance or the rightness of an action or the appropriateness of the underlying norm. Habermas distinguishes theoretical discourse, in which consensus regarding the truth of utterances is under discussion, and practical discourse, in which consensus about the rightness of norms is at stake.

For discourse ethics, the practical discourse is of specific interest. Apel points out that discourse ethics is not at all a "special ethics for argumentative discourses, but an ethics of the responsibility in solidarity of all those who are able to enter into argumentation, an ethics for all the problems of the lifeworld which can be discursive."[9] Discourse ethics is not just an ethics for conducting discourses, but it aims at principles of communicative understanding, which must be satisfied by moral norms, which it reaches by reflecting on the structure of discursive argumentation. In this reflection, the question of how a consensus can be reached and secured becomes central. According to Habermas, the reaching of a consensus is guaranteed by the formal presuppositions of the discourse, which have to fit those of an ideal speech situation "with sufficient approximation."[10] An ideal speech situation, by definition, is one which incidentally provides no limitations with regard to either the number of participants or the number of issues under scrutiny. The concept of an ideal speech situation disregards the constraints that determine actual communication according to a model of pure communication. If a discourse takes place under such conditions, a rationally motivated agreement among the participants is possible, providing that the argumentation is carried on in a sufficiently open manner for a long enough period of time.

According to Habermas, the following rules of procedure are relevant for discourse ethics:

(3.1)   Every subject with the competence to speak and act is allowed to take part in discourse.

(3.2)   a. Everyone is allowed to question any assertion whatever.
        b. Everyone is allowed to introduce any assertion whatever into a discourse.
        c. Everyone is allowed to express his attitudes, desires and needs.

(3.3)   No speaker may be prevented, by internal or external coercion, from exercising his rights as laid down in (3.1) and (3.2).[11]

Most significant for practical discourse is that kind of principle which makes possible the argumentative agreement about controversial norms of action and founds them in an intersubjectively binding manner. That is the principle of universalizability. It is already implied in Kant's categorical imperative, according to which only those norms are accepted as valid which are suitable for a "general law." But whereas Kant relates universalizability to the imagination of the solitary subject, who hypothetically tries to take a general perspective, discourse ethics binds its principle to real argumentation and to factual discourse.

Provided that valid norms must be acceptable to all concerned, the principle of universalizability is to take into account the interests of all and, thus, is to lead to the formulation of general interests. This principle, in the words of Habermas, "is intended to compel the universal exchange of roles that G. H. Mead has called 'ideal role taking' or 'universal discourse.'"[12] In Habermas' view, the principle of universalizability can be summed up in the principle "D," which reads: "Only those norms can claim to be valid that meet (or could meet) with the approval of all affected as participants in a practical discourse."[13]

Habermas considers "D" as a formal-procedural principle and not as an ethical principle itself. For Apel, the principle of universalizability turns out to be "a priori a principle which is oriented at consensual-communicative implementation. Insofar, it is not without content and it cannot be applied arbitrarily, but it points to the possible outcome of universal understanding."[14] Apel recognizes in this principle the "fundamental norm of the equality on principle of all the communication partners."[15] At the same time, it implies the "obligation to take one's responsibility for the argumentative . . . solution of all the problems in the lifeworld which are morally relevant."[16]

Whereas Habermas, in the development of his thinking, has become more and more cautious in view of his claims, and only points out the formal and procedural character of discourse ethics, Apel comprehends his transcendental-pragmatic discourse ethics as a reflection on the norms of an ideal community of argumentation. This community is counterfactually anticipated within the real communication community, and it pleads to apply its norms, which have been grounded in discourses of foundation within the lifeworld, by means of discourses of application. Apel's goal thus is an ethics of responsibility in solidarity, in which the real communication community is oriented and moves toward the realization of the ideal communication community.

## 3. The Challenge of Neo-Pragmatism

In the last decade, a position has moved to the forefront of American philosophical debate that considers itself a genuine heir of American pragmatism. Indeed, it tries to revive and continue the program of the great American pragmatists. The most outspoken representative of neo-pragmatism is Richard Rorty.[17] Others include Richard Bernstein and Cornel West.

Rorty's neo-pragmatism sharply contradicts any transcendental or universal pragmatic approaches. Instead of dealing with the conditions of the possibility of communicative agreement, which he regards as a foundationalist fallacy, his philosophy is devoted to the contextual, contingent, and particular. He thus continues a Wittgensteinean approach, combined with a Deweyan perspective which denies and denounces reflection and replaces it by a philosophical language that comes closer to literature. In fact, it chooses poetry and literature as its main conversation partners and cultural heroes.

For Rorty, the experience that our language, our culture, our society, that we ourselves are contingent, arbitrary, that we are what we are just by chance with no kind of reason, purpose, or overall meaning behind the scene, is a significant experience of postmodern times. "Our language and our culture," writes Rorty, "are as much a contingency, as much a result of thousands of small mutations finding niches (and mutations of others finding no niches) as are the orchids and the anthropoids."[18] To be sure, there is neither an overall purpose nor a direction, there are neither universal conditions nor goals for human existence; everything we know and we have to acknowledge is "sheer contingency."[19]

Rorty describes his position as postmodernist bourgeois liberalism.[20] He denies that there are any criteria by which our language, culture, and community can be judged. He denies that truth can be found in the world outside, and he regards any philosophical approach that looks for foundations of human existence, language, and community as misleading. In fact, he thinks that anybody who tries to do so is still, "in his heart, a theologian, or a metaphysician."[21] For Rorty, as he explicitly states, Habermas belongs to this group, not to speak of Apel. Habermas, Rorty deplores, "goes transcendental and offers principles,"[22] although in other respects he could be regarded as a liberal political ally with whom Rorty has "merely philosophical" differences. The decisive "residual difference" Rorty has with him "is that his universalism makes him substitute such convergence [toward undistorted communication] for ahistorical grounding, whereas my insistence on the contingency of language makes me suspicious of the very idea of 'universal validity' which such convergence is supposed to underwrite."[23] For Rorty, the freedom which liberal anti-metaphysicians, that is ironists, promote, basically consists in "the recognition of contingency."[24] Such recognition, according to him, is the chief virtue of the members of liberal society, and the culture of such a society should aim at curing us of our "deep metaphysical need."[25]

Like Wittgenstein, Rorty understands his conception of philosophy as therapeutic. Philosophy will help to get rid of false metaphysical, foundational, universalistic concerns and concentrate instead on the elucidation of one's own language game, form of life, or context, which, for Rorty, is that of postmodernist bourgeois life. Therein he wants to play the game of ironical criticism.

Such a historicist-pragmatist approach, as Apel and Habermas have repeatedly pointed out, denies its own foundations and takes the facticity of common sense as the unquestioned basis, while it ignores "the conditions of the possibility of practically relevant consensus formation at all."[26] It is, to take up the terminology used before in this book, once more an example of a pragmatism having resort to Deweyan secondness instead of including Peircean thirdness.

Cornel West, in his "Genealogy of Pragmatism," follows a Rortyan thread even if he contradicts Rorty's position of postmodern bourgeois liberalism. What he actually presents as the *American Evasion of Philosophy* is more of a potpourri than a genealogy. It assembles figures ranging from Peirce to Sidney Hook and from Lionel Trilling to Quine. Notwithstanding his sharp-minded characterization of the different figures dealt with, he is engaged in the same dissolution of the distinction between philosophical argumentation, literary criticism, and historical narration that he has adopted from Rorty. He presents a historicist, contextualist reading of American pragmatism in which the "common denominator" "consists of future-oriented instrumentalism that tries to deploy thought as a weapon to enable more effective action."[27] The instrumentalist language West uses is telling enough of how he understands pragmatic thinking. Even if he intends to continue American pragmatism into what he calls "prophetic pragmatism"[28] that will combine cultural criticism and political engagement, the question arises of where this criticism takes its criteria from and how, given the thoroughly historicist approach, prophetic pragmatism will arrive at a "universal consciousness," which West sees as its "distinctive hallmark."[29]

Richard Bernstein is one of the outstanding American philosophers who try to bring together Anglo-American and European thinking. Rooted in the pragmatic tradition, to which he has made important contributions, he has for some decades been focusing on bringing into conversation hermeneutic thinking, practical philosophy, and (post)analytic conceptions, which he sees as moving together beyond the Cartesian legacy of objectivism, on the one hand, and a corresponding relativism, on the other. Over the last decade, Bernstein has become especially interested in showing the common interest of Gadamer, Habermas, and Rorty, who, according to him, coincide in their effort to point to a dialogical, communicative, practical philosophy oriented toward conversation, mutual agreement, and action.

Bernstein realizes, however, that Habermas leaves that conversation and at times "slips into the language of strict dialectics or strict transcendental arguments,"[30] which, for Bernstein, is apparent not only in his "original distinction of the three 'quasi-transcendental' cognitive interests" but also "evident in some of his initial attempts to argue that four different types of validity claims are implicitly raised in communicative action."[31]

Bernstein's reading of Habermas regards these transcendental elements of his thinking as remnants of the Cartesian-Kantian tradition that he has not yet fully overcome. Against that, he calls attention to Habermas' "pragmatic voice and his practice of interpretative dialectics."[32] Thus, with great sympathy and eloquence, he tries to embrace him into the ongoing transatlantic conversation in a pragmatic mode. Habermas and Rorty, Bernstein tells us in his recent book, *The New Constellation*, "both share an understanding of rationality as intrinsically dialogical and communicative. And both pursue the ethical and political consequences of this form of rationality and rationalization."[33] Bernstein is eager to help break the ideological or philosophical boundaries that for decades divided philosophers into segregated camps. At the end of his book, *The New Constellation*, and as an expression of it he pleads for the healing of the wounds of those ideological battles. According to him, such a healing could be achieved by pursuing a pragmatic tradition that is characterized by five contemporary common themes and concerns. The first theme is anti-foundationalism; second, a thoroughgoing fallibilism; third, insistence on the social character of the self and the need to nurture a critical community of inquirers; fourth, awareness and sensitivity to radical contingency; and finally, the theme of plurality.[34]

Despite Habermas' occasional transcendental temptations, Bernstein considers him in general to be part of the pragmatic tradition. This is not so for Apel, whom he keeps out of the game. Maybe Bernstein regards Apel's obsession with transcendental reflection as still another expression of Cartesian anxiety and a case of foundationalism, which according to Bernstein has already been overcome by Peirce. But in fact, there is another reading of Peirce and of pragmatic thinking, of its history, and its logic as well. In this book I have tried to present such a reading.

# *Notes*

1. See, e.g., Murphy, *Pragmatism*; Rosenthal, *Speculative Pragmatism*; Sleeper, *Necessity*; Campbell, *Community*; and the five-volume encyclopedia of pragmatic thinking by Stachowiak, ed., *Pragmatik*.
2. See Apel, *Diskurs*; Habermas, MCCA and *Erläuterungen*.
3. See Rorty, *Mirror*; *Consequences*; and *Contingency*; Bernstein, *Beyond Objectivism*; *Profiles*; and *New Constellation*; West, *American Evasion*.
4. This position differs from that of Ricoeur, who restricts the term "text" to Scripture: see Ricoeur, *Interpretation Theory*.
5. See the discussion of Apel's conception in Hösle, *Krise*. Habermas' approach to discourse ethics is discussed in Benhabib, *Critique*; Benhabib and Dallmayr, eds., *Controversy*; White, *Recent Works*; McCarthy, *Ideals*. See my discussion of discourse ethics and philosophy of liberation in Arens, "Diskursethik." In view of the emerging conversation between these two positions, involving Apel, Dussel, and others, see Fornet-Betancourt, ed., *Ethik*; ed., *Diskursethik*.
6. Habermas, MCCA, p. 196.
7. Ibid., p. 197.
8. Apel, *Transformation II*, p. 163f.
9. Apel, *Diskurs*, p. 116.
10. Habermas, TCT I, p. 71; see MCCA, p. 88. In view of the further-reaching claims he raised in former works, see 6.3.4. above.
11. Habermas, MCCA, p. 89.
12. Ibid., p. 65.
13. Ibid., p. 93.
14. Apel, *Diskurs*, p. 121.
15. Ibid., p. 116.
16. Ibid.
17. See the discussion of Rorty's approach in Malachowski, ed., *Reading Rorty*; Prado, *Limits*; see Habermas' remarks in his *Philosophical Discourse*, p. 206f.
18. Rorty, *Contingency*, p. 16.

19. Ibid., p. 22.
20. See Rorty, *Objectivity*, pp. 197–202.
21. Rorty, *Contingency*, p. xv.
22. Rorty, *Pragmatism, Relativism*, p. 736.
23. Rorty, *Contingency*, p. 67.
24. Ibid.
25. Ibid., p. 46.
26. Apel, *Diskurs*, p. 400.
27. West, *American Evasion*, p. 5.
28. Ibid., pp. 211–239.
29. Ibid., p. 232.
30. Bernstein, *Beyond Objectivism*, p. 184.
31. Ibid.
32. Ibid., p. 195.
33. Bernstein, *New Constellation*, p. 48.
34. Ibid., pp. 323–340.

# Bibliography

Albert, H. *Treatise on Critical Reason*, trans. M. V. Rorty. Princeton, N.J.: Princeton University Press, 1984.

————. *Transzendentale Träumereien. Karl-Otto Apel und sein hermeneutischer Gott*. Munich: R. Piper, 3rd. ed., 1973.

Alexy, R. *Theorie der juristischen Argumentation. Die Theorie des rationalen Diskurses als Theorie der juristischen Begründung*. Frankfurt: Suhrkamp, 1978.

Alston, W. "Pragmatism and the Theory of Signs in Peirce," *Princeton Philosophical Review* 17 (1956/57), pp. 79–88.

————. *Philosophy and Language*. Englewood Cliffs: Prentice-Hall, 2nd. ed., 1965.

Anscombe, G. E. M. *An Introduction to Wittgenstein's "Tractatus."* New York: Hillary House, 1959.

Apel, K.-O. "Das 'Verstehen' (eine Problemgeschichte als Begriffsgeschichte)," *Archiv für Begriffsgeschichte* I (1959), pp. 142–199.

————. *Die Idee der Sprache in der Tradition des Humanismus von Dante bis Vico*. Bonn: Bouvier, 1963.

————. "Die erkenntnisanthropologische Funktion der Kommunikationsgemeinschaft und die Grundlagen der Hermeneutik." In S. Moser and S.J. Schmidt, eds., *Information und Kommunikation*. Munich and Vienna: Fink, 1968, pp. 163–171.

————. "Charles W. Morris und das Program einer pragmatisch integrierten Semiotik." Introduction to C. W. Morris, *Zeichen, Sprache und Verhalten*. Düsseldorf: Schwann, 1973, pp. 9–66.

————. "Programmatische Bemerkungen zur Idee einer transzendentalen Sprach-Pragmatik." In T. Airakinen, ed., *Studia Philosophica in honorem S. Krohn*. Turku: Turku University Press, 1973, pp. 11–36.

————. "Zur Idee einer transzendentalen Sprach-Pragmatik." In J. Simon, ed., *Aspekte und Probleme der Sprachphilosophie*. Freiburg and Munich: Alber, 1974, pp. 283–326.

————. "Der semiotische Pragmatismus von Ch. S. Peirce und die abstractive fallacy in den Grundlagen der Kantschen Erkenntnistheorie und der Carnapschen Wissenschaftslogik." In A. J. Bucher, H. Drüe, and T. M. Seebohm, eds., *bewußt sein. Gerhard Funke zu eigen*. Bonn: Bouvier, 1975, pp. 48–58.

————. "Das Kommunikationsapriori und die Grundlagen der Geisteswissenschaften." In R. Simon-Schäfer and W. C. Zimmerli, eds., *Wissenschaftstheorie der Geisteswissenschaften*. Hamburg: Meiner, 1975, pp. 23–55.

————. *Transformation der Philosophie I. Sprachanalytik, Semiotik, Hermeneutik*. Frankfurt: Suhrkamp, 1976.

————. *Transformation der Philosophie II. Das Apriori der Kommunikationsgemeinschaft*. Frankfurt: Suhrkamp, 1976.

————. "Sprechakttheorie und transzendentale Sprachpragmatik zur Frage ethischer Normen." In K.-O. Apel, ed., *Sprachpragmatik und Philosophie*. Frankfurt: Suhrkamp, 1976, pp. 10–173.

————. "Das Problem der philosophischen Letztbegründung im Lichte einer transzendentalen Sprachpragmatik." In B. Kannitschneider, ed., *Sprache und Erkenntnis*.

Festschrift G. Frey. Innsbruck: Styria 1976, pp. 55–82.

———. "Transcendental Semiotics and the Paradigms of First Philosophy," *Philosophic Exchange* 2 (1978), no. 4, pp. 3–22.

———. "Warum transzendentale Sprachpragmatik?" In H. M. Baumgartner, ed., *Prinzip Freiheit*. Festschrift H. Krings. Freiburg and Munich: Alber 1979, pp. 13–43.

———. "Types of Rationality Today. The Continuum of Reason between Science and Ethics." In T. Geraerts, ed., *Rationality Today*. Ottawa: University Press of Ottawa, 1979, pp. 307–339.

———. *Towards a Transformation of Philosophy*, trans. G. Adey and D. Frisby. London: Routledge & Kegan Paul, 1980.

———. "C. S. Peirce and the Post-Tarskian Problem of an Adequate Explication of the Meaning of Truth. Towards a Transcendental-Pragmatic Theory of Truth I," *The Monist* 63 (1980), pp. 386–407.

———. *Charles S. Peirce. From Pragmatism to Pragmaticism*, trans. J. M. Krois. Amherst, Mass.: University of Massachusetts Press, 1981.

———. "C. S. Peirce and Post-Tarskian Truth." In E. Freeman, ed., *The Relevance of Charles Peirce*. La Salle, Ill.: Open Court, 1983, pp. 189–223.

———. *Understanding and Explanation. A Transcendental-Pragmatic Perspective*, trans. G. Warnke. Cambridge, Mass.: MIT Press, 1984.

———. *Diskurs und Verantwortung*. Frankfurt: Suhrkamp 1988.

Apel, K.-O., et al. *Hermeneutik und Ideologiekritik*. Frankfurt: Suhrkamp, 1971.

Apel, K.-O., J. Manninen, and R. Tuomela, eds. *Neue Versuche über Erklären und Verstehen*. Frankfurt: Suhrkamp, 1978.

Apel, K.-O., ed. *Sprachpragmatik und Philosophie*. Frankfurt: Suhrkamp, 1976.

Apel, K.-O., D. Böhler, A. Berlich, and G. Plumpe, eds. *Reader zum Funk-Kolleg Praktische Philosophie / Ethik I*. Frankfurt: Fischer, 1980.

Arens, E. "Communication as Counter-Power in the Struggle for Democracy," *Media Development* 35 (1988), no. 1, pp. 18–20.

———. "Diskursethik, ein Spiel für Philosophen der ersten Welt?" In R. Fornet-Betancourt, ed., *Diskursethik oder Befreiungsethik?* Aachen: Augustinus 1992, pp. 55–69.

Arens, E., O. John, and P. Rottländer. *Erinnerung, Befreiung, Solidarität. Benjamin, Marcuse, Habermas und die politische Theologie*. Düsseldorf: Patmos Verlag, 1991.

Arens, E., ed. *Habermas und die Theologie. Beiträge zur theologischen Rezeption, Diskussion und Kritik der Theorie kommunikativen Handelns*. Düsseldorf: Patmos Verlag, 1989.

Aristotle. *Metaphysics*, ed. W. D. Ross. Oxford: Clarendon, 1953.

Austin, J. L. *Philosophical Papers*. Oxford: Clarendon, 1962.

———. *How to Do Things with Words*. Cambridge., Mass.: Harvard University Press, 2nd ed., 1975.

———. "Performative Utterances." In *Philosophical Papers*. Oxford: Clarendon, 1962.

Ayer, A. J. *The Origins of Pragmatism*. San Francisco: Freeman Cooper, 1968.

Baumanns, P. "Sprechakttheorie—Universalpragmatik—Ethik. Zur linguistischen Wende der kritischen Theorie," *Allgemeine Zeitschrift für Philosophie* 3 (1978) H. 2, pp. 45–70.

Beckermann, A. "Die realistischen Voraussetzungen der Konsensustheorie von J. Habermas," *Zeitschrift für allgemeine Wissenschaftstheorie* 3 (1972) pp. 63–80.

Benhabib, S. *Critique, Norm and Utopia. A Study of the Foundations of Critical Theory*. New York: Columbia University Press, 1986.

Benhabib, S., and F. Dallmayr, eds. *The Communicative Ethics Controversy*. Cambridge, Mass.: MIT Press, 1990.

Berlin, I., et al. *Essays on J. L. Austin*. Oxford: Clarendon, 1973.

Bernstein, R. *Praxis and Action*. Philadelphia: University of Pennsylvania Press, 1971.

———. *Beyond Objectivism and Relativism. Science, Hermeneutics and Praxis*. Philadelphia: University of Pennsylvania Press, 1983.

———. *Philosophical Profiles. Essays in a Pragmatic Mode*. Philadelphia: University of Pennsylvania Press, 1986.

———. *The New Constellation. The Ethical-Political Horizons of Modernity / Postmodernity*. Cambridge, Mass.: MIT Press, 1992.

Bernstein, R., ed. *Habermas and Modernity*. Cambridge, Mass.: MIT Press, 1985.

Bittner, R. "Transzendental." In *Handbuch philosophischer Grundbegriffe* 5, pp. 1524–1539.

Black, M. "The Semiotics of Charles Morris." In *Language and Philosophy*. Ithaca: Cornell University Press, 1963.

———. *Models and Metaphors*. Ithaca: Cornell University Press, 1962.

———. *A Companion to Wittgenstein's "Tractatus."* Ithaca: Cornell University Press, 1964.

Blau, J. L. "Royce's Theory of Community," *The Journal of Philosophy* 53 (1956), pp. 92–98.

Blumenberg, H. "Wirklichkeitsbegriff und Möglichkeit des Romans." In H. R. Jauss, ed., *Nachahmung und Wirklichkeit*. Munich: Fink, 1964, pp. 9–27.

Breuer, D. "Vorüberlegungen zu einer pragmatischen Texttheorie," *Wirkendes Wort* 22 (1972), pp. 1–23.

———. *Einführung in die pragmatische Texttheorie*. Munich: Fink, 1974.

———. "Schulrhetorik im 19. Jahrhundert." In H. Schanze, ed., *Rhetorik*. Frankfurt: Athenaeum, 1974, pp. 145–179.

Bühler, K. *Theory of Language. The Representational Functional of Language*, trans. D. F. Goodwin. Amsterdam and Philadelphia: J. Benjamins, 1990.

———. *Semiotic Foundations of Language*, ed. R. E. Innis. New York: Plenum, 1982.

Campbell, J. *The Community Reconstructs. The Meaning of Pragmatic Social Thought*. Urbana and Chicago: University of Illinois Press, 1992.

Cohen, J. L. "Do Illocutionary Forces Exist?" *Philosophical Quarterly* 14 (1964), pp. 118–137.

Cohen, T. "Illocutions and Perlocutions," *Foundations of Language* 9 (1973), pp. 492–503.

Cooper, D. E. "Meaning and Illocutions," *American Philosophical Quarterly* 9 (1972), pp. 69–77.

Corti, W. R., ed. *The Philosophy of George Herbert Mead*. Amriswil: Amriswiler Bücherei, 1973.

Dallmayr, F., ed. *Materialien zu Habermas' "Erkenntnis und Interesse."* Frankfurt: Suhrkamp, 1974.

Dewey, J. "The Reflex Are Concept in Psychology," *Psychological Review* 3 (1896), pp. 357–370.

———. "The Realism of Pragmatism," *The Journal of Philosophy* 2 (1905), pp. 324–327.

———. "Reality and the Criterion for the Truth of Ideas," *Mind* 16 (1907), pp. 317–342.

———. "What Does Pragmatism Mean by Practical?" *The Journal of Philosophy* 5 (1908), pp. 85–99.

———. "The Dilemma of the Intellectualist Theory of Truth," *The Journal of Philosophy* 6 (1909), pp. 433–434.

———. "A Reply to Professor Royce's Critique of Instrumentalism," *Philosophical Review* 21 (1912), pp. 69–81.

———. "The Pragmatism of Peirce," *The Journal of Philosophy* 21 (1916), pp. 709–715.

———. *Reconstruction in Philosophy*. Boston: Beacon, 1948.

———. *The Quest for Certainty*. New York: Minton, Balch, 1931.

———. *Experience and Nature*. New York: Macmillan, 1949.

———. *Philosophy and Civilization*. New York: Minton, Balch, 1931.

———. "Peirce's Theory of Quality," *The Journal of Philosophy* 32 (1935), pp. 701–708.

———. *Logic. The Theory of Inquiry*. New York: H. Holt, 1938.

———. "Peirce's Theory of Linguistic Signs, Thought, and Meaning," *The Journal of Philosophy* 43 (1946), pp. 95–96.

———. "Letter to the Editors of the Journal of Philosophy," *The Journal of Philosophy* 43 (1946), p. 280.

———. "Syllabus. The Pragmatic Movement of Contemporary Thought." In J. A. Boydston, ed., *John Dewey. The Middle Works*, 1899–1924. IV. 1907–1909. Carbondale, Ill.: Southern Illinois University Press, 1977, pp. 251–263.

Döbert, R. *Systemtheorie und die Entwicklung religiöser Deutungssysteme*. Frankfurt: Suhrkamp, 1973.

———. "Zur Logik des Übergangs von archaischen zu hochkulturellen Religionssystemen." In K. Eder, ed., *Seminar. Die Entstehung von Klassengesellschaften*. Frankfurt: Suhrkamp, 1973, pp. 330–363.

Döbert, R., and G. Nunner-Winkler. *Adoleszenzkrisen und Identitätsbildung*. Frankfurt: Suhrkamp, 1975.

Dressler, W., ed. *Textlinguistik*. Darmstadt: Wissenschaftliche Buchgesellschaft, 1978.

Eder, K. *Seminar. Die Entstehung von Klassengesellschaften*. Frankfurt: Suhrkamp, 1973.

———. *Die Entstehung staatlich organisierter Gesellschaften*. Frankfurt: Suhrkamp, 1976.

Eschbach, A. "Charles W. Morris' dreidimensionale Semiotik und Texttheorie." Introduction to C. W. Morris, *Zeichen, Wert, Ästhetik*. Frankfurt: Suhrkamp, 1975, pp. 7–68.

———. "Pragmatische Semiotik und Handlungstheorie." Introduction to C. W. Morris, *Pragmatische Semiotik und Handlungstheorie*. Frankfurt: Suhrkamp, 1977, pp. 11–76.

Fann, K. T., ed. *Symposium on J. L. Austin*. Atlantic Highlands, N.J.: Humanities Press, 1969.

———. *Ludwig Wittgenstein*. New York: Dell, 1967.

Feibleman, J. K. *An Introduction to Peirce's Philosophy*. New York and London: Harper, 1960.

Fitzgerald, J. J. *Peirces's Theory of Signs as Foundation of Pragmatism*. The Hague and Paris: Nijhoff, 1966.

Fornet-Betancourt, R., ed. *Ethik und Befreiung*. Aachen: Augustinus, 1990.

———. *Diskursethik oder Befreiungsethik?* Aachen: Augustinus, 1992.

Frege, G. *Logical Investigations*, ed. P. T. Geach, trans. P. T. Geach and R. H. Stoothoff. New Haven: Yale University Press, 1977.

Furberg, M. *Saying and Meaning*. Totowa, N.J.: Rowman and Littlefield, 1971.

Gardiner, A. *The Theory of Speech and Language*. Oxford: Clarendon, 2nd ed., 1960.

Gebauer, G. *wortgebrauch, sprachbedeutung*. Munich: Fink, 1971.

Goffman, E. *Asylums*. New York: Doubleday, 1990.

———. *Stigma*. New York: Simon & Schuster, 1986.

Gordon, D., and G. Lakoff. "Conversational Postulates." In P. Cole and J. L. Morgan, eds., *Syntax and Semantics III. Speech Acts*. New York: Academic Press, 1975, pp. 83–106.

Graham, K. *Austin. A Critique of Ordinary Language*. Atlantic Highlands, N.J.: Humanities Press, 1977.

Greenlee, D. *Peirce's Concept of Sign*. The Hague: Mouton, 1973.

Grice, P. "Meaning," *Philosophical Review* 66 (1957), pp. 377–388.

———. "Utterer's Meaning, Sentence-Meaning, and Word-Meaning," *Foundations of Language* 4 (1968), pp. 1–18.

———. "Logic and Conversation." In P. Cole and J. L. Morgan, eds., *Syntax and Semantics III. Speech Acts*. New York: Academic Press, 1975, pp. 41–58.

Habermas, J. "On Systematically Distorted Communication," *Inquiry* 13 (1970), pp. 205–218.

———. "Towards a Theory of Communicative Competence," *Inquiry* 13 (1970), pp. 360–375.

———. *Knowledge and Human Interest*, trans. J. J. Shapiro. Boston: Beacon, 1971.

———. *Toward a Rational Society*, trans. J. J. Shapiro. Boston: Beacon, 1971.

———. "Vorbereitende Bemerkungen zu einer Theorie der kommunikativen Kompetenz." In J. Habermas and N. Luhmann, *Theorie der Gesellschaft oder Sozialtechnologie*. Frankfurt: Suhrkamp 1971, pp. 101–141.

———. "Theorie der Gesellschaft oder Sozialtechnologie? Eine Auseinandersetzung mit Niklas Luhmann." In J. Habermas and N. Luhmann, *Theorie der Gesellschaft oder Sozialtechnologie*. Frankfurt: Suhrkamp 1971, pp. 142–190.

———. *Theory and Practice*, trans. J. Viertel. Boston: Beacon, 1973.

———. *Kultur und Kritik*. Frankfurt: Suhrkamp, 1973.

———. "Wahrheitstheorien." In H. Fahrenbach, ed., *Wirklichkeit und Reflexion*. Festschrift W. Schulz. Pfullingen: Neske, 1973, pp. 211–265.

———. *Legitimation Crisis*, trans. T. McCarthy. Boston: Beacon, 1975.

———. "Aspects of the Rationality of Action." In T. F. Geraerts, ed., *Rationality Today*. Ottawa: University of Ottawa Press, 1979, pp. 185–205.

———. *Communication and the Evolution of Society*, trans. T. McCarthy. Boston: Beacon, 1979.

———. *Philosophical-Political Profiles*, trans. F. Lawrence. Cambridge, Mass.: MIT Press, 1983.

———. *The Philosophical Discourse of Modernity*, trans. F. Lawrence. Cambridge, Mass.: MIT Press, 1987.

———. *The Theory of Communicative Action*, 2 vols, trans. T. McCarthy. Boston: Beacon, 1984, 1988.

———. *On the Logic of the Social Sciences*, trans. S. Weber Nicholson and J. A. Stark. Cambridge, Mass.: MIT Press, 1988.

———. *The Structural Transformation of the Public Sphere*, trans. T. Burger. Cambridge, Mass.: MIT Press, 1989.

———. *Moral Consciousness and Communicative Action*, trans. C. Lenhardt and S. Weber Nicholson. Cambridge, Mass.: MIT Press, 1990.

———. *Texte und Kontexte*. Frankfurt: Suhrkamp, 1991.

———. *Erläuterungen zur Diskursethik*. Frankfurt: Suhrkamp, 1991.

———. *Postmetaphysical Thinking. Philosophical Essays*, trans. W. M. Hohengarten. Cambridge, Mass.: MIT Press, 1992.

Hacker, P. M. S. *Insight and Illusion. Wittgenstein on Philosophy and the Metaphysics of Experience*. Oxford: Clarendon, 1972.

Hartmann, P. "Zum Begriff des sprachlichen Zeichens," *Zeitschrift für Phonetik, Sprachwissenschaft und Kommunikationsforschung* 21 (1968), pp. 205–222.

———. "Text als linguistisches Objekt." In W. D. Stempel, ed., *Beiträge zur Textlinguistik*. Munich: Fink, 1971, pp. 9–29.

Höffe, O. "Kritische Überlegungen zur Konsensustheorie der Wahrheit," *Philosophisches Jahrbuch* 83 (1976), pp. 313–332.

Hösle, V. *Die Krise der Gegenwart und die Verantwortung der Philosophie.* München: Hanser, 1990.

Holdcroft, D. "Meaning and Illocutionary Acts," *Ratio* 6 (1964), pp. 128–143.

———. "Performatices and Statements," *Mind* 83 (1974), pp. 1–18.

Humboldt, W. von. *On Language*, trans. P. Heath, intro. by H. Aarsteff. Cambridge and New York: Cambridge University Press, 1988.

Ingram, D. *Habermas and the Dialectics of Reason.* New Haven: Yale University Press, 1987.

James, W. *The Will to Believe and Other Essays in Popular Philosophy* (1892). New York: Dover, 1956.

———. *Essays in Radical Empiricism and A Pluralistic Universe* (1909), ed. R. B. Perry. New York, 2nd ed., 1958.

———. *The Meaning of Truth. A Sequel to "Pragmatism"* (1909). New York: Longmans, 1968.

———. Philosophical Conceptions and Practical Results. In *Pragmatism* (The Works of William James, Appendix I). Cambridge, Mass.: Harvard University Press, 1975, pp. 257–270.

Kallmeyer, W., et al. *Lektürekolleg zur Textlinguistik*, 2 vols. Frankfurt: Fischer, 1974.

Kamlah, W. "Sprachliche Handlungsschemata." In H.-G. Gadamer, ed., *Das Problem der Sprache*. Munich: Hanser, 1967, pp. 427–484.

Kamlah, W., and P. Lorenzen. *Logical Propaedeutic. Pre-School for Reasonable Discourse.* Lanham, Md.: University Press of America, 1984.

Keane, J. "On Tools and Language. Habermas on Work and Interaction," *New German Critique* 3 (1975) no. 6, pp. 82–100.

Kempski, J. V. *Charles Sanders Peirce und der Pragmatismus.* Stuttgart and Cologne: Kohlhammer, 1952.

Kenny, A. *Wittgenstein.* Cambridge, Mass.: Harvard University Press, 1973.

Klaus, G. *Semiotik und Erkenntnistheorie.* Berlin: Deutscher Verlag der Wissenschaften, 4th ed., 1973.

Kopperschmidt, J. *Allgemeine Rhetorik. Einführung in die Theorie der persuasiven Kommunikation.* Stuttgart: Kohlhammer, 1977.

Krausser, P. "Die drei fundamentalen Strukturkategorien bei Charles Sanders Peirce," *Philosophia Naturalis* 6 (1960), pp. 3–31.

Kuhlmann, W. *Reflexion und Erfahrung.* Frankfurt: Suhrkamp, 1975.

Kummer, W. *Grundlagen der Texttheorie.* Reinbek: Rowohlt, 1975.

Kunstmann, W. *Emanzipation, Gesellschaft, Diskurs. Darstellung und Kritik der Gesellschaftstheorie von Jürgen Habermas.* Munich: Fink, 1977.

Ladd-Franklin, C. "Charles S. Peirce at the John Hopkins," *The Journal of Philosophy* 21 (1916), pp. 715–722.

Lewis, D. *Conventions. A Philosophical Study.* Cambridge, Mass.: Harvard University Press, 1969.

Lorenz, K. *Elemente der Sprachkritik.* Frankfurt: Suhrkamp, 1975.

Luhmann, N. *Soziologische Aufklärung.* Cologne and Opladen: Westdeutscher Verlag, 1970.

——. *Soziologische Aufklärung II.* Cologne and Opladen: Westdeutscher Verlag, 1975.

Luhmann, N., and J. Habermas. *Theorie der Gesellschaft oder Sozialtechnologie.* Frankfurt: Suhrkamp, 1971.

Maas, U. *Argumente für die Emanzipation von Sprachstudium und Sprachunterricht.* Frankfurt: Athenaeum, 1974.

——. *Kann man Sprache lehren? Für einen anderen Sprachunterricht.* Frankfurt: Syndikat, 1976.

Maas, U., and W. Wunderlich. *Pragmatik und sprachliches Handeln.* Frankfurt: Suhrkamp, 3rd ed., 1974.

Mahowald, M. B. *An Idealistic Pragmatism. The Development of the Pragmatic Element in the Philosophy of Josiah Royce.* The Hague: Nijhoff, 1972.

Malachowski, A., ed. *Reading Rorty.* Cambridge, Mass.: Basil Blackwell, 1990.

Malcolm, N. "Wittgenstein's 'Philosophical Investigations.'" In *Knowledge and Certainty.* Englewood Cliffs: Prentice-Hall, 1963, pp. 96–129.

Mans, D. *Intersubjektivitätstheorien der Wahrheit.* Ph.D. Diss., Frankfurt, 1975.

Matejka, L. "On the First Russian Prolegomena to Semiotics." In V. Vološinov, *Marxism and the Philosophy of Language.* Cambridge, Mass.: Harvard University Press, 1986, pp. 161–174.

McCarthy, T. *The Critical Theory of Jürgen Habermas.* Cambridge: MIT Press, 1978.

——. *Ideals and Illusions. On Reconstruction and Deconstruction in Contemporary Critical Theory.* Cambridge, Mass.: MIT Press, 1991.

Mead, G. H. "A Behavioristic Account of the Significant Symbol," *The Journal of Philosophy* 19 (1922), pp. 157–163.

——. "A Pragmatic Theory of Truth," *UCPP* 11 (1929), pp. 65–88.

——. "The Philosophies of Royce, James, and Dewey in their American Setting," *International Journal of Ethics* 40 (1929/30), pp. 211–231.

——. *The Philosophy of the Present,* intro. and ed. A. E. Murphy. Chicago: University of Chicago Press, 1932.

——. *Movements of Thought in the Nineteenth Century.* Chicago: University of Chicago Press, 1936.

——. "The Philosophy of John Dewey," *International Journal of Ethics* 46 (1936), pp. 64–81.

——. *The Philosophy of the Act.* University of Chicago Press, 1938.

——. *Selected Writings.* Indianapolis: Bobbs-Merrill, 1964.

——. *Mind, Self, and Society.* Chicago: University of Chicago Press, 5th ed., 1967.

Meyer, M. *Formale und handlungstheoretische Sprachbetrachtung.* Stuttgart: Klett, 1976.

Meyer, T. *Zwischen Spekulation und Erfahrung. Zwei Bemerkungen zur Wissenschaftstheorie von Jürgen Habermas.* Frankfurt: Makol, 1972.

Moore, E. C. American Pragmatism. Peirce, James, and Dewey. Westport, Conn.: Greenwood Press, 1985.

Morris, C. W. "Peirce, Mead, and Pragmatism," *Philosophical Review* 47 (1938), pp. 109–127.

——. "Letter to the Editors of the Journal of Philosophy," *The Journal of Philosophy* 43 (1946), p. 196.

——. "Letter to the Editors of the Journal of Philosophy," *The Journal of Philosophy* 43 (1946), pp. 363–364.

——. "Pragmatism and Logical Empiricism." In R. A. Schilpp, ed., *The Philosophy of Rudolf Carnap.* New York, 1963.

——. "On the Unity of the Pragmatic Movement," *Rice University Studies* 51 (1965), pp. 109–119.

————. Introduction to G. H. Mead, *Mind, Self, and Society.* Chicago: University of Chicago Press, 5th ed., 1976.

————. *The Pragmatic Movement in American Philosophy.* New York: G. Braziller, 1970.

————. *Writings on the General Theory of Signs.* The Hague and Paris: Mouton, 1971.

Müller, A. *Probleme einer beavioristischen Semiotik.* Ph.D. Diss., Frankfurt, 1970.

Murphey, M. G. *The Developments of Peirce's Philosophy.* Cambridge, Mass.: Harvard University Press, 1961.

Murphy, J. P. *Pragmatism. From Peirce to Davidson.* Boulder: Westview, 1990.

Nolte, R. B. *Einführung in die Sprechakttheorie John R. Searles. Darstellung und Prüfung am Beispiel der Ethik.* Freiburg and Munich: Alber, 1978.

Oelmüller, W., ed. *Transzendentalphilosophische Normenbegründungen.* Paderborn: Schöningh, 1978.

————. *Normenbegründung–Normendurchsetzung.* Paderborn: Schöningh, 1978.

Pears, D. F. "Wittgenstein and Austin." In B. Williams and A. Montefiore, eds., *British Analytical Philosophy.* London: Routledge & Kegan Paul, 1966, pp. 17–39.

————. *Ludwig Wittgenstein.* New York: Viking, 1970.

Peirce, C. S. *Collected Papers I-VI,* ed. C. Hartshorne and P. Weiss (1931–1935). Cambridge, Mass.: Harvard University Press, 1975.

————. *Collected Papers VII-VIII,* ed. A. W. Burkes. Cambridge, Mass.: Harvard University Press, 1958.

————. *Charles Sanders Peirce's Letters to Lady Welby,* ed. I. C. Lieb. New Haven: Yale University Press, 1953.

Perry, R. B. *The Thought and Character of William James,* 2 vols. Boston: Little, Brown, 1935.

Petöfi, J. S., and D. Frank, eds. *Präsuppositionen in Philosophie und Linguistik.* Hamburg: Meiner, 1973.

Peukert, H. "Bemerkungen zur Theorie der Übersetzung und zum Verständnis von umgangssprachlicher Kommunikation und Fachsprache der Theologie." In J. S. Petöfi, A. Podlech, and E. von Savigny, eds., *Fachsprache–Umgangssprache.* Kronberg: Athenaeum, 1975, pp. 303–315.

————. Universal Solidarity as Goal of Communication," *Media Development* 28 (1981) no. 4, pp. 10–11.

————. *Science, Action, and Fundamental Theology. Toward a Theology of Communicative Action,* trans. J. Bohman. Cambridge: MIT Press, 1984.

Peukert, U. *Interaktive Kompetenz und Identität. Zum Vorrang sozialen Lernens im Vorschulalter.* Düsseldorf: Patmos, 1979.

Pieper. A. "Ethik als Verhältnis von Moralphilosophie und Anthropologie. Kants Entwurf einer Transzendentalpragmatik und ihre Transformation durch Apel," *Kant-Studien* 69 (1978), pp. 314–329.

Pike, K. L. *Language in Relation to a Unified Theory of the Structure of Human Behavior.* The Hague: Mouton, 2nd rev. ed., 1967.

Pitcher, G. *The Philosophy of Wittgenstein.* Englewood Cliffs: Prentice-Hall, 1964.

Pole, D. *The Later Philosophy of Wittgenstein.* London: Athlone, 1958.

Popper, K. R. *The Open Society and Its Enemies.* London: Routledge & Kegan Paul, 5th ed., 1966.

Prado, C. G. *The Limits of Pragmatism.* Atlantic Highlands, N.J.: Humanities Press, 2nd ed., 1989.

Puntel, L. B. *Wahrheitstheorien in der neueren Philosophie.* Darmstadt: Wissenschaftliche Buchgesellschaft, 1978.

Rasmussen, T. *Reading Habermas.* Cambridge, Mass.: Basil Blackwell, 1990.

Rasmussen, T., ed. *Universalism vs. Communitarianism. Contemporary Debates in Ethics.* Cambridge, Mass.: MIT Press, 1990.

Reck, A. J. *Recent American Philosophy*. New York: Pantheon, 1964.

Ricoeur, P. *Interpretation Theory*. Fort Worth: Texas Christian University Press, 1976.

Roderick, R. *Habermas and the Foundations of Critical Theory*. London: Macmillan, 1986.

Römer, R. "Pragmatische Dimension und sprachliche Wirkungen," *Linguistische Berichte* 18 (1972), pp. 19–26.

Rorty, A., ed. *Pragmatic Philosophy*. Garden City: Doubleday, 1968.

Rorty, R. "Pragmatism, Categories, and Language," *Philosophical Review* 70 (1961), pp. 197–223.

———. *Philosophy and the Mirror of Nature*. Princeton: Princeton University Press, 1979.

———. "Pragmatism, Relativism, and Irrationalism," *Proceedings and Addresses of the American Philosophical Association* 53 (1980), pp. 719–738.

———. *Consequences of Pragmatism*. Minneapolis: University of Minnesota Press, 1983.

———. *Contingency, Irony, and Solidarity*. Cambridge: Cambridge University Press, 1989.

———, ed. *The Linguistic Turn*. Chicago: University of Chicago Press, 1967.

Rosenthal, S. B. *Speculative Pragmatism*. Amherst: University of Massachusetts Press, 1986.

Rossi-Landi, F. *Language as Work and Trade*. South Hadley, Mass.: Bergin & Garvey, 1983.

Royce, J. *The World and the Individual*. Gloucester, Mass.: P. Smith, 1976.

———. *The Problem of Christianity*, intro. and ed. S. Smith. Chicago and London: University of Chicago Press, 1968.

Ryle, G. *The Concept of Mind*. New York: Barnes & Noble, 1949.

Saussure, F. de. *Course in General Linguistics*, ed. C. Bally and A. Sechehaye, trans. R. Harnis. La Salle, Ill.: Open Court, 1986.

Savigny, E. v. *Die Philosophie der normalen Sprache*. Frankfurt: Suhrkamp, 1974.

Schapp, W. *In Geschichten verstrickt*. Wiesbaden: Heymann, 1972.

Schlieben-Lange, B. *Linguistische Pragmatik*. Stuttgart: Kohlhammer, 1975.

———. "Perlokution—Eine Skizze," *Sprache im technischen Zeitalter* 52 (1974), pp. 319–333.

Schmidt, S. J. *Bedeutung und Begriff*. Braunschweig: Westermann, 1969.

———. "'Text' und 'Geschichte' als Fundierungskategorien. Sprachphilosophische Grundlagen einer transphrasistischen Analyse." In W. D. Stempel, ed., *Beiträge zur Textlinguistik*. Munich: Fink, 1971, pp. 31–52.

———. "Texttheorie und Pragmatik," *Studia Leibnitiana*, Special Number 3 (1973), pp. 1–57.

———. *Texttheorie*. Munich: Fink, 1974.

———. "Das 'kommunikative Handlungsspiel' als Kategorie der Wirklichkeitskonstitution." In *Pragmatik I*. Munich: Fink, 1974, pp. 103–117.

Schmidt, S. J., ed. *Pragmatik I. Interdisziplinäre Beiträge zur Erforschung der sprachlichen Kommunikation*. Munich: Fink, 1974.

———. *Pragmatik / Pragmatics II. Zur Grundlegung einer expliziten Pragmatik*. Munich: Fink, 1976.

Schnädelbach, H. "Über den Realismus," *Zeitschrift für allgemeine Wissenschaftstheorie* 3 (1972), pp. 88–112.

———. *Reflexion und Diskurs. Fragen nach einer Logik der Philosophie*. Frankfurt: Suhrkamp, 1977.

Schnelle, H. *Sprachphilosophie und Linguistik*. Reinbek: Rowohlt, 1973.

Schrader-Klebert, K. "Der Begriff des Transzendentalen bei Jürgen Habermas," *Soziale Welt* 19 (1968), pp. 342–359.

Schulz, W. *Wittgenstein. Die Negation der Philosophie.* Pfullingen: Neske, 1967.

Searle, J. "How to Derive 'Ought' from 'Is'," *Philosophical Review* 77 (1968), pp. 53–59.

———. "Austin on Locutionary and Illocutionary Acts," *Philosophical Review* 77 (1968), pp. 405–424.

———. *Speech Acts. An Essay in the Philosophy of Language.* London: Cambridge University Press, 1969.

———. "A Taxonomy of Illocutionary Acts." In K. Underson, ed., *Minnesota Studies in the Philosophy of Science III. Language, Mind, and Knowledge.* Minneapolis: University of Minnesota Press, 1975, pp. 344–369.

Shibles, W. A. *Wittgenstein. Language and Philosophy.* Dubuque, Iowa: W. C. Brown, 1969.

Simons, E. "Transzendentalphilosophie und Sprachpragmatik. Zur Methodik der Auseinandersetzung von Hermann Krings mit der transzendentalen Sprachpragmatik Karl-Otto Apels." In H. M. Baumgartner, ed., *Prinzip Freiheit.* Festschrift H. Krings. Freiburg and Munich: Alber, 1979, pp. 44–72.

Sleeper, R. W. *The Necessity of Pragmatism. John Dewey's Conception of Philosophy.* New Haven and London: Yale University Press, 1986.

Smith, J. E. *Royce's Social Infinite. The Community of Interpretation.* New York: Liberal Arts, 1950.

———. Introduction to J. Royce, *The Problem of Christianity.* Chicago and London: University of Chicago Press, 1968, pp. 1–36.

Specht, E. K. "Die sprachphilosophischen und ontologischen Grundlagen im Spätwerk Wittgensteins," *Kant-Studien,* Supplementary Number 84, 1963.

Stachowiak, H., ed. *Pragmatik. Handbuch pragmatischen Denkens,* 5 vols. Hamburg: Meiner, 1986—.

Stalnaker, R. C. "Pragmatics," *Synthese* 22 (1970/71), pp. 272–280.

Stegmüller, W. *Das Wahrheitsproblem und die Idee der Semantik.* Vienna: Springer, 1957.

———. *Hauptströmungen der Gegenwartsphilosophie,* I. Stuttgart: Kröner, 6th ed., 1978; II. Stuttgart: Kröner, 1975.

Stenius, E. *Wittgenstein's Tractatus.* Oxford: Basil Blackwell, 1960.

Strawson, P. F. "Critical Notice. 'Philosophical Investigations,' by Ludwig Wittgenstein," *Mind* 63 (1954), pp. 70–99.

———. *Logico-Linguistic Papers.* London: Methuen, 1971.

Thayer, H. *Meaning and Action. A Critical History of Pragmatism.* Indianapolis: Hackett, 1982.

———. Introduction to W. James, *Pragmatism* (The Works of William James, Vol. I). Cambridge, Mass., and London: Harvard University Press, 1975, pp. xi–xxxviii.

Thompson, J., and D. Held, eds. *Habermas: Critical Debates.* Cambridge, Mass.: MIT Press, 1982.

Titunik, I. R. "The Formal and the Sociological Method (M. M. Bachtin, P. N. Medvedev, V. N. Vološinov) in Russian Theory and Study of Literature." In V. N. Vološinov, *Marxism and the Philosophy of Language,* trans. and ed. I. R. Titunik. Cambridge, Mass.: Harvard University Press, 1986, pp. 175–200.

Tugendhat, E. *Selbstbewußtsein und Selbstbestimmung. Sprachanalytische Interpretationen.* Frankfurt: Suhrkamp, 1979.

Vološinov, V. N. *Marxism and the Philosophy of Language,* trans. L. Matejka and I. R. Titunik. Cambridge, Mass.: Harvard University Press, 1986.

———. *Freudianism. A Marxist Critique,* ed. I. R. Titunik and N. H. Bruss. Bloomington, Ind.: Indiana University Press, 1987.

Walther, E. *Allgemeine Zeichenlehre. Einführung in die Grundlagen der Semiotik.* Stuttgart: Kohlhammer, 2nd ed., 1979.

Warnock, G. J. *English Philosophy Since 1900.* London: Oxford University Press, 1958.

Wartenberg, G. *Logischer Sozialismus.* Frankfurt: Suhrkamp, 1971.

Weber, M. *Economy and Society,* ed. G. Roth and C. Wittich. New York: Bedminster, 1968.

Weber, S. M. "Der Einschnitt. Zur Aktualität Vološinovs." In V. N. Vološinov, *Marxismus und Sprachphilosophie.* Frankfurt, Berlin, and Vienna: Ullstein, 1975, pp. 9–45.

Wennerberg, H. *The Pragmatism of Peirce. An Analytic Study.* Uppsala: Uppsala University Press, 1962.

West, C. *The American Evasion of Philosophy. A Genealogy of Pragmatism.* Madison: University of Wisconsin Press, 1989.

White, S. K. *The Recent Work of Jürgen Habermas.* Cambridge: Cambridge University Press, 1988.

Wiggershaus, R. *Zum Begriff der Regel in der Philosophie der Umgangssprache—Über Wittgenstein, Austin und Searle.* Ph.D. Diss., Frankfurt, 1974.

Wiggershaus, R., ed. *Sprachanalyse und Soziologie. Die sozialwissenschaftliche Relevanz von Wittgensteins Spätphilosophie.* Frankfurt: Suhrkamp, 1975.

Winch, P. "The Unity of Wittgenstein's Philosophy." In P. Winch, ed., *Studies in the Philosophy of Wittgenstein.* London: Routledge & Kegan Paul, 1969, pp. 1–19.

———. *The Idea of Social Science in Relation to Philosophy.* Atlantic Highlands, N.J.: Humanities Press, 2nd ed., 1991.

———. "Apel's 'Transcendental Pragmatics,'" In S. C. Brown, ed., *Philosophical Disputes in the Social Sciences.* Sussex, N.J.: Harvester; Atlantic Highlands, N.J.: Humanities Press, 1979, pp. 51–73.

Wittgenstein, L. *Philosophical Remarks,* ed. R. Rhees. Chicago: University of Chicago Press, 1980.

———. *Philosophical Investigations.* Oxford: Basil Blackwell, 8th ed., 1978.

———. *Tractatus Logico-Philosophicus.* Atlantic Highlands, N.J.: Humanities Press, 1992.

———. "A Lecture on Ethics," *Philosophical Review* 75 (1965), pp. 3–12.

———. *Lectures and Conversations on Aesthetics, Psychology and Religious Belief,* ed. C. Barrett. Oxford: Basil Blackwell, 1966.

———. *Philosophical Grammar,* ed. R. Rhees. Berkeley: University of California Press, 1974.

———. *On Certainty,* ed. G. E. M. Anscombe and H. von Wright. New York: Harper & Row, 1972.

———. *Culture and Value,* ed. H. von Wright in collaboration with H. Nyman. Oxford: Basil Blackwell, 1980.

Wright, H. von. *Norm and Action. A Logical Inquiry.* New York: Humanities Press, 1963.

———. "Logic of Action." In N. Rescher, ed., *The Logic of Decision and Action.* Pittsburgh: University of Pittsburgh Press, 1966, pp. 121–136.

———. *Explanation and Understanding.* Ithaca: Cornell University Press, 1971.

Wuchterl, K. *Struktur und Sprachspiel bei Wittgenstein.* Frankfurt: Suhrkamp, 1969.

Wunderlich, D. *Grundlagen der Linguistik.* Reinbek: Rowohlt, 1974.

———. *Studien zur Sprechakttheorie.* Frankfurt: Suhrkamp, 1976.

———. "Was ist das für ein Sprechakt?" In G. Grewendorf, ed., *Sprechakttheorie und Semantik.* Frankfurt: Suhrkamp, 1979, pp. 275–324.

Wunderlich, D., ed. *Linguistische Pragmatik*. Frankfurt: Suhrkamp, 1972.

Zimmermann, J. *Wittgensteins sprachphilosophische Hermeneutik*. Frankfurt: V. Klostermann, 1975.

Zimmermann, R. "Sprache und Praxis. Der späte Wittgenstein und die Frage nach einer materialistischen Sprachtheorie." In A. Leist, ed., *Ansätze zur materialistischen Sprachtheorie*. Kronberg: Athenaeum, 1975, pp. 292–324.

# Index

Act, illocutionary, 51–54, 64 n.47, 65 n.51, 140; linguistic, 69, 74; locutionary, 51; perlocutionary, 51–53, 64 n.47, 140; philosophy of the, 15, 18; propositional, 52, 83, 140; social, 38; question, 60; utterance, 53

Action, communicative, 94–102; Habermas' concept of, 93–97; innovatory, 132; instrumental, 93–94; strategic, 94–95, 96–97; theory of, 17–18, 58–60

Agreement, 47, 50, 79, 83, 86, 96, 101, 105, 128, 130, 141, 147; argumentative, 144; communicative, 55, 124, 127. *See also* Consensus

Albert, Hans, 89 n.25

Alston, William, 27 n.4

Apel, Karl-Otto, 2, 10, 11, 20, 27 n.10, 28 n.16, 29 nn.20, 28, 33 n.117, 43, 55, 78–88, 90, 124–29, 133, 137, 139, 141–43, 145–46, 148; argumentative discourse, 85, 125, 143; communication community, real and ideal, 80, 85–88, 145; discourse ethics, 141–43; ethics of communication, 85–86; on Austin, 83–84; on Morris, 81–82; on Peirce, 80–82; on Searle, 83–85; on Wittgenstein, 82–83; transformation of transcendental philosophy, 78–80; transcendental language-game, 82–83, 85–86; transcendental pragmatics, 85–88; transcendental semiotics, 79, 81–82; ultimate philosophical foundation, 86, 142

Aporia, in Morris' semiotics, 24–27, 82, 136; in Wittgenstein's conception of philosophy, 47–50

Arens, Edmund, *Kommunikative Handlungen*, 139

Aristotle, 89 n.24

Austin, John L., 33 n.117, 50–53, 56–57, 60, 66 n.86, 80, 99, 102–4, 121 n.27; *How to Do Things with Words*, 50, 52; on constative and performative utterances, 50–51; speech act theory, 50–52

Bakhtine, Mikhail, 39 n.2

Beckermann, Ansgar, 129

Behaviorism, 15, 21, 31 n.83, 33 n.117

Bernstein, Richard, 139, 145, 147–48; *The New Constellation*, 147

Blumenberg, Hans, 70

Bühler, Karl, 33 n.117, 58

Carnap, Rudolf, 19

Category, doctrine of, 2–3, 27 n.10

Chomsky, Noam, 80, 91, 124

Community, communication, 11, 80, 85–88, 117, 123, 145; of interpretation, 10, 80–81; of investigators, 6–11, 81; sign 38

Competence, cognitive, 100, 117; communicative, 74, 84, 91, 98, 114, 123–24, 145; interactive, 98, 100, 114, 117; linguistic, 84, 91, 100, 114, 117, 123–24

Consensus, 11, 47, 49, 81, 87, 97–101, 104–6, 111, 127, 129–30, 143. *See also* Agreement

Contingency, 109, 145–48

Conventionalism, transcendental, 46, 48–49, 83

Correctness. *See* Rightness

Croce, Benedetto, 36

Descartes, René, 36, 83

Dewey, John, 11, 16–18

Dijk, T. A. van, 74

Discourse, 100–106, 127; of application, 145; argumentative, 85, 125, 143; of foundation, 145;

163

language, 41–42; language-game
theory, 41–45, 61 n.6; on meaning,
44–45; on ordinary language, 41–42;
on philosophical language, 44,
47–49; on rules, 46–47; *Philosophical
Investigations*, 41–43; *Tractatus logico-
philosophicus* 41–42
World view, cosmological, 109;
ideologies as a replacement of, 110;

mythical, 109
Wunderlich, Dieter, 55–59; speech act
theory, 55–58; types of speech acts,
56–57; consequences of speech acts,
56–58
Wundt, Wilhelm, 36

Zimmermann, Rolf, 43–44, 61 n.64

## DATE DUE

| 4/2/15 | | | |
|---|---|---|---|
| | | | |
| | | | |
| | | | |
| | | | |
| | | | |
| | | | |
| | | | |
| | | | |
| | | | |
| | | | |
| | | | |
| | | | |
| | | | |
| | | | |
| | | | |
| | | | |
| | | | |
| | | | Printed in USA |